chapter one

the tri-ask technique and how it works

As I have explained, in order to present this course to you with the same informality that I use in the classroom, I shall use first person. I'll describe some of the letters that my students and I have written and the answers we have received. First, I should like to dispel your dread of writing letters and to assure you that this form of communication can be not only easy but exciting.

This is, of course, a program in business communication, but you will find, as many of my students have, that a letter-writing ability will serve you well in a personal way. I don't mean by this that you will be given instruction in writing your most personal letters. I always tell my students that they are on their own for love letters and "Dear John" letters, but even the latter can be turned out more readily by an application of the TRI-ASK TECHNIQUE. You will, however, have training and experience in writing inquiries and answers to inquiries, claim and adjustment letters, letters of refusal, credit and collection letters, sales letters, and most important to you personally, the application letter and resume. Then there will be the fun project, the "out" letter, a real letter from which you may expect an answer. You will be made aware of the over-and-above-and-beyond-the-call-of-duty letter which could place you in that rare position of having an awareness that few in business have.

If you don't like to write letters, you are in the majority. You seldom meet anyone who can honestly say, "I like to write letters." I always ask my students this question at the beginning of each term: "How many of you like to write letters?" The answer is usually the sound of muffled groans. Once in a while a girl will raise her hand, but she usually admits that the letters she enjoys writing are those to her boy friend. If it would mean writing a claim letter, an inquiry, or an application letter, even this girl would admit a real dislike. No male in my classes has ever admitted that he likes to write letters. The married men admit that their wives do the letter writing, and those men who are not married confess that they will expect their wives to carry on this part of the family responsibility. Almost all men plan to look for secretaries who are proficient enough to handle the letter writing for them.

Before we start, I'd like to make it clear that I am not going to write letters for you, and I am not going to present model letters for you to copy. If I did that, the letters wouldn't even sound like you. The very thing to avoid in written communication is stereotyping.

Remember that you are in the majority if you don't like the idea of business communication and that no one is born with a special talent in this area. This is a learned skill that anyone may acquire.

If this skill is so readily available to anyone, why do most people avoid it and dislike it? Usually the reason is that they have not stopped to figure out a short cut, a key, and no one has given one to them. I'll give you in these lessons a technique for attacking any letter you may have to write—and you will be able to write it easily and quickly. Remember that writing effective letters is not a talent bestowed on some and denied to others. You will develop this skill, and it will not be necessary for you to write hundreds of letters to test it. This has been done for you.

If you will follow the TRI-ASK TECHNIQUE with every letter you write, you will not only learn to enjoy letter writing, you will willingly write letters you don't HAVE to write—those over-and-above-and-beyond-the-call-of-duty letters which will enhance your progress, or your company's, far beyond expectations.

If a recipe were to be handed to a chef, he would follow it step by step, using the proper ingredients in the precise amounts and in the correct order specified, and he would cook the mixture at a given temperature. If he made this dish often, he likely would no longer need to look at the recipe. It would be in his mind; he would remember the ingredients and the technique and then he would improve the recipe by experimenting with his own ideas to enhance the flavor and to satisfy his most discriminating clientele.

This course is literally a recipe for effective communication. It is one of those never-fail recipes. You will apply it to every letter that you write until its use becomes second nature—and then you will begin to see how unfounded were your dread and fear of writing letters. You will even add a little spice and flavor of your own to give your letters your very personal touch.

I repeat: this formula will ALWAYS work if you use it as outlined. No longer will your letters be stuffy and dull. They will be easy to turn out, and they will be effective. Without any question, you will see the proof of these statements. If you are looking for model letters, forget it. Nearly every company in the country has a guide book for model letters. They don't work for two reasons. They are stereotyped, and they do not fit a *precise* need.

Before I give you the TRI-ASK TECHNIQUE which you will use with every business letter you write, let's define a business letter. Some might say that it is a communication between businesses. In a sense this is true, but a good business letter, an effective one, attempts to INFLUENCE the recipient to accept something that is said by the writer. INFLUENCE here is the key word. No matter what kind of letter you write, you want the person who receives it to accept what you have said. This involves good will, and good will is conveyed in written communication by using the YOU attitude. With this in mind, here is the TRI-ASK TECHNIQUE OF LETTER WRITING.

When you have a business letter to compose, ALWAYS ask yourself these three questions:

No. 1   WHAT DO I WANT TO ACCOMPLISH?

The answer to this is always the specific goal AND good will.

No. 2   HOW CAN I DO THIS MOST EFFECTIVELY?

If you have something negative to convey—perhaps turning a person down or telling him you cannot do what he asks—you have a boom to lower, so when you answer this question, "How can I do this effectively?" remember to SOFTEN THE BLOW BEFORE YOU LOWER THE BOOM. Say something soothing before you express the negative message. At this point, write the letter, then as you read what you have written, ask yourself the third question:

No. 3   HOW WOULD I FEEL IF I WERE TO RECEIVE THIS LETTER?

If you can consistently get into the habit of asking yourself these three questions, and if you answer them with good will in mind, the letter cannot help being effective.

So here, again, are the three questions—the TRI-ASK TECHNIQUE:

No.. 1   WHAT DO I WANT TO ACCOMPLISH?

(The specific goal AND good will.)

No. 2   HOW CAN I DO THIS?

(Soften the blow first if you have a boom to lower.)

****

(At this point write the letter.)

No. 3   HOW WOULD I FEEL IF I WERE TO RECEIVE THIS LETTER?

This is the TRI-ASK TECHNIQUE.

Perhaps the use of these questions could be clarified by an example. Let's suppose that you are a merchant and your men's department received the following letter:

Gentlemen:

On March 29 I purchased from your Men's Department a Charles Evans sport coat for my husband. For this coat I paid $75. This was for his birthday, but he really needed it for a business trip which he took shortly after his birthday. Two weeks later, you advertised in the Morning Herald the identical coat on sale for $60.

I think it is simply outrageous that I should have to pay $15 more for this coat just because it was purchased two weeks before the sale which I couldn't have known anything about.

I fully expect you to send me a credit slip for the difference in prices; otherwise, I'll never do business with your store again.

Yours truly,

Mary K. Johnson
(Mrs. Roland Johnson)

If you were to receive this letter, your first reaction would be, "Good grief! How could anyone be so stupid! Doesn't this woman know that seasonal sales occur and that merchandise is always marked down? I could do nicely without customers like her, and I just hope she doesn't do business with us again." But wait a minute. Are you going to say this in a letter? There are times in our relationships with people when we must suppress our immediate reactions, especially if those people are our customers or clients. To say to Mrs. Johnson what we think, would be both undiplomatic and unethical. Remember that Mrs. Johnson may have a wide circle of friends and acquaintances. Imagine her, if you will, showing your letter and suggesting that your shoddy treatment of her would be what others could expect.

Businesses deal repeatedly with clients and customers who seem to be unreasonable, yes, even stupid, but we resist any temptation to point this fact out to them. It is always far better not to lose your composure or compromise your dignity.

I like to tell the story of a secretary who was selected over other applicants because she professed an ability at composing letters. Her boss disliked this chore (as most men do); so he would simply say, "Write 'em and tell 'em. . ." and she would compose the letter. When he said, "Write and give them hell," she knew that this meant a letter of complaint in diplomatic terminology.

4

One day this employer was furious with a wholesaler who had not filled an order according to specifications. This man indicated to his secretary that HE would dictate this letter, and that she was not to "doctor it up" with any softened expressions as she usually did. So he did. He dictated that letter with all the vitriolic and even profane expressions he could use, and the secretary took his dictation verbatim. He stood over her while she typed it, and when she had ripped it out of the typewriter, he signed it and folded it with an emphatic flourish and handed it to his secretary to put with the outgoing mail.

The next day when he had cooled down, he said to his secretary, "You know, Sue, I wish we hadn't sent that letter." And the girl smiled and said, "You know—we didn't." I am not suggesting that secretaries should assume this license, but this secretary knew her boss. She knew that he was a bombastic short-tempered man who was completely intolerant of what he considered inefficiency. She knew that much of his business depended on supplies from this wholesaler and that the service had been excellent. She realized that her boss was temporarily inconvenienced by a delay in an order which she was sure was unavoidable. This *was* the case, and the chances of good future service would have been jeopardized if the letter had been sent as dictated.

Losing one's temper and telling a person off has, I suppose, a certain therapeutic value. It soothes the irritation and eases the nerves. So, if you are angry, go ahead and lose your temper. Write that nasty letter if it makes you feel better, but don't mail it. Put it in your bottom drawer; get it out the next day; read it, then tear it up and put it in the round file.

All right, now, let's go back to Mrs. Johnson with her unreasonable claim. Let's just simmer down and use the TRI-ASK TECHNIQUE. (*Try asking* these questions.) First, WHAT DO I WANT TO ACCOMPLISH? The answer to this is that I want to turn down Mrs. Johnson's request for credit on the coat she purchased, but this isn't all. I must do all I can to create the good will that will INFLUENCE her to accept my refusal. Her annoyance must not be reflected in my answer.

5

How about the second question? HOW AM I GOING TO DO THIS?—turn her down and create good will? Well, I do have a boom to lower; so I must soften the blow first. I can do this by appreciating her patronage and complimenting her on her choice of merchandise. THEN I can lower the boom. Let's try.

Dear Mrs. Johnson:

We appreciate your thinking of Easton's when you selected a sport coat for your husband. You showed excellent taste in choosing a Charles Evans coat, since this name represents the finest in quality and workmanship. I am sure that your husband appreciated his birthday present and that he enjoyed wearing the coat on his recent trip. I know he will continue to enjoy it for a long time.

We always have spring sales, particularly after Easter, to make way for summer merchandise. If you had waited until the sale, you wouldn't have been able to get the size that your husband needs, since it is usually the odd sizes that are put on sale. Size 40 is among the first to be sold from regular stock.

If, of course, you had returned the coat within three days because it didn't fit, or because the color didn't suit your husband, we would have been glad to exchange it or give you credit for it. Two weeks, however, exceeds the time limit of our policy for returning merchandise. We are sure you understand.

We have put your name on a preferred list to receive advanced notice of special sales we shall be having. As a matter of fact, we are having sales in our household goods and appliance departments next Friday. You'll find some excellent bargains.

We do appreciate your patronage, and we shall be looking forward to seeing you at Easton's again soon.

Sincerely,

John W. Vincent, Manager
EASTON'S

The writer of this letter has resisted all temptation to use sarcasm in any form. He has complimented Mrs. Johnson on her good taste and has expressed appreciation for her patronage. He has explained the fact that it was to her advantage to purchase the coat when she did. He has refused her request so subtly that no negative words were used—such words as "regret," "refuse," "unfortunately," etc. These words have no place in business letters. He has put her on an intellectual level by saying, "I am sure you understand." He has offered her an alternative, of sorts, in placing her name on a preferred list so that she may be apprised of sales in advance. He has turned her down, and yet he has not written one word to which she could take exception.

Let's suppose, now, that it is you who are making a claim. Perhaps you are upset about your electric power bill, which has been going up and up. You might be prompted to write something like this to the power company.

Gentlemen:

Every time we get a bill from your company, it is higher than the bill for the month before. We haven't done anything different from what we have ever done, yet the bills go up and up. No one uses our office at night; we have added no electrical equipment of any kind, and we do not have electric heat.

It beats me how on earth our bill could climb the way it does. No wonder you big power companies make such huge profits.

It just seems that $54.60 for one month's bill is completely out of order. I shall expect someone to come out and adjust our meter so that our bills will not be so high.

Yours truly,

Does this letter follow the TRI-ASK TECHNIQUE? Does it soften the blow before it lowers the boom? Does it have any semblance of YOU attitude? Would you feel prompted to rush right out and check the meter?

Let's use the TRI-ASK TECHNIQUE with this claim letter.

Gentlemen:

We have appreciated your good service for many years. I don't know what we would do without electricity, as much of our office equipment is electrical, and we depend upon it to make our work easier.

However, for the last four months our bills have been increasing steadily. We do not depend on electric heat, and our office is not open at night. We have the same electrical equipment that we have had for several years. We have added no new machines in the last three years, and we were told that our machines would add very little to our bill.

Our bill has gone up steadily for several months, and we feel that this last bill of $54.60 is unreasonably high. This is nearly $10 more than the charge for the same month last year.

We wonder if something could be wrong with the meter, or if there could be an error in billing. We'd appreciate it if you would check and let us know. I'll be in the office all day Tuesday and Wednesday of next week. I'd appreciate it if one of your representatives would discuss this with me on one of these days. Please call me so that we may set a convenient time and place to discuss this.

Sincerely,

Dennis Ritchie
Craig and Ritchie Associates

No one could possibly take exception to a letter like this, and chances are it would bring results. The first paragraph softens the blow; it paves the way for the complaint which comes in the next paragraph. The claim itself comes in the form of an explanation of why the writer feels that a mistake could have been made. There are no negative words, no name calling, no sarcasm—those words which semanticist H. I. Hayakawa calls "snarl words." A definite time for checking has been suggested, thus increasing the chance of an early investigation.

Notice in the preceding TRI-ASK TECHNIQUE letter that the transition word *however* is used *after* the blow has been softened. This word paves the way for lowering the boom.

There are, of course, many types of boom-lowering letters, and these, normally, are the hardest kinds of letters to write. With the TRI-ASK TECHNIQUE, the most difficult letter can be a breeze because you know how to start and how to proceed.

STUDY REVIEW — WORDS

Explanation: While this is not a course in English or spelling, a review of common types of errors will prevent making errors in letter assignments. For thirteen years, I have kept a list of the kinds of errors that have been made most frequently in my classes. I pass these on to you in small doses of review so that your letters may be more nearly perfect. Study your own errors carefully; keep a list of them in your book. Never make the same error twice, either in this review or in the letters you write for assignments.

1. convenient convenience

This word comes out convient too frequently. This means that a whole syllable has been omitted. I suggest that you divide this word into syllables. Try to remember that the "i" says "y," con-ven-ient. Write it three times dividing it into syllables, then you will never forget it.

2. its

Without the apostrophe, this word is a possessive pronoun, meaning "belonging to it." Just remember that NO possessive pronoun uses an apostrophe (theirs, hers, his, ours—no apostrophes). It's with the apostrophe means either "it is" or "it has."

3. definite

Just remember de + finite = definite. There is no "a" in the word.

4. all right

All right is always two words. You wouldn't say "alwrong," would you?

5. all ready

All ready means completely ready. He is all ready to go.

6. already

Already means previously. Joe had already gone.

7. occasion

Only one "s." (Only a jackass would put two s's in occasion. Perhaps this memory aid isn't very proper, but I bet it will make you remember the proper spelling.)·

8. surprise

That second "s" may sound like a "z." Prize and surprise come from the same Latin root word prehendere, meaning to take, which has neither an "s" nor a "z" in it; so you are on your own for this word. No "z" in surprise.

9. principal

Too many people use the wrong memory aid to help them remember the principal of a school. (A principal wants to be a pal to his students.) They seem to think that this is the only use of the word principal. Principal refers to the main thing, whether it is the main person in a school, the main reason, or the main amount of money on which interest is figured. Think of the "a" in main.

10. principle

An underlying truth. The principle on which this business is founded is honesty.

9

SENTENCE STRUCTURE

The following sentences illustrate typical errors that occur in business letters. Rewrite each sentence correctly in the space provided.

1. Having sent the order yesterday, it should arrive at your plant by March 4.

2. Included in our package offer is a camera, a projector, and a screen.

3. A typewriter, that has such heavy daily use, should be cleaned and checked annually.

4. Does the XYZ Company have it's phone number listed on the letterhead?

5. Neither the price of our product nor the change in design have effected it's sale.

6. If I was you, I would wait until the price is right.

7. Replying to your letter of April 26, the information you requested will be sent May 2.

8. Please direct my inquiry to whomever is in charge of investments.

9. Your letter of March 12, as well as your two previous inquiries, have been answered.

10. Please send me the names of all those whom you think will be interested.

Assignment 1

Suppose you are a retail merchant who has received the following letter. Write a letter refusing Mrs. Hewitt's request using the TRI-ASK TECHNIQUE. (Fill in addresses for all letter assignments.)

Dear Sir:

I have just read in the Daily News of the big sale you are having next Friday when everything in the store will be reduced by 20 percent during that one day.

Three weeks ago, I purchased a Sure Cold electric refrigerator for $435, for which I agreed to pay $50 a month plus interest. Since it has been so recently that I made this large purchase, surely you will give me the benefit of the 20 percent reduction in price, especially since I have made only one payment.

May I please have the discount on the balance I owe. Just credit this amount to my contract balance.

Very truly yours,

Grace Hewitt
(Mrs. Ralph Hewitt)

Assignment 2

Suppose you are employed by the telephone company to answer written complaints. Write a tactful letter in answer to the following complaint:

Dear Sir:

I just about blew my stack when I saw the telephone bill this month. I seem to have $65 charged to my bill for long distance calls. I have checked this carefully, and there are several calls which I can't account for. One of them alone is for $14.65.

I have checked with everyone in the office, and no one here was responsible for the calls that I have indicated on the enclosed bill.

Please check these numbers and revise my bill to a more realistic figure. I'll be glad to pay my bill when you have adjusted it.

Very truly yours,

George Trask

11

Assignment 3

Suppose that your telephone bill is high, that you have checked the call-out book used by employees for recording long distance calls, and that you have double-checked by conferring with each employee. You cannot account for the large charge of $14.65 and three other smaller charges. Write a letter to the telephone company, asking for cooperation in checking these numbers and examining your bill.

chapter two

words and other things

I have before me a letter which I received just this month from my insurance agent. On a beautiful letterhead this man misspelled my name, used no title before my name—not even Ms., and misspelled the name of the street in the address. Here is the context of the letter itself:

> "Please find enclosed your policy. If I can be of any further service to you, please be sure to call me at 632-7884."

Since no initials indicate a typist, I presume that he typed it himself; so he can blame no one else for the errors or the stuffiness of the context.

This young man took infinite pains to explain in person the terms and details of the policy he sold me, and he was gracious and patient in his explanations. He made two trips to my home to provide answers for all the questions I had. I was favorably impressed with his service and with him; so I bought his policy and paid the premium. After I received his letter, I felt like writing to him to say, "You have intelligence, good looks, personality, youth, and a fine education. How is it possible that you have never learned how to write a letter?" Ethics and diplomacy prevent one from being this blunt. I could add in my communication to him, however, "I could show you how to double your business." I honestly believe that letter-writing ability can do just that. As important as the sale are the service and goodwill provided a customer and the word-of-mouth reputation that will result.

What he should have done in sending my policy was to express appreciation for my business and my confidence in him and to assure me of his willingness to help if I have questions or problems relative to the policy.

Inaccuracy in the spelling of a policyholder's name is inexcusable, but the thing that offends me most about this letter is that stuffy cliche, "Please find enclosed." This expression and those like it should have gone out with the horse and buggy. For a young man, presumably up-to-date and intelligent, to use such a stilted and unnatural expression is incredible.

Amy Vanderbilt, renowned authority on business and social etiquette, has repeatedly deplored stuffy business letters. The following question and answer appeared recently in her *Ladies' Home Journal* column:

> **"Business Correspondence**
> In its correspondence, my firm uses a lot of old terms such as 'Yours of the 15th inst. received and contents noted.' We also must put a period after Miss. How can I convince them that this is out of date?
>
> "Tell them, very tactfully, that it is. Say that using such old-fashioned language projects the wrong image if they want to be considered a progressive firm. Good business correspondence should read like clear conversation—brief and to the point."

Actually, words are magic. They can mean the difference between success and failure. An indifferent letter writer seldom realizes what havoc he can create by the use of wrong words. Words like *unsatisfactory, ignore, failure,* and *misunderstanding* have no place in today's business letters. These and words like them simply turn people off—they make people feel that someone is snarling at them. Little better than the snarler is the gookler. A gookler is a person who writes gobbledegook—a stuffed shirt. Here is a typical gookler letter:

Dear Mr. Zilch:

We have at hand your letter of April 14 in which you claim that we made a mistake in your order. We cannot understand this, since all orders are checked carefully before they leave the store, and we have received no complai   from other customers.

You state that when you made your phone order you specified grey tw   cover and upholstery for the card table and chairs that were on   al. However, our employee who took the order wrote on the slip that   u failed to indicate the color; so we sent to you the color beige marble, which is popular with most people. We are sorry that you are dissatisfied.

Unfortunately, the grey tweed is sold out, and although we expect another order within the next three weeks, the cost to you will be the regular price and not the sale price that was a special the day you placed your order.

If you decide that you don't want to keep the card table and chairs we delivered to your home, let us know and we'll let you know just when you may expect us to pick them up. If you do want to substitute the set in grey tweed, let us know and we'll reserve a set for you (at the regular price, of course).

If there is anything else we can do for you, please let us know.

Very truly yours,

James Huff
Customer Service
Newell's

While it is true that adjustments are trouble, a customer's goodwill is always important, and a letter like this one would do nothing but irritate and antagonize. Mr. Zilch would have every right to say, "What customer service?" Mr. Huff is not servicing his customers by the kind of recriminations he suggests in his letter.

While some businessmen are beginning to realize the importance of word choice in letters in order to create goodwill, many have not. Too many regard letter writing as an unpleasant duty, and they proceed to sound as unpleasant as they feel.

Let's take a look at James Huff's letter. Obviously he has "at hand" the letter he is answering—it is not necessary to say so. After this unnecessary gookler start, Mr. Huff implies that Mr. Zilch's claim is so unreasonable that it passed understanding, and then he compares him unfavorably to other more exemplary customers. He questions his customer's honesty by saying, "You state..." which implies a question of the statement. Then Mr. Huff outright accuses his customer of "failure," a snarl word if there ever was one, and he adds insult to injury by dragging out another negative word, "dissatisfied."

He prefaces the next blow with "unfortunately," an unfortunate word to use in any letter—ever. He lowers the boom by telling Mr. Zilch that he will not only have to wait three weeks to get the merchandise he ordered, but he will be penalized further by having to pay the full price.

He then places the responsibility of the next move on his customer, by asking him to make a decision and then suggests that if he doesn't want the merchandise, he will be expected to be on hand so that it may be picked up at the convenience of the store. At this point Mr. Zilch will read the last paragraph with disdain, and, if he is not boiling over at this point, he may ask himself facetiously, "Anything else???? What HAVE you done for me? Customer Service? In what way, Mr. Huff, have you served me?"

This may sound like an exaggeration, but it is all too typical. Unless a customer is unreasonable, anyone in charge of customer service should do all he can to right a mistake, and he should never point an accusing finger at his client. Any inconvenience his firm might suffer would be more than compensated for if the adjustment is made willingly and with language that will soothe.

Let's try eliminating all the gobbledegook and use the TRI-ASK TECHNIQUE:

Dear Mr. Zilch:

I am sorry that you have been inconvenienced by a mix-up in your order. We try to avoid such blunders, but I am sure you understand that mistakes do occasionally happen, especially when a "special" such as you ordered proves to be popular with so many customers. Somewhere between the phone and the shipping room, we goofed.

This "special" resulted in a sellout, but we have reordered and we expect a new shipment within the next three weeks. We'll reserve a card table and chairs for you in the grey tweed design that you want. While this shipment will not be put on special sale, the price to you will be the sale price quoted in the advertisement from which you made your order. If you prefer, you may keep the set in the beige marble finish. We shall credit your account with $3 to partly compensate for your inconvenience.

Just let us know which alternative you would prefer or whether you simply want to return the set to us for credit. We will pick it up at your convenience, if this is what you want.

We shall make every effort, Mr. Zilch, to be more careful in the future. We do appreciate your business, and we look forward to hearing from you soon.

Sincerely,

James Huff
Customer Service
Newell's

Any reasonable customer understands that mistakes do occur, and if he receives an apology, an explanation, and an adjustment such as those in this revised letter, he quite likely will accept it in good grace.

Let's look at another poor (and all too typical) example: .

> Dear Sir:
>
> We have received your letter of May 14 in which you asked about the balance of your account. This is to inform you that our records show that your account with us is in the amount of $78.65. Please be advised that this account is payable on or before the 10th of June. It will be appreciated by us if you will give this your attention before the due date at which time your account should be paid in full.
>
> We wish to take this opportunity to express our sincere appreciation for your kind patronage. We look forward to the pleasure of serving you again in the near future.
>
> We shall, in the meantime, await the receipt of the balance of your current account. Hoping to serve you again soon, we remain.
>
> Very truly yours,

Now the person who composed this letter may be a personable sort of fellow, a good Joe, and a friendly direct conversationalist. Why does he feel that it is necessary to become pompous and stuffy when he writes a letter? The only answer to this is that somehow letter writing is a hangover from the dark ages. This is one phase of business which has not met the pace of technical and economic progress. People dislike writing letters; so they stick with the format and jargon that was popular years ago. Too few businessmen have updated their written communication.

Employees in one state department rejected the services of a young correspondent consultant because those whom she was trying to teach claimed that they had been writing letters before she was born. This is exactly what their letters sounded like—the kinds our grandfathers wrote.

If the writer of the aforementioned typical letter were to SAY his letter instead of reciting it in words of his ancestors, the communication might be something like this:

> Dear Mr. Harris:
>
> The balance of your account, about which you inquired May 14, is $78.65. Of course, this is not due until June 10.
>
> We have certainly enjoyed doing business with you, and we look forward to serving you again soon. Be sure to let us know if we can help you in any way.
>
> Sincerely,

Notice the difference in the two letters. Let's analyze the first one. To say that a letter has been received is unnecessary. Obviously, it has been received, or the writer wouldn't be answering it. Neither is it necessary to refer to records. Anyone in business keeps records. Any amount that is due, is, of course, a matter of record.

"Please be advised," or similar cliches—even "This is to advise you"—are unnecessary. The only person qualified to give advice is an attorney, and even an up-to-date attorney would not fall into a "please be advised" pattern. He likely would say, "I advise you to. . ." but let's leave the advising to attorneys. There is no need to say, "This is to inform you." Just go ahead and say what you have to say without all this completely unnatural warm-up. When you converse, do you say, "I am about to tell you something?" Of course not. You go ahead and say what you have to say.

Good writers avoid passive voice in letters. This means that such expressions as "It will be appreciated by us. . ." or "It has been decided by our committee. . ." are stuffy, since this is not the way we talk. "We shall appreciate it. . ." and "Our committee has decided. . ." are more natural. In this particular letter, however, the writer appears to express concern about the payment of the bill. Since the bill is not due for about 20 days, and since the writer is merely answering a question about the amount, he will create goodwill more readily if he mentions the amount casually and emphasizes a desire to be of service. This is the YOU attitude. BUSINESSES WHICH PLACE SERVICE AND CUSTOMER CONCERN AHEAD OF OBSESSION WITH PROFIT USUALLY MAKE MORE PROFIT IN THE LONG RUN. Good letters contribute to this service.

What opportunity is the writer talking about in the beginning of the second paragraph? There is no need for this kind of warm-up. If a person wants to express appreciation, he should go ahead and do it, without announcing his intent. "The near future" means soon.

The final paragraph in the gookler letter expresses again an urgency for the payment of the bill. This urgency need never be expressed in any but a final collection letter, the formula for which is given in Chapter 11 of this text.

"Hoping to serve you again soon," is grammatically poor construction since no closing in a business letter should start with a participle—an i-n-g verbal. This is not a course in English: so suffice to say that such constructions as "Hoping to hear from you," "Acknowledging the receipt of your letter," "Referring to yours of May 12. .," "Thanking you for your reply. . ." are expressions which are not used in good letters. Of course, any such wind-up as "We remain" should have remained in grandfather's files.

The writing of today's business letters should reflect today's world, where there would be no place for outdated, outmoded, pompous language.

Many companies are making the effort to update their letter-writing policies, but change is always difficult. One very large insurance company has invested a great deal of time, effort, and money in creating a policy which has been described and admired editorially in a number of widely read publications. I suspect, however, that this effort has resulted in little more than lip-service, since I have seen a series of letters to a policyholder which would indicate that this company is just as vague as ever in its written communication. One series of letters I have in my files is so stereotyped that it could have been ground out by a robot. The poor policyholder had to write repeatedly in an effort

to get clear-cut answers. These letters from this company which had made a study of written communication were so obtuse that they were ludicrous, but such failure at communication is really not funny.

My research proved that for most insurance companies letter writing poses a perennial problem. The Director of the Policyowners Service Bureau of a large and prestigious insurance company wrote, "I wish I could tell you that we have an effective letter-writing program, but, unfortunately, our efforts to improve our communications are not as well organized as we would like. Ours is an unusually technical field and if, in our correspondence, we have any one problem more than another, it is the elimination of the use of technical terms which are meaningful within the business but which do not convey ideas to the layman and may even result in misunderstanding."

This Director closes his four-page letter (in answer to my questions) this way: "You have asked whether we agree that a 'friendly, interested approach in communication with policyholders would be directly responsible for increasing volume and reducing cancellations.' I couldn't agree with you more. Such an approach not only serves these purposes but helps policyowners to understand that we are more than a billion dollar company and they are more than a number in our files—that we are interested in them and their present and future financial needs, and in helping them to plan their life insurance so it will be of maximum usefulness in their individual situations.

"From our personal experience in trying to recruit well-trained correspondents there is undoubtedly a real opportunity in industry for your students in business communication. We would be delighted to have them call on us to discuss the possibility of an association with our company."

The person who can write a good letter is a rarity in the business world, and the young man or woman who can prove an ability in this area is regarded by businessmen as a "find." Just today, as I write this, one of our graduates who has worked for two years in a top Government agency in Washington, D.C., stressed, in speaking to my class, the importance of letter-writing ability. She said, in effect, "My letter and my resume got my job for me, and my ability to write letters resulted in my promotions." It delights me to have my students hear such testimonials from our graduates. They realize then, I hope, that I am not "putting them on."

Grammar and spelling should be correct, but the good business letter should sound as if one human being is talking to another. Even pertinent, up-to-date slang expressions are acceptable if they are appropriate and if they add to the clarity and friendliness of informal communication.

Since business letters should be versatile and adaptable, an easy, friendly, casual style is quite appropriate with acquaintances of long standing. Picture the recipient, if possible, and adapt the tone of the letter to this person. Following the formulas outlined in this course will result in letters that are not stereotyped. The formulas make planning any letter easy and quick, and, above all, enable anyone to know how to start any kind of letter and how to proceed effectively.

Many companies know their customers or clientele only through correspondence, and the success of a business depends largely on this relationship. Conversely, the failure of an organization can actually be attributed to an inefficient and indifferent letter-writing policy. Before we go into formulas for definite kinds of letters, let's discuss some details which tend to make letters more attractive. The first is letterhead. This, you might say, is a matter of personal choice. True, but whose choice? Are you selecting a letterhead to impress yourself or those who will be receiving your letters?

It is a fallacy to assume that money will be saved by having several names of executives printed on letterheads to avoid ordering personal stationery for each one. Invariably a change in personnel makes this paper out-of-date before it is all used.

The worst letterhead I have seen is that of a realty company dealing in rural property. Printed on green paper and covering the entire page is a landscape featuring a man on a horse. The figures and the letterhead itself are darker green. How a person could read a letter typed on this is anyone's guess. Another poor example is that of a chain store which lists in the left margin the names of 16 stores in the chain and the manager of each.

Some businessmen go to the other extreme in insisting on a simple, conservative, black letterhead on white bond paper. This, of course, is more desirable than a cluttered, too colorful letterhead, but the wise move is to consult a good printer for suggestions. His expertise in this area is part of his service, and he will gladly show you a folio of samples, or custom design several letterheads for your selection. Chances are that you will be delighted with his professional suggestions and that your customer will be impressed with your choice.

Any good secretarial handbook will give information on letter format. The complete block with date, inside address, salutation, paragraphs, and complimentary close at the complete left is the more efficient from the typist's standpoint. This will save the most time, if time is a factor. Statistics have shown, however, that most people prefer the semi-block, which means a five- or ten-space indentation for paragraphs, and this seems to be preferred by most businesses. Usually, the date and complimentary close are aligned two or three spaces to the right of center, unless the date is placed to conform with the letterhead.

The U.S. Postal Service is requiring the outside address to use the two-letter state abbreviation with two spaces between it and the zip code. Scanners will throw out and delay letters which are not addressed according to these instructions. It is wise, then, for the inside address to correspond to the one on the envelope.

I wouldn't mention these technicalities except that many businessmen are careless about details.

Research indicates that most business letters use the complimentary close Sincerely instead of the more formal ones such as Very truly yours, Yours truly, etc. Respectfully is preferred for the closing of letters written to persons of high rank or prestige. Except for very short one-sentence letters, single spacing should be used. Use a name in the salutation whenever possible. A letter to a company calls for Gentlemen as a salutation. Dear Sir should be used rarely—only when a letter is directed to a man whose name is not known. I never use it, but direct my letter To the President, To the Author, To the Registrar, or To the Editor.

Since trends and policies change, however, an individual, in business or not, should select the style and format that he feels is the most effective and efficient. Many businesses are using the simplified form which places the inside address at the lower left of the letter, and which uses no salutation or complimentary close. This is practical and attractive, and if the context of the letter is friendly, the recipient will not miss these rather meaningless and time-worn customs. One very successful and friendly businessman never uses a salutation. He starts his letter with conversational comment, then uses the name of the recipient in the body of the letter. He closes most of his letters with, very simply, Regards. His secretary uses only her initials as the typist since his name is both typed and signed—another sensible practice. See the example at the end of this chapter. Note that simplifying this letter tends to make it seem more friendly.

These details of format are relatively unimportant if the context of the letter is clear, sincere, and friendly. Both sentences and paragraphs should be short without being terse or curt. People get bogged down in reading long sentences, and they simply do not read long paragraphs. The letter should look like a picture on the page.

A secretary should be her boss's good right arm. He should be able to depend on her to turn out letters that are attractive. If she is that jewel who can compose letters, she is truly a Girl Friday. However, any letter that goes out over a signature speaks for the person who signs it, and it is his responsibility.

Following is a list of expressions to avoid in a well-written letter. There may be others, but if, when you ask yourself, "Would I say this if I were talking?" the answer is "No," then don't write it.

1. I have received your letter. Your letter is at hand. Since you are answering the letter, no warm-up is necessary. However, the date of the letter being answered should almost always be mentioned in passing. This is for filing purposes. If carbon copies of several letters are in one file, knowing the date of each reference is a matter of convenience. Say something like this: "Mr. John White, about whom you inquired October 2, has a good credit record with us." "The order you mentioned in your letter of April 4 was sent April 2."

2. Under separate cover   What kind of cover? Exactly what do you mean? Say what you mean. If something is being sent separately, say how. "I am sending our samples by parcel post." "Our contract will be sent by registered mail." "We shall send the results of our research by air mail."

3. Enclosed please find   If you have remembered to enclose what you say you have, the recipient will find it. Why should he have to search, and why say, "please?"   Simply say, "I enclose a check for $50." or "Our brochure is enclosed."

4. Thank you again   Once is enough. If your letter has been friendly and explicit, there is no need to be redundant with your thanks. This expression may remind us of that horror, the Christmas thank-you letter, in which we expressed thanks at the beginning and again at the close of the letter because we didn't know what else to say.

5. Thanking you in advance   Don't. You are being very presumptuous when you ask someone to do something for you and then thank him before he does it. Say instead, "I shall appreciate it if you will. . ."

6. We regret to inform you   Unless you are sorry for something that you or your company has done, DON'T APOLOGIZE. If you do have to apologize for a blunder, simply write (as you would say), "I am sorry." Perhaps something like this: "You are quite right. We did send the wrong order, and we are sorry that we have inconvenienced you. The right order is on its way." Don't regret unless you really mean it, and then express your apology as you would say it.

7. In the amount of   Not this: "We enclose our check in the amount of $54," but "We enclose our check for $54."

8. Kindly   as in "Thank you kindly." "Will you kindly send me your samples." What does kindness have to do in either of these situations? How can you send something either kindly or unkindly? What is meant here is "please." Just be kind in all of your letters by forgetting the gobbledegook.

9. At your earliest convenience   Be very careful about rushing a favor. If you have asked someone to do something for you and you are in a hurry, be specific. "I should certainly appreciate receiving this order by September 9." If there is really no great rush, say simply ". . .at your convenience" or "soon." This policy would apply to such expressions as ". . .at the earliest possible moment" or "at an early date." Avoid them.

10. In the near future   Say either soon or be specific—say when.

11. My personal opinion   Say "I think," or "my opinion."

12. <u>Consensus of opinion</u>   Just say "consensus."

13. <u>Beg to inform</u>   Don't beg in a business letter.

14. <u>Unfortunately</u>   This word has no place at all in the business letter. Forget it. We want our relationships to be fortunate, not unfortunate.

15. <u>You claim</u>   <u>You state</u>   What do these imply? Simply that the person to whom you are writing has not told the truth. How tactless.

16. <u>The undersigned, the writer, myself</u>   Don't say, "John, Joe, and myself were appointed to the committee." Use I. <u>Myself</u> is a reflexive pronoun used in a sentence as "I hurt myself." or for emphasis, "I did it myself." <u>The undersigned</u> and <u>the writer</u> are pompous and unnatural. When you are speaking would you refer to yourself as <u>the speaker</u>? Don't be afraid of the pronouns <u>I</u> and <u>me</u> as long as the context of your letter has the YOU attitude.

17. <u>The present time</u>   Just say "now."

18. <u>We cannot understand</u>   What this implies is that it is hard for us to understand how anyone could possibly do or say what you have. We imply, "How could you be so stupid?"

19. <u>I hope you will answer in the affirmative</u>.   "I hope you will say 'yes.' "

20. <u>Failure, neglect, carelessness</u>   These words accuse. Specific examples of avoiding these expressions are given in the chapter on adjustment letters.

21. <u>Permit me to say</u>   You are writing the letter—no permission is needed.

22. <u>Entirely complete</u>   Complete is enough.

There are dozens of useless expressions and redundancies which have crept into the business writer's communications. Think before you write, and ask yourself if you would say this if you were talking. You don't impress people by being pompous and unnatural.

Avoid expressions that are negative or accusing. Far better than negative expressions is the very diplomatic one, "I am sure you understand." This places the recipient of the letter on an intellectual level with the writer. It plants a positive seed of suggestion which usually nurtures understanding.

A person who loses his dignity in a letter loses good relationship with the person to whom he is writing. If blowing off steam in a letter makes you feel better, go ahead and write that letter, but don't mail it. Words you use reflect you. Use them wisely. They can be magic.

LETTERHEAD HERE

ADDRESS

September 20, 1973

Congratulations, Mr. Garver

on the fine talk you made at Rotary Club yesterday. I agree with everything you said, and I especially admire you for expressing yourself so clearly on the importance of service before profit. Too many of us in business are inclined to be blinded by dollar signs.

The noon hour passed all too quickly, and I am sure that you must be aware that your talk was received most enthusiastically.

Your talk was so exemplary from the standpoint of enthusiasm, knowledge of subject matter, voice, eye contact, and all the other factors that make public speeches excellent, that I should like to ask you to repeat this talk at the Allendale Speakers' Club. This group convenes the second and fourth Tuesdays for dinner meetings at 6:30 p.m. in the East Room at the Shannon Hotel. Would it be possible for you to make it on October 9 or 23?

I'd like the members of our club to hear both what you say and how you say it. You would, I'm sure, serve as an inspiration for some of us who are not so polished in the speaking area. As you know, the Speaker's Club is designed to give its members the opportunity for practice in making various kinds of talks. We learn, also, by hearing good speakers such as you.

Will you call me at 643-8964 to let me know your decision? If you say "Yes," I'll be. . . . . .most grateful.

Marlin Moore

Mr. Dwight Garver
Garver Services, Inc.
346 NE Vine Ave.
Allendale, MI   49401

Letter Formats (a matter of choice)

Complete block

September 20, 1973

Mr. Dwight Garver
Garver Services, Inc.
346 NE Vine Ave.
Allendale, MI   49401

Dear Mr. Garver:

Body of letter here. No paragraph indentation.

Sincerely,   (or Very sincerely yours, Yours truly, etc.)

Marlin Moore
(title here, if any)

Standard block is the same as complete block except that the date and complimentary close are placed just to the right of center. (This depends on the length of the name or company.) The date may be placed conveniently to tie in with the letterhead.

Semi-block

                                          September 20, 1973

Mr. Dwight Garver
Garver Services, Inc.
346 NE Vine Ave.
Allendale, MI 49401

Dear Mr. Garver:

     Body of letter starts here with five or ten-space indentation for the beginning of each paragraph. Two spaces, of course, between paragraphs with all formats. (placement of typist's initials optional)

                                   Sincerely,

sh   Merlin Moore

25

These directions were printed in 1971 and were widely distributed at Customer Cooperation Programs during 1971 and 1972. Since, as a matter of efficiency, so many businesses are using the windowed envelope, this means that this format will appear as the inside address on the letter itself. Since it is human nature to oppose change, this format has not been widely accepted. However, when business finds that electronic scanners will "accept" more readily mail which is properly addressed, the trend will change. The United States Postal Service has every right to make suggestions for more efficient service, and if "customers" value speed and priority, they will follow these suggestions.

Here is an example of an address as suggested by the USPS.

```
                      GENERAL XYZ CORP
(2) ———————— ATTN MR C P JONES
(3) ———————— 1000 MAIN ST  ROOM 4325———— (4)
              DETROIT MI  48217———————————— (5)
```

1.   BASIC FORMAT

The address area should be in block form with all of the lines having a uniform left margin. It should be at least 1 inch from the left edge of the envelope and at least ½ inch up from the bottom of the envelope. No print should appear to the right or below it.

2.   ACCOUNT NUMBERS, DATES, ATTENTION LINES, etc.

Enter these on any line of the address block above the second line from the bottom.

3.   STREET ADDRESS OR BOX NUMBER

These should be placed on the line immediately above the city, state, and ZIP Code. When a box number at a particular station is indicated, the box number should precede the station name.

Correct spelling of street names is essential, since some machines match the names in the address to those like it in the machine's memory.

4.   UNIT NUMBER

Mail addressed to occupants of multi-unit buildings should include the number of the apartment, room, suite, or other unit. The unit number should appear immediately after the street address on the same line—never above, below, or in front of the street address.

5.   CITY, STATE, AND ZIP CODE

These should appear in that sequence on the bottom line of the address block. This is where automatic sorting equipment is instructed to look for this information.

6.   WINDOW ENVELOPES

Inserts and envelopes must be matched so that the address will show through the window no matter how much the insert slides around in the envelope. There should be at least ¼ inch between the address and the left, right, and bottom edges of the window whatever the position of the insert.

Companies or businesses which use envelopes imprinted with anything at all in the lower left part of the envelope will be wise to change the imprinting format with their next orders.

The Postal Service has published the two-letter state abbreviations, and these have been widely accepted. Not so widely accepted or even known is the list of abbreviations for street designators and for words that appear frequently in place names.

For example:	Academy	—	ACAD	Boulevard	—	BLVD
	Causeway	—	CWSY	College	—	CLG
	Crossing	—	XING	Falls	—	FLS
	Highlands	—	HGLDS	Junction	—	JCT
	Memorial	—	MEM	Mountain	—	MTN
	Parkway	—	PKY	Place	—	PL
	Village	—	VLG	Vista	—	VIS

The complete list of abbreviations may be obtained from the United States Postal Service, Washington, DC 20260. This list also includes specific abbreviations for postal names which cannot be abbreviated to 13 positions by use of the standard list. For instance, Petrified Forest National Park (in Arizona) becomes PET FOR NT PK; Cold Springs-Highland Heights (in Kentucky) becomes CLD SP-HLD HT; and Los Ranchos De Albuquerque becomes LS RANCHS ALB. Long names of cities, villages, Air Force bases, Naval Stations, etc. have been abbreviated and programed into postal electronic equipment.

Psychologically, we resist the inconvenience of change, but for efficiency in communication, we would do well to comply.

TWO-LETTER STATE ABBREVIATIONS

Alabama	AL	Montana	MT
Alaska	AK	Nebraska	NE
Arizona	AZ	Nevada	NV
Arkansas	AR	New Hampshire	NH
California	CA	New Jersey	NJ
Canal Zone	CZ	New Mexico	NM
Colorado	CO	New York	NY
Connecticut	CT	North Carolina	NC
Delaware	DE	North Dakota	ND
District of Columbia	DC	Ohio	OH
Florida	FL	Oklahoma	OK
Georgia	GA	Oregon	OR
Guam	GU	Pennsylvania	PA
Hawaii	HI	Puerto Rico	PR
Idaho	ID	Rhode Island	RI
Illinois	IL	South Carolina	SC
Indiana	IN	South Dakota	SD
Iowa	IA	Tennessee	TN
Kansas	KS	Texas	TX
Kentucky	KY	Utah	UT
Louisiana	LA	Vermont	VT
Maine	ME	Virginia	VA
Maryland	MD	Virgin Islands	VI
Massachusetts	MA	Washington	WA
Michigan	MI	West Virginia	WV
Minnesota	MN	Wisconsin	WI
Mississippi	MS	Wyoming	WY
Missouri	MO		

Observe the following in good, precise writing.

1. High school, as: He went to high school in New York.

   High school is capitalized within a sentence only when it refers to a particular school, and is preceded by its name. Otherwise it is lower case.

   John went to Central High School.

2. The same applies to college or university.

   Mary is a graduate of Willamette University.

   She is a university graduate.

3. Ordinarily, names of school subjects are not capitalized unless they are followed by a number:

   History 203,   Typing III,   Psychology 405

   but: He took psychology at the university.

         Her favorite subject was chemistry.

4. College or high school classes are usually not capitalized.

   John was a junior in high school.

   The senior class had its picnic in May.

   Class names are sometimes capitalized in news titles or stories or on programs, etc. Used as adjectives for particular events they would be capitalized:

         The Junior Prom   Senior Skip Day

5. Vice President

   In writing this word, particularly in business letters, I suggest we lean heavily on the YOU attitude and use psychology rather than adhering strictly to the dictionary. In the dictionary, we find this word lower case and hyphened. However, I have never known a vice-president to follow this usage, and in deference to his position, let us remember to omit the hyphen and capitalize the word: Vice President. After all this IS an important position.

6. Enthuse: This is one of my pet aversions. Most dictionaries indicate that this word is colloquial. One dictionary describes it as a "back" formation of enthusiasm. My new Random House dictionary concedes that this word is widely used in speech and writing, but it is felt by many to be poor writing, and it is best to paraphrase it.

   She became enthusiastic about her new position.

   Not: She was enthused over her job.

7. Complected: While this word is not frequently used in business correspondence, I place it in the same category as enthuse. It is classified in dictionaries as dialectical or colloquial. The right word is complexioned.

She was dark complexioned.

8. Heighth: There is no such word. There is width, but not heighth. The word is height without the third h.

9. The reason is because, as in:

The reason he didn't go is because he wasn't invited.

Say instead: The reason he didn't go is that he wasn't invited.

Never- - - -The reason is because. . .

10. Try and come, as in Try and come to the meeting.

Technically, this implies two verbs, whereas you (understood) is the subject, try is the only verb, and to come (an infinitive) is the direct object. If you don't understand all that, just take my word for it. Don't try AND do anything. TRY TO.

Assignment

1. Revise in the space provided the following group of sentences:

a. We are in receipt of your letter of 7/15/72. We regret to inform you that because of a reorganization in our production department, your order was delayed. It is being sent under separate cover today.

I am sorry your order was delayed.
It is being sent under separate cover
today.

30

b. Thank you for your letter of August 21. In response permit me to say that our representative will be glad to call on you September 12 in accordance with your request. Thank you again for your letter.

In response to your letter of August 21 permit me to say that our representative will be glad to call on you September 12 in accordance with your request.

Thank You

c. This letter is for the purpose of requesting your permission to use your latest sales letter in our company publication, "The Sentinel." Thanking you for your assistance, it is our hope that we can return the favor.

d. This is to advise you that our catalogue is being sent to you at an early date. Enclosed please find a special sales sheet for the month of September.

e. Thank you for your letter of October 2. Unfortunately, we regret to inform you that we are unable to supply you with No. 5018 business forms. We are no longer printing this particular number. Consult our catalogue for a substitution. Thank you again for your inquiry.

I am sorry that we are unable to supply you with No. 5018 business forms. We are no longer printing this particular number. Consult our catalogue for a substitution.

Thank you for your inquiry.

31

2. Rewrite the following letter:

Dear Mr. Young:

This is to tell you that we received your letter of July 15. I wish to state that the printing order that you inquired about was delayed because of the breakdown of one of our presses.

As per your request, this is being sent C.O.D. within the next two or three days. Enclosed please find is a copy of your original order. Thanking you in advance for your patience.

Respectfully yours,

3. Write a letter to Rite-Flight Air Lines claiming that your luggage arrived in Portland two days after you did. Explain that you were attending a 3-day conference during which you were guest lecturer at one of the sessions. The slip-up necessitated the expense and inconvenience of having to shop for and purchase a new suit and accessories for the occasion. Your luggage arrived on the day before your departure. Fortunately, lecture notes were in your brief case, which you carried. In lieu of punitive damages, ask for reimbursement for the amount spent for the clothes plus taxi fares to the shopping area and to and from the airport to pick up the luggage.

4. Write a letter to Jerry Arthur refusing permission to return a diamond engagement ring and wedding band six months after it had been purchased. Jerry's reason for the request was a broken engagement.

5. Write a letter to Mrs. Stanley Russell refusing to exchange her single-oven range for a double-oven model four months after purchase. Your salesman has informed you that he urged her to select the larger range because of the size of her family, but price had been the determining factor in her decision. Handle this in an appropriate manner or make fitting suggestions, but refuse her suggestion that she return the used range and pay only the difference between it and the larger one.

6. Write a claim letter complaining to the printer about a letterhead order which was correct in every detail except the style of type—which was different from that which you had selected.

chapter three

ask and you shall receive
(the letter of inquiry)

No one has all the answers, but the person who has the most answers is the one who asks questions. I tell my students that it is never stupid to ask questions—it is stupid not to ask; and in a classroom situation if the instructor doesn't have the answer—and if the question is a legitimate one—he will make every attempt to find out the answer and impart this answer, not only to the one who posed the question, but to the entire class. It makes sense to write letters that ask questions; yet, regrettably, too many people are too lazy to take the time to write. The way to develop a good habit—like writing letters—is to repeat the process until it becomes a pleasure instead of a chore. The real pleasure of writing letters is getting the answers. Everyone likes to receive letters.

In my research for information on correspondence practices, my students and I have written literally hundreds of letters. We have found out a good many things about letter-writing policies that otherwise we would never have known. In studying the answers, we have not been very much surprised to determine that the companies and individuals who attach the most importance to written communication are those who are the most successful. It is conclusive, actually, that there is a direct correlation between a good correspondence policy and success. This will be illustrated more fully in the chapter on the over-and-above-and-beyond-the-call-of-duty letters. We have received most gratifying and informative letters from men who not only do not resent our inquiries, but who are most gracious and helpful in their responses. Our experiences proved over and over that big people really do have time for little people.

In business, letters of inquiry could readily be inspired by articles in trade or professional publications. Suppose a businessman reads an article about a company similar to his with low turnover in salesmen who have an enviable record of high production. He cannot help thinking, "I wonder how they do it? What do you suppose is the incentive program?" If this company is not in his area and is not in direct competition with his, it would be quite ethical for this man to write and ask. Many businessmen would consider this kind of inquiry a compliment.

There are, of course, two kinds of letters of inquiry—one in which you initiate the inquiry and one which has solicited your inquiry. The solicited letter of inquiry is usually one in answer to an advertisement or a sales letter. The one, however, which occurs to people less frequently is the unsolicited letter of inquiry—the one a person writes to find out something he wants to know—the one similar to the one just described. This idea may

occur to a person, but because of his innate distaste for writing letters and because writing is something that can be put off or neglected entirely, too often the idea is dissipated by inaction.

The formula for this letter is very simple. First, of course, use the TRI-ASK TECHNIQUE:

1.　WHAT DO I WANT TO ACCOMPLISH?

The answer to this is the specific inquiry.

2.　HOW CAN I DO THIS?

Now here is the formula:

    a.　Make the inquiry easy to answer.

    b.　Make the recipient of the letter feel that it is to his advantage to do what you ask.

Then, of course, after you have written the letter, you read it and ask yourself the third question:

3.　HOW WOULD I FEEL IF I WERE TO RECEIVE THIS LETTER?

Let's illustrate this technique. Suppose you are very curious about a company's salesman incentive program, and perhaps you would like to know the details of handling salesmen's pay. You have no boom to lower in this letter, but you do have to think of goodwill—your first thought, actually, in starting any letter. Then, in making the inquiry easy to answer, questions could be tabulated with space for answers to be checked or filled in. Next, ask yourself, "Why would the recipient of this letter want to answer it? How can I make him feel that it is to his advantage to do what I ask?" This may not always be possible, but always think of the possibility.

Here is how such a letter *could* be written:

EXAMPLE OF LETTER OF INQUIRY
(Full Block)

October 4, 1973

Mr. Darwin Skelton
950 Parkway Blvd.
East Saint Louis, IL   62201

Dear Mr. Skelton:

I enjoyed reading the article in the October issue of Effective Management about the success of your company in the production and sales of business forms. It is really amazing that your sales have actually increased 200 percent within such a short period of time.

While my company does not deal in business forms, we do sell office machines and equipment, and we frequently service the same clientele that your company does.

The thing that impresses me most about your company is the low turnover in salesmen, and quite frankly, I should like to know the basis of this success. If you will answer the following questions, I shall not divulge this information. I fully realize, considering your enviable record, that your plan is unique.

1. Do you always employ men who have had previous selling experience?

    Yes_____   No_____   Usually, but not always_____

2. Do you have any preference as to age? If so, what age?

    _____

3. Do you pay your men salary plus commission, or commission only?

    Salary plus commission_____

    Commission only_____

4. Do you have any form of profit sharing or bonus?

    Yes_____   No_____

    If so, will you describe it briefly?

35

5.   Do you have any system of salary or commission increments?

6.   How do you determine the territory of each man?

7.   Do you provide health insurance or life insurance benefits?

8.   What do you consider the most effective factor of your sales incentive program?

You appreciate, I know, that any improvement in sales incentives will increase sales, and that is what we are all looking for. Our company has worked out a very successful program for handling salesmen's expenses which has not only saved us money, but which is heartily endorsed by the salesmen themselves. If you feel that this technique would help your company in any way, I should be happy to outline it for you.

I look forward to your response.

Sincerely,

Glenn Marlowe
Marlowe Associates

The format of this letter makes it easy to answer, the tone is complimentary, and something has been offered in return for the requested favor. An answer has not been rushed. Too often writers appear to be in a hurry with such cliches as "Please answer at your earliest convenience," or similar such urgent requests. Remember, NEVER RUSH A FAVOR.

A similar letter requesting information could be sent out on a research basis to many companies, with the YOU attitude being fulfilled by promising to send results of the survey.

Sometimes it is just not possible to have something to offer in return. In this event, remember you have nothing whatever to lose by asking and possibly much to gain.

Back in 1960, Life Magazine carried the story of a young married girl who wrote a letter of inquiry to President Eisenhower. She told him that she had just turned 21 and had not yet made up her mind whether to register as a Republican or a Democrat, and she asked President Eisenhower why she should be a Republican. She explained that her father had always told her that if she wanted to know anything, she should go to the man at the top. She wrote a similar letter to a prominent Democrat. President Eisenhower sent the young lady a brief note telling her that he was making arrangements to answer her. His ultimate answer was in the form of making this young lady the guest of honor at a $100-a-plate Republican dinner at which he answered her question in a talk that was heard on closed circuit television by 100,000 Republicans in 83 cities. What an exciting reward for a simple letter of inquiry!

Using this as an incentive, one of my students wrote similar inquiries in trying to determine how he should register politically. He explained that his mother was registered as a Democrat and his father, as a Republican; so he was somewhat undecided. He received excellent and definitive letters from Clay Myers, Republican, Oregon's State Secretary of State, and from Robert Straub, Democrat, Oregon's State Treasurer. Both letters were sincere and clear, and they served as bases for discussion among young people who knew little about differences in party philosophy.

Businesses or individuals who are considering investing money in a service or a product should take the opportunity to write a letter of inquiry asking for specific information. Several similar letters will give a fine opportunity for making comparisons. Sometimes, perusing information at leisure is preferable to making a snap decision during a personal presentation. Such perusal may be followed by further letters of inquiry which will result in the comparison which leads to a wise choice.

Usually, written inquiries are more satisfactory than personal or telephoned ones. The written word is a matter of record which may be filed, while the spoken word may be misunderstood or forgotten. This is the reason that most important telephoned communications in business, especially orders, are confirmed by letter.

How about answering inquiries? An inquiry should never be ignored, since each one is important to the person who made it. My research has shown that emphasis is placed on sales letters, many of which solicit inquiries, and that then, too often, answers to the inquiries are delayed or the inquiries are ignored entirely. Sales letters and advertisements frequently carry the message, "If you have any further questions, don't hesitate to write." Inquiries which have been solicited should be answered immediately. Neglecting them will nullify the most extensive sales program.

My students and I found that of 50 solicited inquiries to which we responded we received only five answers within a week and 12 within three weeks; six were not even answered, and the rest took more than 30 days to answer. Names or addresses were incorrect on 11 of the letters. While these were solicited inquiries, more than half enclosed only brochures or advertising literature, and 18 of these included a form letter. Only four enclosed a personal letter, and these were prompted by specific questions. Since our letters were justified answers to inquiries—each person asked about something in which he was actually interested—opportunities for selling or promotion were actually sacrificed in 80 percent of the answers.

Letters of inquiry should not be regarded as a nuisance, nor should they be routinely answered. Too many times letters of solicited inquiry are answered in the following manner:

> Dear Sir:
>
> Enclosed is our brochure on promotional gifts. You will find an order blank on the last page to assist you in listing items you may desire.
>
> Very sincerely yours,

Such an answer to an inquiry says in effect, "Here is the catalogue you asked for. We've done you a big favor by sending it; we couldn't care less whether or not you use it."

Whether you are in the business of selling a product or performing a service, if someone has risen to the bait, you should hook him if you feel you can serve him legitimately. In any event, your answer should be prompt, courteous, and personal. Even if you cannot provide the service or product requested, you should answer promptly.

Suppose a woman has seen your advertisement for office furniture in her husband's professional journal, and she writes asking about description and prices of captains' chairs. It may be a nuisance to write explaining that you are not in the household furniture business, and it would be easy to ignore her request or cut her off with a "Sorry, we cannot help you" letter. Observe the difference in the following letters.

> Dear Mrs. Miller:
>
> We regret to advise you that we do not carry the kind of captain's chair about which you recently inquired. Our business is limited to office furniture and equipment. This is the reason that our advertising is carried by professional publication.
>
> Very sincerely yours,

This implies that she should know the nature of the business, since she obviously found the ad in a business magazine. The writer of this letter has failed to consider the fact that this rebuff may influence Mrs. Miller's husband to cut this service from his list.

Compare the following letter:

Dear Mrs. Miller:

We appreciate your inquiry of June 14 about captains' chairs, and we wish we could help you. We do have a chair similar to the one you asked about, but since our furniture and equipment is designed for office use, you might find our chairs a little heavy for your home. We have enclosed a brochure with a picture of the nearest thing we have to the kind of chair you want, and if you feel this is suitable we'll be delighted to fill your order. Note that this is available in walnut or oak, but not in the maple you mentioned.

I suggest that you write to the Acme Furniture Company, 123 Garth Avenue, Plainsville, Ohio, for information, or that you call on the Weddle Furniture Company in your city. I feel sure you would find the chairs at either of these companies to suit your needs.

However, if you feel that our chairs are what you want, we'll fill your order promptly. One thing I should like to point out is that, although they cost more than household furniture, they are made to last for many years. We hope that when your husband has need for office equipment or furniture he will think of us.

Sincerely,

You never know when the person you cut off, because you regard the inquiry a nuisance, might have a wide circle of friends, relatives, or acquaintances who could use your service or product. Who knows, Mrs. Miller might be a business woman herself, or perhaps her husband seeks her advice in furnishing his office. Even if she cannot use in her home the product you sell, your courteous letter could prompt her to use her influence in your direction.

The very fact that the letter to Mrs. Miller is rather long and detailed will make her appreciate all the more the fact that interest has been shown in her inquiry.

You may have heard the story of the shabby couple who asked the president of Harvard University how much it cost to run a university. The president must have looked down his aristocratic nose when he made it plain to them that they could not understand such high finance. So instead of giving money to Harvard as they had planned, the Leland Stanfords returned to California and started their own university.

The simple law of human relations requires anyone in business to be courteous to all who make inquiries.

The formula, then, for writing a letter of inquiry is this:

1. Make the letter easy to answer.

2. If possible, make the one who receives the letter feel that it is to his advantage to do what you ask.

3. Be natural and friendly; create goodwill.

4. Don't ever be too reluctant or too lazy to ask. A good letter of inquiry usually brings a good response.

The directions for *granting* an inquiry are:

1. Answer the inquiry promptly. If it has to do with your service, give it priority.

2. Answer the inquiry in terms of the advantage of your service or product to the inquirer.

3. Positively expect the recipient to accept your service.

4. Even if you regard the inquiry as a nuisance, answer it graciously.

In refusing an inquiry, use the following formula:

1. Soften the blow before you lower the boom.

2. Refuse.

3. Explain.

4. Offer an alternative, if possible.

5. Create goodwill.

Whether you write a letter of inquiry or answer an inquiry, make your letter clear, conversational, and friendly. Emphasize the YOU attitude until writing this kind of letter becomes a habit—a habit for which you'll be grateful. Ask and you shall receive.

Remember that no attempt is made here to cover *all* rules of English or spelling. I include those rules which apply to the mistakes which seem to be most frequently made in letters and papers that I have proofread and corrected for the last 14 years. Most of my students maintain that they have a preponderance of literature in high school but very little grammar and spelling. Evidence prompts me to believe them.

Here are some common mistakes in punctuation. Study them carefully and try to apply what you learn here to your letter assignments.

1. The period is ALWAYS inside the quotation marks. ALWAYS.

   Joe said, "I like to write letters."

   Even if there are double quotes, the period is ALWAYS inside.

   The teacher explained, "I heard him say, 'I must be at the airport at two o'clock.' "

2. Likewise, the comma is ALWAYS inside the quotation marks.

   "Thank you," Roberta said, "I'll be happy to go."

3. The question mark and the exclamation point "float." They may be either outside or inside the quotes, depending on their use.

   If the quotation is a question, the question mark is inside the quotation marks:

   Bill exclaimed, "Have you heard the news?"

   If the sentence itself is a question, the question mark is placed outside the quotes.

   Did you hear her say, "I'll be home by four o'clock"?

4. Policies regarding use of the period with abbreviations are changing so rapidly that it behooves anyone simply to "keep up." For instance, most government agencies and bureaus use neither spacing nor periods with abbreviations:

   OPA,   FBI,   FHA,   etc.

   The two-letter state abbreviations (capitalized with no periods) are recommended by the United States Postal Service. However, this use is accepted only on the envelope and on the inside address. It is not (at this writing) acceptable in the body of the letter. I would be inclined to violate this rule if several addresses were quoted in the letter. Newspapers seem to have set a trend of their own, but don't use them as models for abbreviations, punctuation, spelling, or division of words.

41

5. When the name of a city and its state occur within a sentence, both the city and the state are followed by commas. (This rule is one of the most frequently violated ones in my classes. Few students have ever heard of this.)

The contract was signed in Pittsburgh, Pennsylvania, October 17, 1973.

6. When the year is preceded by the month and the day of the month, the year is preceded and followed by commas.

The contract was signed October 17, 1973, in Pittsburgh, Pennsylvania.

7. A compound adjective is hyphenated when it occurs before the noun that it modifies, but not when it is used as a predicate adjective and follows the noun.

Jason's is an up-to-date store.

Jason's store is up to date.

8. Percent is now written as one word. (I'll have to admit that I am reluctant to accept this relatively new form, since this seems to be a perversion of the correct Latin form, but there it is.) Unless statistical information is enumerated or itemized in a letter, the percent symbol (%) is not used.

The store gave a 20 percent discount to employees.

9. Use the word *percentage* when no numeral occurs.

A large percentage of the membership opposed the plan.

10. The latest handbooks permit the use of figures in written communication, even figures under 10. (This has not been accepted as general usage; so determine the policy of the place where you work. Remember that a sentence never starts with a figure. You may, however, rearrange the sentence to get around this rule.)

Forty men and 25 women were present for the meeting.

Present for the meeting were 40 men and 25 women.

(Some authorities would insist that the 25 in the first sentence should be written out for parallel construction.)

11. Indefinite amounts or periods of time are expressed in words.

The car cost about four thousand dollars.

He is about forty years old.

12. Write time in figures if <u>a.m.</u> or <u>p.m.</u> are used. Use words with <u>o'clock</u>.

8 p.m. five o'clock

1.   Assume that you are conducting research on business correspondence. Write a letter to the Acme Insurance Company requesting information on this company's letter-writing policy. Formulate questions which will be easy to answer. Use the YOU attitude.

2.   Revise the following letter:

Dear Mrs. Powell:

    I have received your request for information about our Speed Heat electric range. You will find enclosed a brochure about this appliance.

    If you are interested in purchasing a range, I suggest that you consult the ABC Appliance Center in your city.

               Yours very truly,

               Donald A. Hall
               Speed Heat Corporation

3.   Revise the following letter:

Dear Mr. Henry:

    This is in answer to your letter of July 15. I regret to advise you that it will be impossible for me to give you the information you asked for.

    To divulge to you our procedure for paying our salesmen would violate our policy of confidential relationship with our representatives. I suggest that you work out your own plan with your salesmen.

4.   Mrs. Jake Bowman, 242 Grand Street, Arkela, Oregon, has sent you a check for $19.75 for a spray-steam iron advertised in a national woman's magazine.

Since your company sells only to dealers, write to Mrs. Bowman that you have forwarded her order to your dealer in her area, the Rawlins Appliance Shop in Salem, Oregon. Suggest that she go there to make her selection.

chapter four

if you are hurt, scream
(the claim letter)

I know a man who says, "If I'm hurt, I scream—it always makes me feel better." There is, of course, a certain therapeutic value in letting off steam when you are hurt. The thing is, most people seem to enjoy screaming, but usually they are either too lazy or too scared to turn their screams in the right direction. Now, however, society not only is making it easy for those who are hurt to scream, but is making loud complaints seem like a duty. We are urged by Ralph Nader, by Sylvia Porter, by the Departments of Commerce and Agriculture, and by Congress itself to expect good service and to complain if we fail to get less than we expect.

Many states have set up Consumer Service Divisions under the Department of Commerce, and complaints which are not adjusted to the satisfaction of the consumer will be handled by officials whose authority has "teeth." As I write this, students in my class have just heard a talk by Wanda Merrill, Administrator of the Consumer Division of Oregon's Department of Commerce. (See the chapter on reports for an outline of this talk.) Mrs. Merrill explained how complaints should be made, and she cited instances in which her office has effected satisfactory settlements in behalf of consumers. She stressed, however, that while the consumer should expect good service and products, a complainer should always tell the truth and should not expect adjustments for products he has abused or services for which he has not paid. There are always the chronic complainers who make the handling of legitimate complaints more difficult.

What does all this have to do with written communication? Complaints should be written, that's what. The problem, of course, lies in the fact that making a complaint is trouble, and most people imagine double trouble when a letter is involved. Too many people rationalize themselves out of asking for what is rightfully theirs simply because they procrastinate writing the letter which could bring a very satisfactory adjustment.

The truth is that those who serve business or the public would usually far rather have complaints made to them than to others, whom they might lose as customers. Actually, it is only fair that consumers provide a chance for an explanation or amends to be made. Business is complex, and since perfection is rare, errors are bound to occur. No one in business would be naive enough to promise that mistakes would never be made. The trouble is that when anyone has been inconvenienced, he is likely to feel personally slighted—that he has been singled out to be taken advantage of.

Claim letters are usually more effective than telephone calls for three reasons: First, the claimant is less likely to lose control of himself by letter than by phone. A hot-under-the-collar attitude results too frequently in accusations and recriminations for which the claimant is sorry later. Because a person hasn't had time to formulate a logical criticism, he will express himself poorly and fail to get the response he seeks. Second, a telephone call will seldom reach the person he wants. Too frequently a secretary or assistant who is acting as a buffer for the man at the top will brush a person off. A well-written letter directed to a specific person or a title will land on that person's desk as a constant reminder of the claim until it is answered. Third, a more explicit claim may be made by letter with less likelihood for misunderstandings.

Now, this type of letter can be illustrated after a fashion, but model letters are virtually useless because of the unlimited variety of claims. This is a very definite and personal type of letter, but it is never difficult because, here again, you have a specific formula.

First, of course, as with every letter, the good old three-questions TRI-ASK TECHNIQUE is used, but the sub-goal is specific. Here it is:

First, what do I want to accomplish?

The answer to this is that I want an adjustment.

Second, how am I going to do this?

Well, I'll never inspire an adjustment by pointing a finger, so here is the specific sub-formula:

1. If possible, soften the blow before you lower the boom. Make some remark about the good quality of previous service or about the good reputation of the company, or in some way pay a sincere compliment.

2. Explain the claim.

3. Tell how you have been inconvenienced, if you have been.

4. Try to motivate action by way of some adjustment.

5. If you feel it is feasible, suggest a specific adjustment.

Next write the letter, following this sub-formula, and then ask yourself the third question:

How would I feel if I were to receive this letter?

If it would make you angry or resentful, tear it up and try again. If, when you read your claim letter, you can honestly say that it is clear, precise, yet firm, and that if you were to receive it you would be prompted to make an adjustment or an explanation, then seal it and send it.

Notice that under the sub-formula the final direction is *IF it is feasible, suggest an adjustment.* There are times, in an effort to make amends, when the adjuster will impose on himself what is comparable to punitive damages, and the adjustment will be greater than is expected.

A case in point is that of the woman who purchased an expensive pair of shoes at a fine store in a city some distance from her home town. She wore the pair of shoes for a few days, and the soles separated from the tops. She bundled up the shoes and returned them with a firm, unruffled request for a replacement or credit. Within a few days she received a replacement. Then the same problem occurred with the second pair of shoes—they were defective, also. She found the address of the manufacturer and returned the shoes to this source with an explanation of her experience. By air mail, she received a reply from the president of the company apologizing profusely for the inconvenience she had experienced, along with an explanation that this particular number had been defective and every attempt had been made to withdraw the shoes from the shelves. The letter enclosed a brochure picturing and describing several new styles of shoes, and the president of this prestigious shoe manufacturing company asked the woman to select TWO pairs of her choice—the extra pair to make up for the trouble and inconvenience she had been caused.

Some women would have been angry at the store as a result of the apparent double inconvenience. Some likely would have returned the shoes with a threat of never patronizing the store again. Yet here is an example of a person who firmly pursued her rightful claim and was rewarded for making a reasonable request. The president of the shoe company actually seemed grateful for a chance to explain the problem and make amends.

All adjustments are not this cheerfully made, and some claims must be pressed. If the claim is legitimate, don't give up after the first rebuff. As a matter of principle and duty to your fellow consumers, keep after what is rightfully yours. The nearest I ever came to giving up in disgust had to do with an order for natural vitamins that I made to an Eastern firm on October 30, 1971. I had filled out an order blank and enclosed my check for $28.70. Fortunately, I kept a copy of the order. Although the check was processed November 5, 1971, I did not receive my order; so on December 11 I wrote a letter enclosing a copy of the order and asked why I had not received it. In answer to my letter I received a form card asking me to list my order and to indicate the amount of the check, the date of the order, etc. Although I had indicated all of this in my first follow-up, I repeated the order. I went through this procedure three times, December 11, December 23, and January 9. On February 1, 1972, I wrote to the president of the firm and to the bank where my check was processed to see if the company was still in business. This brought a letter from the company's Director of Consumer Affairs. Here it is:

Dear Mrs. Hallock:

This responds to your February 1 letter concerning the non-receipt of an October order.

If you will be kind enough to advise me what type of products were involved, as well as sizes, we will be in a more intelligent position to assist you.

We have been in business for over 40 years, and it certainly is not our policy to accept a customer's money and not ship the merchandise.

My personal envelope is enclosed for your convenience in replying.

We deeply regret the inconvenience caused.

Sincerely,

Since I had sent a copy of the order three times, it was obvious to me that this company had a problem of the right hand's not knowing what the left hand was doing. I made another copy and received no reply to my letter; so I turned a history of my problem over to the Administrator of Consumer Services at the Oregon Department of Commerce. This brought action. Finally, after more than three months, I received a refund check along with this letter:

Dear Mrs. Hallock:

Thank you for your letter of February 9.

A check reveals that a refund check for $28.70 was sent to you on February 8 by another department to cover the loss of your original order. It is assumed that the package was lost enroute. It is, as you know, a long trip from the East to the West coast.

Sincerely,

This Director of Consumer Affairs also sent a letter to the Department of Commerce reporting that the refund check had been sent to me. I resisted the temptation to write one more letter in response to the "long trip" bit, saying that I didn't realize that they were still using Pony Express.

The Consumer Service Division reports that by far the most problems are with mail order businesses.

Before this service had been set up by the Oregon State Legislature, I made reports to local or national Better Business Bureaus, and I have found the service to be excellent.

One response from the National Better Business Bureau brought me an explanation, but not an adjustment. Here is this story in brief. I had ordered a tree from an Eastern firm from an advertisement in a city newspaper. The tree cost $6 and was guaranteed to grow the "height of the eaves" in two seasons. This was just what we needed in front of a large picture window. The small tree arrived all right in a tube, and we very carefully followed directions and planted it in just the right spot. Our friends and neighbors wondered about our "twig" in the ground, and we received a good deal of ribbing. A stick is exactly what it was; the Better Business Bureau reported that the two men who had perpetrated this hoax of sending out twigs in response to tree orders were resting in the penitentiary. They were apprehended as a result of complaints, and if it hadn't been for those complaints, these men would still be sending out twigs at $6 each.

Even small orders should be pursued to the point of settlement. The theory has been advanced that frequently small orders are not sent until an inquiry is made, for many people actually forget that they have made the order, or it is too small to be worth writing a letter about.

Nothing is more frustrating than to have some purchase or service be unsatisfactory. Merchants and other businesses spend millions of dollars developing their products or services and then advertising them. If they are reputable organizations, they welcome legitimate claims. How else would they know that their products are unsatisfactory? They are eager for a second chance to prove themselves, and if the volume of similar complaints is high, they are quick to make necessary changes.

Except for the formula for writing a claim letter, there are no specific rules to follow, but here are some suggestions worth considering:

1.   Be very sure that your claim is justified. Don't attempt to get an adjustment if you are responsible for damage to a product, and don't try to take advantage of a service. Don't, for instance, complain about charges on a long distance telephone call unless you are absolutely sure that you or someone in your office or household did not make the call. Don't try to get a new watch for one you have accidentally dropped.

2.   Be sure to include all facts with regard to your claim. If it involves a product, cite the date of purchase, the price, and any identifying information. If it is a service, give dates and complete information and state specifically how the service deviated from your idea of what it should have been.

3.   If you feel that you know exactly what adjustment you should have, propose a specific remedy. Do you want a replacement, repairs, refund, credit? Be realistic, but be specific. Remember, if you feel reasonably sure that the person who receives your letter will agree with your claim, he might not only make an adjustment, but he might also compensate you for your inconvenience. Don't, for instance, be like the irate customer who complained about a rollaway bed's being sent to her residence instead of to her summer cottage. She said in her letter, "Now, just what are you going to do about this?" How would the recipient know what she wants? Her abusive accusation told how she had needed it for a guest, and she implied this need had passed. Did she want to return it for credit? Did she want it taken from her residence to the summer home, or was she just letting off steam? How was the adjuster to know what to do? All he could do was to apologize and wait for further instructions.

48

4. Tell the truth—don't exaggerate, but tell the whole truth including specifically how you have been inconvenienced. Don't overstate or understate.

5. Be calm. Don't threaten. Remember, no one is prompted to regard your claim favorably if you lose your temper or call names.

6. Don't procrastinate. Your prompt complaint will result in a quicker adjustment or explanation and will prevent other consumers from having similar experiences.

7. If you feel that your claim is completely justified and that there should be no question about an adjustment, direct your letter to the customer relations department or to the department that is directly involved. If it is serious, if an immediate adjustment is important, if a great deal of money is involved, or if the customer relations department has not responded satisfactorily, direct your letter to some executive—to the owner himself in the case of a smaller business.

8. If you feel that you are being given the run-around, go to the VERY top. If, for instance, your problem has to do with your car, and your local dealer has failed to give you the service you feel your warranty promises, write to the manufacturer. One young businessman, for instance, who received poor service on his new car, compiled a two-page chronological list of his failure to get proper service and sent this to the president of the car manufacturing corporation. The letter was so articulate that the president determined that the car must be one of those infrequent "lemons," and the complainer was given a new car. The dealer could very well have handled this adjustment and created goodwill on the local level, but he gave the car owner the run-around. Even after the adjustment was made, this businessman felt that he would not be willing to take a chance of subjecting himself to the indignities he had gone through with the dealer. Next time, he would buy another make of car. Car manufacturers and local dealers don't seem to realize that although car performance is important, service is the determining factor in repeat business. People frequently pass up buying the car of their choice because of a dealer's reputation for poor service. Legitimate letters of complaint might prompt better service on the local level. This very legitimate technique could apply to appliances or any nationally advertised product which is subject to service.

9. If going to the top brings no satisfaction, write to the local Better Business Bureau if there is one. This Bureau will handle complaints only after they have been submitted to the company involved. If a town has no Better Business Bureau, the local Chamber of Commerce will frequently investigate legitimate dissatisfaction. One such Chamber has been known to look into complaints of tourists who write after having shopped in a town that service or merchandise was poor. One local Chamber investigated a new concern which made collections on the basis of telephone solicitations for a service not yet set up in the area. Innumerable inquiries prompted this investigation, whereas one complaint might not have been considered significant. A legitimate complaint protects not only the complainer but other consumers as well. Such complaints are, actually, a civic duty.

10.   Complaints need not be limited to services or products but could well include deceptive advertising, broken promises resulting in inconveniences, rude salespeople, situations which jeopardize safety, unseemly noise, or any other situation which warrants a valid gripe. You are not being big-hearted to suffer in silence; actually, you are being a bit of a coward.

11.   If a serious complaint involves loss of money, time, or a reputation, you are wise to consult an attorney. Frequently a claim letter stating such intentions will bring a response and a subsequent adjustment. However, unless you are actually prepared to go to an attorney, don't bluff—be prepared to carry out your threat. This kind of situation would call for a statement such as: "If I do not hear from you by March 12, I shall turn this matter over to my attorney." If you receive no response by March 12, then let the attorney take it from there. Your communication with the attorney, whether it be personal or by writing, should be preceded by careful notation of all facts in the case. Such attention to detail will expedite the attorney's responsibility and will save you money.

However, before you go to an attorney, remember to seek satisfaction at the source of the problem; and, then, if this results in no adjustment or response, go first to the top, then to the Better Business Bureau or the Chamber of Commerce. If your state is fortunate enough to have a Consumer Services Division of the Department of Commerce, use this as your source for help. This service will relieve the Council of Better Business Bureaus in New York of wide-spread claims. This Council, however, will usually provide reports on services or products which have been investigated previously.

In making a report to any source, follow directions in Chapter 3 for the letter of inquiry. State all facts clearly and make the letter easy to answer. Avoid the "tattling" approach of a too personal complaint. It might help if your complaint is stated in such a way that you seem to be concerned about protecting other consumers. Remember, you are protected by other consumers' complaints. Above all, be honest and objective. A self-addressed and stamped envelope may be more likely to assure you of a prompt answer.

Reliable United States manufacturers and retailers agree that individuals and businesses do not complain enough. How else, except by complaints, will they know if their products are unsatisfactory? Executives of large companies agree that their millions of dollars spent in advertising each year should be followed by a careful evaluation of consumer reaction. Some of them send out questionnaires to determine this, but they would much rather have consumers be more sophisticated in their complaints. Remember the example in Chapter 1 of the man who complained about his light bill. The accusatory letter—pointing a finger at big companies which take advantage of their customers—would never bring the desired investigation. Utility companies provide invaluable services, and, although like any other businesses, they can make mistakes, they admit that they receive far more letters of complaint than of appreciation. It is so easy to "soften the blow" with compliments of good service, and this type of letter is more likely to get the desired response.

Follow carefully the preceding directions. If you ever receive less than the best in service, complain. If you are hurt, SCREAM.

Nothing is easier to understand than the apostrophe if it is presented correctly. For some reason many people seem to take a handful of apostrophes and throw them at the written page. Perhaps the written or typed sheet looks bare; so, when writers come across words that end with the letter s, they simply decorate that word with a little apostrophe. This mark of punctuation serves a real purpose, and its purpose is specific. Use it only where it belongs. Let's take the first use.

This is the contraction. This use of the apostrophe simply means that something has been left out. We talk contractions more than we write them. We seldom say I shall or you are. We say I'll and you're. Written correspondence is usually a little more precise than spoken communication. The trend for friendly informality in business letters, however, has allowed some use of contractions.

Here are some typical examples of most frequently used contractions. Where the apostrophe is, something has been left out.

I'm — I am		we're — we are	
I'll — I shall or I will		it's — it is, it has	
you've — you have		*(never* belonging to it)	
he'll — he will		wouldn't — would not	
can't — cannot		would've — would have	
won't — will not		should've — should have	
(Dictionaries, even my large new Random House, fail to explain this irregularity.)		it'll — it will (seldom write this)	

To form the possessive of a word, add an apostrophe and an s ('s) if the word does not end with s. Add only the apostrophe if the word does end with s. There is no sense in fooling around with plurals in this rule; simply determine whether or not the word ends with s. Notice the correct use of the apostrophe in the following possessives: boy's, boys', lady's, ladies', instructor's, instructors', attorney's, attorneys', man's, men's, children's. Note that the rule follows on these last two plural words. They do not end with s.

While it is never wrong to add an apostrophe and an s to a name that ends with s, custom and sound have accepted as a general rule the following: A one-syllable name that ends with s adds the apostrophe and s ('s) to make it possessive. A two or more syllable name ending in s adds only the apostrophe ('):
Mr. Jones's house, Mr. Hopkins' car, Miss Fitzgibbons' books

To form the possessive of a compound noun like sister-in-law, simply add the apostrophe and s ('s) to the last word: sister-in-law's. If you refer to two sisters—in—law the apostrophe and s still go at the end of the word: sisters-in-law's.

Usually avoid the apostrophe and <u>s</u> with an inanimate object: the blue of the sky (not the sky's blue), the door of the house (not the house's door).

When two or more names are thought of as one organization, the <u>'s</u> is used only on the final name: Meier and Frank's, Miller and Park's.

Have a reason for using the apostrophe. Don't throw this punctuation mark at the page indiscriminately. Try not to suffer from a bad case of the misplaced apostrophe.

Assignments

1.   Revise the following letter using the TRI-ASK TECHNIQUE:

Gentlemen:

On February 16 I ordered 3200 square yards of carpeting from your company. Your representative promised that this would be delivered and installed by April 1 in time for an open house to be held April 10.

I really think that your salesman was so eager to make the sale on the large order that he made promises he knew his company couldn't fulfill.

Well, just tell that salesman that unless all of the carpeting is installed by not later than April 3, you might just as well rip out the carpeting installed in the three apartments, because I won't pay for any of it unless all of it is installed as promised.

Please let me know your intentions.

Yours truly,

Ray Banfield
(Banfield Enterprises)

2.   Answer the preceding letter with a counter claim explaining that twice your carpet layers had delivered carpeting and were prevented from proceding with the job because workmen had not finished plastering and wiring. Tell Mr. Banfield that if your men are further prevented from proceding with the work he will receive a bill not only for the carpeting installed in the three apartments, but for the trips his installers made when they were prevented from working.

3. Revise the following letter:

Gentlemen:

On January 5 I received a bill from your company for plumbing service which took place in October. I received the first bill for this early in November and it was paid November 9. I have the canceled check to prove it.

I received another statement December 1—after I had already paid the bill, mind you. I returned the statement to you with a notation that it had already been paid.

And now I have received another bill for this service which, may I remind you, was performed in October and paid for in November within five days of receipt of the statement. This last statement indicates extra charge for late payment.

Now, I just wonder what kind of game you are playing. I suppose some people might be stupid enough to pay a bill twice, but not me. I keep my books straight and I pay my bills on time. If your plumbing service is no better than your bookkeeping, I'd better get another plumber next time.

Now get this paid bill straightened out and quit sending me duplicate statements or you'll have trouble on your hands.

Emphatically,

Richard Meier

Study Review Test

Indicate in the space below each word the correct possessive of that word:

1. attorney

2. men

3. directors

4. children

5. lady

6. Jones and Jackson (store)

7. Moore Co.

8. hours

9. sons-in-law

10. pharmacist

11. months

12. cities

13. Mr. Glass

14. Mr. Phillips

15. women

16. hours

17. notary public

18. manager

19. countries

20. companies

Study Review Test

Study the underscored phrases in the following sentences.

If the possessive is correct, write C in front of the sentence number.

If the possessive is not correct, draw a line through the word(s) and write the correct form above the sentence.

1. Her <u>mother-in-laws'</u> car was parked near the store.

2. The <u>treasurers'</u> report was made on time.

3. He did four <u>months'</u> work.

4. John received his <u>master's</u> degree.

5. <u>Mens' and boy's</u> suits were on sale.

6. He retired after forty <u>years'</u> work with the company.

7. The decision was a result of four <u>mens'</u> opinions.

8. <u>Franklyn's and Roger's</u> store had a sale every Friday.

9. The money yielded a <u>year-and-a-halfs'</u> interest.

10. Mr. Rogers gladly answered <u>customers'</u> complaints.

chapter five

when someone screams at you
(the adjustment letter — or refusal)

A claim letter is, in a way, a kind of criticism—and no one likes to be criticized. The immediate and natural response is to be defensive. How is it possible that I could be accused of doing something wrong? Most claim letters are directed to business or branches of the Government, but it is entirely possible that they could be directed on a very personal basis. You could, you know, receive a letter claiming that your dog had ruined a newly planted garden, or that your son had damaged, with his birthday knife, a choice three-year-old tree. These claims cannot be answered with blunt denials. Whether or not the claim is true, it must have a response.

When criticism involves your business, your life blood so to speak, the natural reaction is resentment. Quite likely you may react emotionally when a claim is made and when your business is questioned. Your response will be one of two—you will grant the adjustment or you will refuse it. Either of these involves personal consideration, but either is accomplished easily with the formulas you will study in this chapter.

Four considerations will precede your actual answer. Here they are:

1. Any complaint should be answered promptly, preferably within 24 hours.

2. Remember that even though you may regard your answer as time-consuming, the letter you are about to answer is important to the person who wrote it, and your answer is important to you.

3. The answer should avoid being arrogant or critical. Don't condescend; don't point your finger.

4. The answer should be honest and courteous, with no hint of compromising the dignity of either the writer or the recipient.

Bearing in mind these considerations, you must next decide the specific course of your response. A claim will either be granted or it will be refused, and company policy largely determines the nature of the response. Relatively few businesses follow the "customer is always right" policy. Such companies deal largely in very expensive merchandise designed for an exclusive clientele. Losses incurred by the use of such a general practice would result in higher prices' being absorbed by the customer, a policy which could drive customers to competitors.

59

Another impractical response, at the other end of the spectrum, is the "caveat emptor" policy—let the buyer beware—which means, "If you avail yourself of our services, and you have paid for it, you've had it; don't come back complaining." Such a policy would result in a word-of-mouth reputation which would break a company in short order.

Any practical person would consider neither the "customer is always right" policy nor the "caveat emptor" one. By far the most prevalent and practical policy is to grant adjustments when the claim seems fair. This means refusing ridiculous requests like the one in the first chapter of the woman who wanted credit for the difference in the price she paid for a sport jacket and a sale price two weeks later. Any claim should be considered carefully with the decision made on the merit of the specific case. It is difficult not to be paranoid about criticism, particularly of your own service or product. Your equitable response, however, could be an opportunity to create good human relations—a challenge to lose neither your dignity nor your customer. Success in business depends not only on wooing customers and friends but in keeping them.

Your reaction to a claim will be reflex. Your client will tell his friends that your response was good or that it was poor, and of such reports will your image be created. Yielding to an urge to tell a person off or to cut him down will damage your image and hurt you and your business.

Let's imagine that you or your company has made a mistake and that a client is perfectly justified in his claim. Your first reaction may quite likely be one of impatience with yourself or your employees, with the result that you hasten to provide a scapegoat or offer a rationalization. Such excuses may make you feel better, but they are not readily accepted by your claimant. Ask yourself what he wants to hear, and if you are objective and honest, the answer to this is twofold. First, he wants to hear that you admit the responsibility for the error, and then he wants to be quite sure that he will receive an adjustment.

In granting an adjustment, think first of the TRI-ASK TECHNIQUE, and then the specific formula:

First: What do I want to accomplish?

The answer to this is to make the adjustment acceptable to the claimant.

Second: How am I going to do this? Here we have the specific formula, and it's very simple:

1. Apologize.
2. Adjust.
3. Explain. (Include any necessary directions.)
4. Create goodwill.

Now write the letter; then ask the last question: How would I feel if I were to receive this letter?

Actually put yourself in the place of the person receiving the letter. If, for any reason, you feel that it expresses any reluctance in making the adjustment or any rationalization in the explanation, then quite likely the letter should be re-written. Remember that re-writing letters may seem unpleasant at first, but achieving a desirable effect will come naturally with a little practice.

Suppose that you receive a letter from a retailer complaining that he had received six dozen men's shirts which appeared to be water damaged. The retailer was both unhappy and disappointed, since the dress shirts he ordered were to be featured at a spring showing. Suppose, on checking, you found that a new employee in the shipping department was responsible for the mistake. Your first reaction, very likely, would be annoyance at the new employee, but your chastisement of him would in no way lessen the inconvenience to your customer, nor would it make amends. The discussion of the seriousness of such an error with the employee can wait. The first responsibility is a letter with an adjustment. Such a letter could be something like this:

Dear Mr. Thomas:

I was dismayed to learn from your letter of March 11 that we had blundered on your order. You will be relieved, I know, to learn that the correct order is being rushed to you by United Parcel, and it will reach you well in advance of your spring showing.

The shirts sent to you by mistake were some that apparently had been damaged by water en route to us. Like you, we were unhappy to receive such merchandise, and it had been put in our stock room awaiting orders for disposal of it. Since the size of the box was similar to your order, a new employee mistakenly sent it to you instead. I believe, in all the years that we have been serving you, that this is the first time we have made a mistake in filling your orders. These things happen occasionally, and we are especially sorry that it should have happened to a favored customer like you.

Will you please hand the damaged shirts to United Parcel when your order is delivered? We have made arrangements for them to be picked up and shipped back to us collect.

To make up for your inconvenience, we have included in your order, as a gift, one dozen color-coordinated ties to accessorize the shirts. We have enclosed an order blank and a price list in the event that you should want more of these colorful ties, which are being featured in several men's magazines.

You will be receiving our new catalogue soon so that you may place your fall order early. We'll make every effort to be especially careful with your next shipment.

Sincerely,

Note how the formula has been used. The apology is followed in the first paragraph by a notice of adjustment. A full and satisfactory explanation is given, and goodwill is expressed by a gift to make up for the inconvenience. Note that directions for disposition of the damaged goods are fully explained. While this may not appear to be part of the formula, any letter should cover each situation carefully so that further correspondence is not necessary. If directions for returning the damaged shirts had not been included, two more letters would have been involved—one asking for directions and another answering this inquiry. Careful handling of each situation will save time and money. So, under the third part of the formula, remember to explain not only the reason for the error but also to outline any necessary directions to the claimant.

Any time a letter is received claiming that merchandise is faulty, the adjustment should be handled on the merit of the claim. In the case of mechanical equipment, the apparent defect may be a case of the client's not knowing how to handle it. Actually, many service calls on electrical appliances are made because electrical connections have come unplugged. Suggestions and explanations should be made with an offer of personal inspection in the event that suggestions don't work. Customers appreciate an understanding and patient explanation, and they especially appreciate saving the cost of a service call. Such a letter, adapted in every case to the specific situation, would follow this formula:

1.   Acknowledgment of the complaint with the claim re-worded

2.   Possible suggestions which could simplify the remedy

3.   An offer to make a prompt check if the suggestions do not solve the problem

(Depending on the situation, this offer could be instructions for returning the product for repair, or promise of a service call. The claimant should be reminded of the terms of the guarantee—which might include charges for shipping or for parts. If the products still fall under the time limit for unconditional guarantee, a prompt and full offer of restitution should be made. Nothing will hurt business more than a client who feels that the guarantee is not valid and that he has been "taken." His friends will learn about this in short order. A satisfied customer is the best advertising in the world. Time spent on adjustment letters and money spent on adjustments are worth more than any elaborate advertising program. Remember to make amends graciously, never grudgingly.)

Occasionally there are situations in which a customer may be placated by a compromise on an adjustment, even though this is neither a legal nor a moral obligation. Suppose a customer has purchased a watch from your jewelry department and, within a month after the purchase, he returns the watch because it has stopped running. Because of a guarantee, he says he expects a full adjustment. On examining the watch, your jeweler determines that it has been dropped or severely jarred and a part has actually been broken. There is no reason for an apology in such a situation, since the merchandise was not defective. However, you do understand the customer's dismay at having a new watch stop running. A formula for this type of situation is as follows:

1.   An attempt to relate to the claimant's problem and agree with him in some way

2.   An explanation of the situation

3.   A gentle refusal of complete adjustment, with the concession you will make

4.   A request for acceptance of the concession

5.   An expression of goodwill

62

The following is an example of this type of letter:

Dear Mr. Arthur:

We quite understand how lost you must feel without your fine Executive watch which we received in the mail this morning. You will be relieved to know that nothing is seriously wrong with it.

Our jeweler has already examined the watch carefully, and he found that it appears to have been dropped or jarred, and a small but important part of the mechanism has been broken. You understand, of course, although the watch is guaranteed for two years against all defects in workmanship or materials, this type of damage is not covered.

We shall, however, be glad to put your watch in brand new condition for the actual cost of the broken part, $4.95, with no charge to you for the labor involved.

Just mail the enclosed card today, authorizing us to go ahead with repairs, and your watch will be back on your wrist within a week. We know that you will have many years of service from your fine Executive.

Sincerely,

Notice the tenor of this letter. A finger has not been pointed accusing Mr. Arthur of handling his watch carelessly. He has been placed on an intellectual level with the writer, and complete understanding of the situation is implied. The application of the guarantee is explained without an undiplomatic reminder of the terms. The seriousness of the damage is minimized, and a concession in not charging for labor is granted. Authorization for repairing the watch is requested with an easy answer insured by enclosing a self-addressed postcard. A promise of prompt service is assured. Nothing has been left out, and Mr. Arthur, who could possibly have dropped his watch from a window ledge to the pavement below, is likely quite relieved to learn that the situation is not serious and that an inexpensive repair is forthcoming. Another satisfied, unruffled customer.

Now let us consider that most difficult of all letters, the refusal of adjustment. This is the situation in which the claim has been considered and no adjustment can be granted. Some claims are made by those who do not really expect an adjustment, but who operate on the "nothing ventured, nothing gained" philosophy. They feel it never hurts to try.

Regardless of the intent or justification of the claimant, the refusal of adjustment follows a definite formula, and here it is:

1. Soften the blow before you lower the boom.

2. Refuse.

3. Explain.

4. Give an alternative.

5. Create goodwill.

It is that simple. Psychologically, a person will accept a rebuff or a refusal if the blow is softened. This comes first, always. Then the refusal should be made, although sometimes this is made so subtly that no negative words are used. As Chapter 2 outlined, such negative words as unfortunately, sorry, and refuse are simply not used. If something is unfortunate, attention should not be called to this fact. You are never sorry unless you have done something for which you must apologize, and refuse is a harsh word that can be averted by such an expression as "I cannot grant your request. . ." with an explanation following immediately.

This type of letter was illustrated in the first chapter, but another example might impress the importance of the formula. Suppose you are the owner of a sports equipment store or that your general store carries this type of merchandise and that Mrs. Conrad has responded to your special sale by selecting a golf equipment set including clubs—four woods, eight irons, and a putter, plus a bag and cart for the total price of $249. She has paid $25 down and has signed a contract agreeing to pay $25 a month plus interest for the balance. She agreed to pick up the clubs after the first of the next month in time for her husband's birthday. Now, three weeks later, you have received a letter from her asking for a refund of the $25 with the explanation that she has found a similar set of different make for $200. Since the special has been off for more than two weeks, and since she signed a contract, you are fully justified in refusing her request. Let's tackle it, using the formula:

1.   What do I want to accomplish?

The answer to this is to refuse her request in such a way that she will accept the refusal—we want to keep her goodwill.

2.   How am I going to do this?

First we'll soften the blow, then we'll refuse with an explanation of our refusal, offer her an alternative, if we can, and end with a note of goodwill.

Something like this:

Dear Mrs. Conrad:

You showed excellent judgment in selecting the fine Ellsworth clubs for your husband's birthday. He is sure to be pleased.

Other similar golf equipment, Mrs. Conrad, may cost less, but the quality cannot compare to the Ellsworth name. Our special purchase made this fine set available to you at a price much lower than usual. You were fortunate to be able to take advantage of our sale.

A contract, of course, protects both of us, and prevents either from a change of mind. If someone were to come in and offer to pay cash for your set, we would not be privileged to take his money, since your set is reserved for you. The $25 you paid on it makes it yours. I know you understand.

> We have added to your husband's surprise and pleasure by including half a dozen fine Ellsworth balls in the pocket of the bag. He will be proud to be playing golf with the best equipment, and he will be grateful to you for thinking enough of him to select the best.
>
> We look forward to seeing you when you come in to pick up your husband's clubs next week.
>
> Sincerely,

There is no need in this letter for any negative words. This letter reassured Mrs. Conrad of the wisdom of her choice, and it has explained how the contract protected her as well as the store. A concession by way of the golf balls adds to this reassurance, and a definite reference to her picking up the clubs and the resulting pleasure of her husband leaves no room for argument or doubt in her mind.

You see, the TRI-ASK TECHNIQUE takes the dread out of writing even the most difficult letter. Always use the specific formula, and never forget that third question: How would I feel if I were to receive this letter? This is the YOU attitude. If, when you put yourself in the place of the person receiving your letter, you find that you are willing to accept what has been said with no feeling of resentment, the letter is a success.

Study Review — 1

Study each of the following spelling rules and their explanations.

(This is not a complete course in spelling. The rules cited here will be useful to you in spelling correctly words that are frequently misspelled.)

A two-syllable word ending in a consonant preceded by a vowel doubles the final consonant when a suffix is added that begins with a vowel IF (and this is the important clue) the accent of that word is on the second syllable.

For example, take the word defer. Divide it into syllables:

de-fer

The word ends in a consonant (r) which is preceded by a vowel (e).

Now let's add a suffix (which means ending) — ed.

But before we add this ending, check the accent. Pronounce the word, and we find that the accent IS on the second syllable: de-fer'; so, by adding the ed, the word becomes deferred.

On the other hand, if a two-syllable word ending in a consonant preceded by a vowel has the accent on the first syllable, the final consonant is not doubled when the suffix that starts with a vowel is added.

Take the word differ, which, in a way, is similar to defer.

Each of these words ends in a consonant preceded by a vowel, and each word has two syllables. But here the similarity ends. The accent in differ is on the first syllable:

dif'fer   By adding ed , it becomes differed.

Be aware of syllables and the kinds of suffixes that are added; then you have it made. This is a useful rule.

Observe:

occur	oc-cur'	occurred	occurring	(the r is doubled)
admit	ad-mit'	admitted	admitting	admittance
allot	al-lot'	allotted	allotting	BUT allotment

Observe that ment, the suffix, does not begin with a vowel.

confer	con-fer'	conferred	conferring	BUT conference

Note in the word con'-fer-ence, the accent is thrown back to the first syllable.

Study Review - 2

The following is a general rule and its exception. This rule and its exception cover a wide range of commonly misspelled words.

Drop the (silent) e when adding a suffix that begins with a vowel:

hope — hoping   love — loving   give — giving
       hoped   lovable

The able words seem to give the most trouble:

believable,   censurable,   likable, etc.

However, there is an exception, and it is easy to identify.

Here it is:

When able or ous are added to words that end with ge or ce (and the ge and c in each case must have the soft sound) the e is retained.

THIS RULE HAS ONLY TO DO WITH WORDS ENDING IN ABLE OR OUS.

changeable   peaceable   courageous   exchangeable
manageable   advantageous   chargeable   serviceable   etc.

66

A LETTER WITH A MISSPELLED WORD IS NOT MAILABLE.

Normally, when a suffix beginning with a consonant is added to a word ending in <u>e</u>, the <u>e</u> is retained:

improvement likely requirement encouragement

However, there are a few exceptions. Memorize the following:

truly	abridgment**
wholly	lodgment**
duly	judgment**
*ninth	acknowledgment**
awful	*argument

*Most frequently missed.
**May be spelled either way.

ASSIGNMENTS

Assignment 1

Revise the following letter:

Gentlemen:

I am so angry and upset it is difficult for me to write this letter.

Ten days ago at your ramp sale I purchased a complete set of patio furniture in green—two loungers, six breakfast chairs, two arm chairs—all upholstered in green, plus one large umbrella table with—you guessed it—a green umbrella.

I selected these personally and was promised by the salesman that they would be delivered to our new summer home in the Winding River area not later than Thursday, August 12, in plenty of time for our open house Saturday the 14th.

Well, they arrived, all right, Thursday afternoon at 4 p.m. And guess what! Everything was in bright blue. This may seem trivial to you, but this ruined the color scheme of the party planned around our house colors, brown and green. Blue just didn't fit into the picture at all.

I called your store immediately, but according to your Summer Shop, no green sets would be available until the next week. Apparently the sample set I saw on the ramp was sent to someone else.

We went ahead with the party and so I wouldn't have to make a personal explanation to each guest, I made a large sign which said: "Rowe and Garnell goofed!!! They sent blue patio furniture instead of green. Suggest threat of boycott or promises in writing to make correct deliveries—with penalties for errors."

We tried to make the best of it, but both my husband and I were irritated.

Now will you please deliver to our summer home the furniture in GREEN as we specified and pick up the blue atrocities. Please call me at my home 391-4767 to let me know the time of delivery so I can be on hand to check the order.

Your disappointed customer,

Jane Gibbons
(Mrs. Rollo Gibbons)

Assignment 2

Answer the preceding claim letter admitting that an error was made by the shipping department and granting a credit amounting to a 10 percent discount on the order and apprising Mrs. Gibbons of the time of delivery on the exchange.

Assignment 3

Refer to Assignment 3 of Chapter 4—the letter of complaint from the man who had received statements for a bill he had already paid. Answer this claim letter assuming that errors were made by an inefficient bookkeeper who has since been replaced.

Assignment 4

Use each of the following words in a sentence. Check the dictionary for precise meaning if you are not absolutely sure.

1. cite
2. sight
3. site
4. stationery
5. stationary
6. to
7. too
8. past
9. passed
10. capitol
11. capital
12. compliment
13. complement
14. forth
15. fourth
16. they're
17. there
18. their
19. appraise
20. apprise

chapter six

the "out" letter

The OUT letter is the real thing. A flyer practices with his instructor or the trainer until he gets the hang of flying, and then he solos. A student driver gets expert instruction and practice, and then he takes off by himself. By the same token, after all this practice and theory of letter writing, you will outline and write a real letter using the technique you have learned.

At the beginning of this term, your class, and quite likely you as a member of the class, readily admitted that letter writing is something that you avoid or put off. If you are like members of my classes, you will also admit that you have actually neglected writing letters that should have been written. Give a little time and thought to the planning of your OUT letter. Above all, it should be not a nuisance letter but some kind of message from which you would really like to have an answer.

I always prime the pump by reading letters written by my former students, and then describing or reading the answers. I keep carbon copies of all the letters that go out, and I have in my files either the answers or the photocopies of most of them. I classify the letter types as follows: claim letters, inquiries, letters to public officials, letters about job responsibilities (not application letters), fan letters, and—well, just special letters. Let me tell you about some of them.

CLAIM LETTERS

First the claim letter—this should be a legitimate claim, and as such, it follows the TRI-ASK TECHNIQUE by softening the blow first, then explaining the claim, citing the inconvenience, if any, and occasionally suggesting an adjustment.

The blow softener need not be extensive or flowery, and if the claim is obviously legitimate with no anticipation of adjustment problems, then perhaps it is better to "get with it." A breakage en route or a product with a missing part so clearly merits an adjustment that a flowery blow-softener would be out of place. Usually, however, a note of appreciation or commendation breaks the blow of the claim that follows.

Students have been surprised to have so little trouble in getting fair adjustments to legitimate claims. One clothing store replaced a defective sweater gladly and thanked the girl for calling the problem to their attention. One girl wrote apprising a large food

69

company that its potato chip bags were only half full. This brought a beautiful letter, signed by the Marketing Planning Manager, expressing appreciation for the opportunity to explain that new automatic control equipment had just been installed to give uniform fill level. He expressed regret that the bags she had purchased had seemed less than full, and he told her that arrangements had been made to send her a package of gift items. The letter was beautifully typed in full block style, and it was perfectly centered on the page.

Another girl wrote to a large appliance manufacturer expressing her disappointment in the operation of an electric spray iron. Her answer was explicit instructions on how to operate the iron by what was called a "home treatment." The fine letter ended: "Thank you for giving us this opportunity of serving you. All of our customers are important to us, and if we can do anything more at any time, please call on us." This was signed by the Company Counselor, another instance of a big company's having time for its customers.

Here is a letter written to a florist which is self-explanatory:

Dear Mr. Florist:

On Monday afternoon, February 21, I was very pleased to receive a lovely floral arrangement of yellow roses and baby's breath.

However, by this morning, February 23, they had completely wilted. They were not in sunlight nor were they near any artificial heat. Also, the temperature of the room in which they were is kept at 68 degrees.

Many times I have received roses and other floral arrangements from your shop, but this is the first time this has happened. If you feel that I have not cared for the flowers properly, I would appreciate suggestions you might have for the care of cut flowers.

Sincerely,

On the afternoon of February 25, the writer of this letter received another arrangement of roses and baby's breath with the following handwritten card: "Sorry the roses didn't hold up for you. Hope you enjoy these." Such response restores faith in human nature and restores the satisfaction of a customer.

One girl wrote to a cookware firm asking about her stainless ware that showed evidences of rusting. Her answer expressed appreciation for the opportunity to explain what had happened, with directions on prevention of rust. The letter ended this way, "Thank you very much for writing to us, and we appreciate the opportunity to be of service." It was signed by the head of the Consumer Service Department.

Another girl received a check from a bus company to reimburse her for taxi expense she incurred by having to make an extra trip for her luggage, which had not been put on her bus.

A young man wrote to a large food processing company, explaining that as a bachelor he enjoyed cooking and particularly appreciated cake mixes which made his cooking easy with professional results. However, (he said, lowering the boom), when he opened a box of his favorite cake mix, he was shocked to find that it was—well, infested. He asked for no adjustment, but simply explained that his ardor for cake making was somewhat dampened. A prompt answer explained that such infestation could not possibly have happened at the production end; this must have occurred on the shelves (possibly in the storeroom) of the market where the product was sold. The answer included coupons for three free cake mixes and a request for the name of the market where the cake mix had been purchased.

One girl explained to a large candy maker that she had found a foreign object in her favorite candy bar, and she wrapped this in a small piece of tissue and enclosed it with her letter. Her answer was signed by no less than the president of the company explaining that a laboratory test proved that the foreign object was a piece of peanut root. The apology included the explanation that "we always attempt to guard against such instances, and we have our own personnel as well as electronic devices to detect such foreign matter as you found. Even with these precautions, sometimes some small objects are overlooked. We are very grateful that you did not incur any damage. Separately we are sending you a box of X bars hoping that you continue to enjoy them every day." The president then even added a handwritten postscript extolling the bar, describing its ingredients are "scrumptuous."

Many letters written to cosmetic companies were personally answered by officers or customer relations representatives. Some offered suggestions for proper use of the product; others offered to replace items that appeared to be unsatisfactory, and a few (very few) sent duplicated letters. A duplicated letter in answer to a claim is the poorest human relations possible, since the necessity for multiple letters would indicate many complaints. A duplicated letter would indicate the line of least resistance in explaining away some prevailing problem. It would indicate no personal interest and thus could be a factor in losing customers.

One young married man wrote to a large motor company complaining that because of his youth he had been "brushed off" by salesmen of several local distributors in the area. He was actually interested in buying this make of car, but he had not been offered the courtesy of a demonstration. One day when he arrived home from school, a beautiful new sport model Car X was sitting in front of his apartment with a salesman behind the wheel. During the ensuing demonstration drive, the salesman confessed that the letter had shaken up the company and had resulted in its calling a Northwest sales meeting to discuss the situation.

This demonstration was followed by a letter from the Vice President and General Manager of the company stating in part, "We found your comments concerning the lack of follow-up demonstrated by several Car X salesmen quite disturbing" with an explanation of notification to the Northwest Division and the local distributor. This letter writer concluded, "Thank you for bringing this matter to our attention."

You see, claim letters are not merely headaches to be adjusted grudgingly; they frequently are favors to the recipients who cannot be aware of a situation unless someone tells them. Usually claims result in better service to the consumer and more profit for the producer. In this sense, they are a duty—a moral obligation.

71

The letter of inquiry, as you know, is a means of asking and receiving. It is the obligation of anyone in business or in government to disseminate pertinent information about his work, and he should be ready to answer questions. Besides disliking to write letters, most people procrastinate when it comes to a letter that does not actually HAVE to be written. This negligence leaves them ignorant of information that might prove to be significant, pertinent, and even profitable.

One young lady in my class wrote as her "out" letter an inquiry to a large corporation explaining that she was a new member of the "do-it-yourself" stock market speculators and that she was interested in a stock with a steady and safe return on investment. She said that before she invested she wanted to examine closely the financial conditions and future possibilities of the corporations in which she planned to invest. She asked for a copy of the annual report to stockholders and other information which would give her a clear and comprehensive picture of the corporation. This was a serious request, since she was married, she had no children, and, with her training nearly behind her, she and her husband, with their two salaries, were seriously thinking of starting a portfolio of investments.

A different kind of inquiry was that of a mother who suspected that her son had dyslexia, a physical condition evidenced by serious reading impairment. She wrote to a prominent pediatrician, requesting information on a clinic or specialist dealing with this condition. Her response was a hand-written note from the physician describing dyslexia as being secondary to hyperactivity-distractibility, and he gave her the name and phone number of a specialist who had been working with the condition.

A young mother wrote to the Consumer Association of New York, asking for a list of dangerous toys about which she had read in a women's magazine. Because of the "overwhelming response to the work of our organization," it was quite natural that she should receive a duplicated letter. This letter was complete in its directions on how to obtain up-to-date lists from a branch of the Government and how to acquire slide presentations. She was apprised of a television program entitled, "Let the Buyer Beware," and was given encouragement in making others aware of the danger of some toys.

One woman who had acquired a ready-made family by marrying a minister who had seven children wrote to Billy Graham for advice on how to handle problems she hadn't anticipated, without resorting to tranquilizers. While the answer did not come from Billy Graham himself, she did receive a personal and definitive reply from a "Spiritual Counselor" and the promise of a copy of Mr. Graham's book *The Christ Centered Home*.

I suppose you might say that the letters written by students run from the sublime to the ridiculous, and a contrast to the Billy Graham letter was one to Hugh Hefner of Playboy fame. This student said she had recently become acquainted with Playboy magazine (she left me to wonder how). Her letter in part is as follows: "Your world-renowned Bunnies are of interest to me, and it is about them that I am writing. I would like to know how one goes about becoming a Playboy Bunny. I much admire you for stressing that your girls are more than just cheesecakes with empty smiles and hollow heads. I am a nineteen-year-old girl of Irish heritage with blue eyes and long blond hair. I weigh 126 pounds, stand 5'7", and measure 38-26-37. I graduated fifth in my high school class of 320 students with a GPA of 3.84, and I maintained a GPA of 3.14 during my one year of college. I am presently enrolled in a fine business college, and I intend to become a legal secretary; but I would very much like to explore the possibilities of pursuing the role of a Bunny while I am still young. Please realize this is not an application. What steps should I take to start me on the road to what I believe would be an exciting and rewarding experience?"

In due time, she received an answer, presumably from the High Mogul himself, thanking her for her interest in Playboy and enclosing an application form along with a questionnaire similar to that of an exclusive girls' school. The letter stressed the high quality of the Bunnies and explained that girls were well chaperoned by Bunny Mothers. Many students have been most generous in giving me their answers for my files (especially if I twist their arms a little), but for some reason, I lost out on this one.

One girl received, in answer to her inquiry about wedding veils, a detailed letter from the Royal Lace Manufactory in Bruxelles, Belgique. (Stamp collectors will recognize this as Brussels, Belgium.) It is interesting to note that while the date and complimentary close were in alignment, closed punctuation was used in the inside address and the paragraph indentation aligned with the salutation (Dear Mademoiselle—17 spaces). The letter opened with "We beg to acknowledge receipt of your letter and thank you for your kind enquiry," and closed with "Hoping to be favoured with your order and assuring you of our best attention, we remain." Apparently, gobbledegook is still the "in" thing in Belgium. We were interested to learn that wedding veils are duty free and that personal checks would be accepted for payment.

A fine explanation was sent by a large paper company in answer to the inquiry of a girl who asked about efforts at controlling water and atmosphere pollution. This two-page letter explained in detail the measures being taken by the company to prevent the release of SO_2 into the atmosphere and the effort to protect fish life. The letter went on to explain about the installation of a new recovery plant. It was interesting to note that 5 copies of this letter were sent out. We couldn't help wondering why, since this was in no way an official inquiry.

At intervals I have requested students to write letters of inquiry about written communication policies. The answers to these letters have added materially to my research and have added greatly to classroom discussion. Consensus is that written communication is of prime importance in any business and that few employees are equipped to turn out good letters. A Vice President of American Can Company wrote, "...correspondence is certainly an integral part of our customer relations program." He added "...a good secretary who can tactfully compose letters of acceptance or refusal or more complicated letters is a jewel beyond price."

The "out" letters asking about correspondence policies frankly expressed a desire to learn from the experience of those in business. Students tried to avoid making their letters seem like run-of-the-mill school assignments, and recipients were selected by the students themselves. Response was most gratifying, and many officials seemed to feel complimented that their opinions had been requested. For instance, an official of a popular fashion magazine wrote that letters to readers were chatty and informative rather than formal, but that letters written strictly for business purposes were less informal in tone. She stressed the importance of correct English and punctuation.

The manager of a large trailer rental organization wrote a detailed two-page letter explaining correspondence policies, stating he does not advocate the use of form letters, as such, but that there are certain areas in the operation of the business that make the use of such letters not only desirable but necessary. Then he enclosed samples of nine form letters. He explained that the organization has certain rules that govern the operation of the members and that duplicated letters expedite the business of reports, reminders, and notices. Occasionally personal notes are handled with the speed letter form, usually written in longhand. However, this manager explained that when the occasion arises, letters are written to answer questions or handle individual cases, and the length and tenor are dictated by the specific situation.

In answer to an "out" letter about correspondence policy, a large Eastern advertising specialty company sent samples of form letters and also a folio of guide letters which secretaries adapt to specific situations. Our class objected, in this case, to the use of the salutation, "Dear Sir," which we avoid, and an initial "We regret to advise you." Regret is a word which we would rarely use, and instead of "advising" the recipients of our letters, we just "get with it." No need to announce what you are going to say—just say it. We did approve, however, of the expression, "We are sure you understand...." We have found that when you tell a person he understands, he usually does.

One letter written to an attorney was answered by his secretary who, we learned, had acquired her basic knowledge of letter writing from my class in correspondence three years before. She did add specific information about reference line and policy of carbons and filing.

A supervisor in the Stenographic Department of Mutual of Omaha wrote a beautiful response exemplifying the modified block style, with the date, reference line, and complimentary close in alignment just a little to the right of center. Since this is my preference, I was happy to see this format. (The exact placement would depend on the length of the name in the closing.) She enclosed a set of general instructions with regard to format, abbreviations, division of words, and directions for second page headings.

A beautiful and dignified letter from the Office Manager of the International Silver

Company indicated that customer relations depend largely on the importance attached to written communication. He stated that, since the company enjoys prestige trade, letters avoid the use of gimmicks and try to exemplify integrity and sincerity. Letters, he said, are friendly without being too familiar, and ". . .our correspondents are allowed to express their personalities, but we insist on correct English and the avoidance of repetition except where necessary to make a specific point."

A recent letter to one of our students from Readers' Service of *TV Guide* indicated that this widely-read and prestigious magazine places a great deal of importance on answering mail, which is divided into three categories: network, TV Guide, and research. Letters received which deal with networks register dismay at shows' cancellations, protests or praise of specific networks or programing, or comments about commercials. Letters dealing with the magazine receive individual attention from the correspondence staff. An unusually large response to a particular article or feature results in the preparation of a specific reply suitable for all letters in question. All letters requesting information (inquiry letters), whether they concern *TV Guide* or programs, are researched. If the answer cannot be provided, the reader is given an address to which he may write for information. All of this requires a great deal of time and attention which includes ". . .complete files, flexible but organized office procedures, a good sense of humor, and a staff of crackerjack letter writers." We felt that the staff member from the Readers' Service of *TV Guide* who provided this information in a page-and-a-half excellently written letter was indeed a crackerjack letter writer himself. We were interested to note that the inside address was at the lower left of the letter several spaces below the complimentary closing, which was centered. The date line was centered just below the very simple letterhead.

One student combined her "out" letter assignment for the correspondence class with a project for her secretarial procedures class by writing to 13 different banks asking for information about letter writing policies. She organized her letters, the answers to each, and her critiques in a binder which she gave to me for my files.

It is interesting to note that the best of these 13 letters came from the larger banks and were signed by the managers. Of the 13, four used full block format (no indentations with date and complimentary close at the left margin), four used block form (no indentations with date and closing aligned near center), and five used semiblock format. Of these five, three used the five-space indentation, two used 10-space, and one, the three-space indentation. Four letters were signed by managers, and with one exception these were excellently written. Other signatures were as follows: two by secretaries, two by assistant cashiers, one by the secretary to the president, one by an executive secretary, one by an assistant manager, and one by a cashier (a woman). Only one, a manager of a very small bank, brushed her off with, "If you will come into the bank at your convenience, we will be glad to discuss this with you and give you any information you might need." Since there were no typist's initials, we surmised that this small-bank manager had typed the letter himself and would rather give the information in person than write a letter. The other three letters from bank managers were excellent, and one even sent samples of letterheads and memo forms. The best letter was written by the Secretary to the President. She typed the letter herself, using neat full block. There were no misspelled words or strikeovers; the letter was perfectly centered on the page. The most complete information came from three managers, all of whom dictated their letters to typists. One of these managers has a reputation for placing great emphasis on writing friendly letters.

These inquiries were, I suppose, nuisance letters of a sort, but the requests explained quite frankly that the questions were asked as part of a research report for school. The recipients might know that the answers would be perused and discussed by members of the classes and that this was an opportunity for goodwill. If the writers could have witnessed the discussion and comparisons, some of them might have taken more care with their answers.

PUBLIC OFFICIALS

Public officials usually make every effort to answer letters promptly and efficiently. If they are elected officials, they consider the importance of pleasing their constituency, and most of them are eager to do a good job. Senators and representatives almost always answer promptly. If the inquiry has to do with a current question which brings a large volume of letters, guide letters are provided for secretaries to use or to adapt as answers. Personal inquiries are handled on an individual basis. One very recent letter was written by a woman veteran who explained to Representative Wendall Wyatt that, when she signed up for the G.I. Bill, she found that she wasn't entitled to the same benefits as a married man. She was married while she was serving in the military. She went on to say that she didn't know why she shouldn't be entitled to the same benefits as a married man in view of the fact that women fall under the same regulations and punishment that men do. The prompt answer from Rep. Wyatt expressed his concern over this inequity in veteran legislation. He stated that he was contacting the House Committee on Veterans Affairs and the House Committee on Armed Services on this matter. He promised that he would have the problem firmly in mind when veterans' legislation came to the floor of the House for consideration. A follow-up indicated that he had not forgotten the matter and was pursuing it.

Among our first "out" letters written for research was one answered by J. Edgar Hoover. I have this letter in my file with the signature of this famous late head of the F.B.I. He explained that because all letters written by the Bureau were of a very confidential nature, he couldn't discuss them; but he did send some pamphlets on correspondence prepared by the General Services Administration which were used by his and other departments and bureaus. Because there were no typist's initials and because it reflected his terse and dignified nature, we assume that he wrote the letter himself. Written on a Federal Bureau of Investigation letterhead, signed by J. E. Hoover, and sent in a shadowed envelope—this letter is one of our favorites.

We have received several letters from the White House. Students cherish these, of course; so I have been privileged to keep only one. This, signed by Ralph Dungan in 1961, was in answer to an inquiry about the White House policy of handling correspondence. Mr. Dungan said in this letter that the President and his staff handle the correspondence, ". . .which ranges from about 30,000 to 40,000 letters each week." He stated that while some form and guide letters are used in reply, ". . .each letter does get individual screening and processing." We noted several interesting things about this letter from the White House. For one thing, the letter was written on note size paper (9¼" by 6¼"), and it was sent in a small envelope (6½" by 3 5/8"). Although the simple letterhead, THE WHITE HOUSE with Washington centered below it, was in the patriotic blue used by Congressmen, the typewriter ribbon was black. Instead of being franked, the envelope carried a 4-cent, July 4, 1960, issue patriotic stamp. The return address was simply THE WHITE HOUSE. The inside address on the letter itself was at the lower left below the letter, and instead of the date's being centered under the letterhead, it was in alignment with the complimentary closing, which started at the center of the page. You'll find, as you study this course, that you will become aware of these details.

Back in 1961 when Arthur Goldberg was Secretary of Labor, a student wrote to him offering his suggestion for alleviating the unemployment situation. He said the solution would be simple, and he suggested the following: "1. Retire all the women workers who do not need jobs and should be home caring for their children. 2. Replace these women with unemployed men and pay them a wage high enough to support their families." He went on to say, "When this is done, you can sit back and watch the unemployment figures drop to an all-time low." His letter was turned over to the Women's Bureau of the Department of Labor, and the answer was signed by Esther Peterson, Director. She wrote a detailed personal answer explaining that "No one would want to dictate blanket job restrictions affecting the free men and women who make up our American labor force. Decisions regarding an individual's right to work based on economic need would necessarily involve careful scrutiny of individual and family budgets and financial resources resulting in a control over personal lives foreign to our society. We believe that the goal of putting this Nation's unemployed back to work will be achieved through an increase in the pace of our economic growth." We must remember that this was written before the active days of Women's Lib. In her last paragraph, Mrs. Peterson said, "Thank you for writing on subjects of concern to you and to us. It is good to know that people like yourself are giving serious thought to these aspects of our national life." She enclosed a prepared statement entitled, "Are Women Taking Men's Jobs" and a page of statistics concerning working mothers.

On the local level, a young married student wrote to the State Police Superintendent reporting that while she was stranded in her car on a freeway, even though she had the hood of her car up and a handkerchief tied to the car's antenna, three state policemen drove by without stopping to give assistance. She gave the exact time and date and the location of the freeway. She received a fine letter from the Captain in charge of the Traffic Division, thanking her for her letter and telling her that she was correct in assuming that troopers are instructed to render public service of the kind about which she inquired. He assured her that members of the force would be instructed accordingly, and his letter included notation of carbon copies sent to members of the force—presumably those who were patrolling the area in question.

Others among letters to public officials which received detailed and personal answers include recent letters to two congressmen and one congresswoman concerning wage limitation on Social Security. Each answer agreed that the allowable outside income of Social Security beneficiaries should be increased. The Congresswoman enclosed a copy of a bill she had introduced on the subject.

Other responses include that of a senator who helped a young lady with the procedure of getting her GI husband home from Vietnam because of the serious illness of his father, who was not expected to live. Another senator gave explicit instructions to a young married student on how to go about getting a job on the base where her Air Force husband was to be stationed. A representative answered a letter about Federal taxation of churches. Another wrote in detail about the challenge of pollution and outlined legislative measures that he had co-sponsored in an effort to solve the problem. Senator Mike Mansfield wrote a personal letter to a student from Montana who had written concerning an article about the Senator, whom both she and her father had known personally. Realizing how subsequent classes would benefit from seeing actual letters from VIP's, students have been most generous in turning many of their letters over to me for my files. Senator Mansfield's letter is one of these.

I reiterate that letters to public officials should be pertinent, significant, and serious. I have a horror of "nuisance" letters. No letter should be written just to be writing, like the little old lady who writes nuisance letters to important people to see how many signatures she can accumulate. Congressmen do want to hear from their constituents. They deplore, however, a "snow" campaign in the form of swarms of letters and cards. Letters should be timely and succinct. Personal inquiries are all right if they are reasonable, and gripes are fine provided that they express honest opinions and are not vitriolic or threatening. Congressmen appreciate as much as anyone letters of commendation, and they are quite willing to accept constructive criticism. Each congressman receives an average of about 250 letters a day, and all answerable letters are handled either by staff members or the Congressman himself. One Representative has admitted that letters have influenced him to introduce bills against pornography, for non-denominational prayer in public facilities, and for boosting personal income tax exemptions.

The pen is indeed mightier than the sword.

LETTERS RELATIVE TO JOBS

While I do not assign actual application letters, I do not discourage "out" letters that have to do with employment. Several students have written letters to employers or personnel directors of the kinds of businesses or professions in which they would like to be employed when they finish their training. Quite a number of our girls studying to be legal secretaries have written to attorneys requesting information on technical and personal qualifications for the legal secretary. Following are some of the responses:

"I consider the most important qualifications as follows: Efficiency in all aspects, including typing, dictation, and general office activities.

I consider the personality of the person involved. In the practice of law, I find it absolutely important that the individual have a personality that enables one to communicate with others and be able to assist people with their problems."

Another attorney said, "First, a secretary must be absolutely discreet in both her actions and in what she may say about the business which goes on in the office. Second, it is necessary that she be proficient in all forms of office management, and particularly in shorthand and typing. Third, she should be able to work well under pressure, since the practice of law creates pressure situations for both lawyers and secretaries. Fourth, a good disposition and a general attitude to give and take within an office setup is a great asset. Last, and certainly not least, she should have an interest in the legal profession and in the practice of law over and above the mere monetary values involved."

Still another attorney responded in this way: "In our office, our secretaries work for all the attorneys and, therefore, get well-rounded experience in all the fields we handle. In many offices where there are several attorneys, each secretary works for just one attorney and therefore is exposed principally to the field in which that attorney specializes. Most of the work of a legal secretary can be gained in on-the-job training, once she is equipped to be a good efficient secretary. All the qualifications of good grooming, neatness (in work as well as appearance), attitude, and attention, which are required in any office, are of great importance in the legal office as well. In addition, the work of a legal secretary is completely confidential and must never be carried from the office. Even the mention of a name or the description of a particular situation can lead to grave problems for the client or the attorney if it happens to come up before the wrong people. The training for a secretary pertaining to the legal end of the job is lengthy and time consuming and requires an intelligent, mature person, who is capable of absorbing and applying instructions quickly."

There are many other letters from attorneys in answer to "out" letters, but they all stress ability, personality, and integrity. We have been most grateful for these responses, but in our class discussion of the letters, we cannot help noting that attorneys, probably more than any other business or professional men, seem to use cliches and time-worn expressions. Legal terminology is technical, and to the layman, stuffy and unnecessary.

We suppose that attorneys find it difficult to shift from "whereas," "hereunto," "notwithstanding," and other such legalese to a more personal tone in their letters. In most of them we found such expressions as "This is to advise you," "Thank you for your letter," "I have received your letter," "please be advised," "In reply to your request," and "Thank you again. . . ." One of our graduates has reported that she has finally convinced her attorney boss that letters to clients should be more friendly, and letters to "the other side" can be firm without being stuffy. A secretary would have to be most tactful in making such suggestions and would have to anticipate a receptive response. Surely, the day will come when attorneys (and government employees) can be persuaded that gobbledegook is stuffy and does not add to their effectiveness. There is no law that says that legal documents or correspondence cannot be written in plain English. The only reason, it seems, for resorting to such blatant forms of circumlocution is to confuse, and to this end it is successful. It is regrettable that more businessmen and government employees don't avail themselves of a very effective little booklet put out by the Superintendent of Documents entitled, *Gobbledygook Has Gotta Go.* This should be required reading for anyone who writes letters or reports.

FAN LETTERS

Fan letters can be line-of-least-resistance letters, or they can have real significance. I frown on insipid sophomoric letters to popular singing or TV stars (David Cassidy, for instance). These letters may be counted to measure popularity, but they are as boring to the recipients as to the secretaries who have to pound out canned responses. Avoid this sort of communication, but some fan letters can be very rewarding. I like to cite my own experience of writing to an instructor who taught a graduate course to 28 English teachers. If you think that grammatical construction is so well defined that all teachers have to do is to follow the rules, you just don't know English teachers. When they get together, they nit-pick over restrictive and non-restrictive clauses, splitting infinitives, dialectal and colloquial words, punctuation, etc. In this particular instance, these teacher-students not only would argue with each other but would question the instructor. Without being autocratic or losing her composure, this excellent teacher handled this difficult class with aplomb. She could very easily have put down one young know-it-all who was especially annoying, but she resisted the temptation; and, in spite of the would-be dissidents, we all learned a great deal about the teaching of English grammar—something too few English teachers know, since teaching literature has become the line of least resistance.

I admired her greatly, and after the class was over and I had received my grade, I wrote her a "fan" letter. I simply told her how much I admired her poise in the face of the obstacle course she had been forced to run, and I expressed appreciation for helping me with many fine points of the teaching of English grammar. Her response, it seemed to me, was touching. She seemed overwhelmed by the fact that I had taken the time to write and express my appreciation; she said this was the first time in the many years of her teaching that she had received a letter of appreciation from a student. This type of neglect is reprehensible.

The manager of a fine restaurant sent a handwritten letter of appreciation to a girl who had complimented his steak dinner. He said, "So few people take the time or make the effort to tell of the good things, but so many are quick to tell of the bad. My sincere thanks for your expression."

One girl was surprised to receive a reply to her letter from the president of a very large publishing house. She had complimented a magazine published by the firm and listed specific features that pleased her. This official expressed his appreciation and said he was sending her fine letter to the editor of the magazine. By double spacing and by indenting 15 spaces, by such expressions as "as per your letter of February 16th," and by winding up the letter with a second "thank you," his letter, however, violated many of our policies. While his name was on the letterhead, it was not typed below his signature.

The manager of the Pacific Coca-Cola Bottling Company took the time to write an answer to a fan letter from a student who raved about low-calorie Tab. She was further rewarded by receiving, as a gift, a case of Tab. We were interested in the paper used for the letterhead, since its watermark is the Coca-Cola trademark.

In answer to a fan letter about a nationally known brand of ice cream, one young lady received a letter stating, "We were so delighted to receive your letter and to know that our ice cream makes you and your friends happy. It's great to get mail from a satisfied customer such as you." And then several gift certificates were enclosed "with our compliments and best wishes for continued happy ice cream eating."

The owner of a popular men's wear store stated in answer to his letter, "In the 40 years that I have been in business, your letter was one of the nicest ever received. My employees also appreciated reading your letter, which was passed around. We seldom hear from the satisfied customer, except for his continued patronage. It is the complaints that usually grace the mail. Thank you for your nice letter."

Although one girl waited four months for an answer to her "fan" letter—long after her class was completed, she was delighted to get a note of appreciation from Michael Chrichton, the author of *The Andromeda Strain.* Her letter, of course, had been sent to the publisher in New York, and the answer came from California.

One very popular student, a young man, wrote his letter to a regional Dairy Princess, telling her how very much he had enjoyed reading about her and seeing her on television, etc., and he asked her if she could really milk a cow. Her very formal answer explained that since she lived on a dairy farm, she did, indeed, milk and feed the cows, although she was presently at college. She explained her duties and how she had won the honor and then suggested that further information could be obtained by writing the Dairy Products Commission, for which she gave the address. It was only when a fellow student "squealed" that we learned that the Dairy Princess was the very best girl friend of the fellow who wrote the "out" letter. We were assured, however, that all communication relative to the inquiry and its answer was by letter.

Any letter of this type gives good practice in written communication, but I feel the most significant letters are those relative to business or to jobs. A fan letter—one expressing admiration for a business or individual—can frequently result in invaluable information and, perhaps, even a job.

SPECIAL LETTERS

Occasionally, students have written letters to the editor, and, in each instance, the letter was published. One expressed his ideas about race prejudice, another wrote in favor of a political candidate, and still another reviewed a local education situation. Any letter which stays within the word limitation and is expressed in good taste has an excellent chance of being published. In every case students were surprised and delighted to see their letters—and their names—in print. The voice of the people is important, and the opportunity to use it via the press should be accepted much more frequently than it is by those who have excellent ideas but seem, somehow, reluctant to express them.

Occasionally, a student seizes the opportunity to use as his "out" letter an obligation which he has been putting off—and letter writing chores seem to be the easiest to procrastinate. Terry composed a beautiful letter to an insurance company which had given him a tuition scholarship to the business school. He explained to the class that this honor was a routine thing at his high school and that he had earned it by his good scholastic record, but aside from a very perfunctory thank-you at the time, he had never communicated with the local insurance agency which generously provided the money. In fulfilling his obligation and his assignment, he really outdid himself. He explained that without the scholarship he would have had to wait another year to pursue his schooling. He described his work to some extent, mentioned his 3.6 G.P.A. and added how very much he was enjoying his work. His letter wound up this way: "I know that you will continue to sponsor such a scholarship for future students. I only hope they are as pleased with such a fine gift as I am. Best wishes to you and your company. I hope your business thrives and continues to grow prosperous." Such a letter would not only be appreciated but would justify the expenditure of effort and money in the granting of further scholarships. Of the thousands of scholarships granted, how many recipients take the trouble to follow up with expressions of appreciation? Such grants should never be taken for granted.

Cheryl D. wrote to Captain Eddie Rickenbacker telling him that as she had recently been leafing through her father's scrapbook, she had come across several clippings of her great-grandfather pictured with Captain Rickenbacker. She said she was interested to learn that while her great-grandfather was vice-president in charge of safety for a large airline, his son (her grandfather) was doing stunt flying. She explained that her brother was soon to receive his wings as a pilot in the United States Air Force and that she and her family would attend his graduation. She expressed her desire to uphold the family interest in flying by obtaining a job as secretary for an airline. She asked Captain Rickenbacker if he would fill in any information about her great-grandfather. The answer was long and personal, and described her great-grandfather as "my good friend." He enclosed a biographical resume which gave a background of his career, and while he made no specific or concrete suggestions for Cheryl's career, he assured her that with her background and interest, "...you will have little difficulty in making a good connection, and I know they are always looking for good people in this line of endeavor." Although this was not specific help, it did a great deal to encourage a young lady interested in the flying business.

One student, a parent, wrote the following letter to the school board of her district:

To the Board of Directors:

As concerned parents, we have felt for some time that we should write to you to tell you that we see a great need for discipline in our schools.

Although the present trend seems to be permissive, we feel that now, more than ever before, a strong authority is desirable at every level of a child's development. Since the school experience fills the better part of a child's time, he should be taught definite guidelines for his behavior to supplement what he learns at home.

We have had the privilege in these past five years of becoming acquainted with some of the more mature teachers in the system who see the problem first hand. Our two oldest children were privileged to be taught by Miss A, Mrs. B, and Mr. C, each of whom taught respect for authority as well as the required curriculum. We believe our children progressed at a better rate under these more authoritative teachers.

It is our sincerest hope that you, who speak for us when the time comes to choose teachers to fill openings in our district, will carefully consider each individual. We ask that you insist on firm discipline, for without that, our children will not learn efficiently.

For the good of the community, as well as our own children's development, please give serious consideration to this request when the School Board convenes again.

Very truly yours,

This kind of letter makes board members and school personnel aware of parents' concern. Too frequently parents are either completely apathetic about school policy or they are openly critical and hostile. A dignified letter of concern cannot help favorably influence educational policy.

One of our choice answers came from J. C. Penney, dated December 20, 1969. A girl had written expressing admiration for him and praise for the stores which bear his name, and she cited specific courtesies accorded her. The page-and-a-half answer stated that "It is naturally a great pleasure to receive such a highly complimentary letter as yours." He went on to say that it was the fine service and quality merchandise that accounted for the success of the company. He added, "As you probably are aware, I celebrated my ninety-fourth birthday last September. I hope to live to reach the century mark. I put in a full day at my office every working day, health permitting. I want the remaining years of my life to be the best and most useful ones of all." He mentioned that he would spend his ninety-fifth birthday in Portland, Oregon, at the H.C.S.C. convention. This organization, he said, comprises retired Penney management men and their wives and the widows of Penney men. He enclosed several reprints of talks he had made and other messages written by him, and he expressed appreciation for the young lady's thoughtfulness in writing. Regrettably, he did not live to reach that century mark.

These examples of "out" letters are neither superficial nor provincial. They are most significant. Written communication is a means of learning by asking, of settling a claim, of finding out about job requirements, of expressing an opinion, but most of all it is a means of positive human interrelationships and goodwill. An "out" letter is more than an assignment. It is a privilege.

Are there ever put-downs, disappointments, or no responses to letters? Of course, but these are rare. There are frequent delays; not everyone answers letters within the ideal 24-hour period. My file of what we call negative response is slim. Compared to the hundreds of answers to "out" letters, the negative file is insignificant. I feel that it is inexcusable that the doctor did not answer the girl with cerebral palsy who wrote a letter of appreciation to him and to the Crippled Children's Division of the hospital where she had undergone surgery. She gave him a report of her progress and told him about her schooling. A note from him would have meant much to her by way of encouragement and morale.

Two letters from attorneys were inexcusably stuffy. One of these wrote, "You must realize that a secretary is an "intrical" part of the law office. Either he did not bother to read the letter he signed, or he did not know how to spell the word himself. He should have realized that correct spelling is an integral part of a business letter.

One girl wrote to a photographer explaining that she was making plans for her wedding in the near future and asking specifically about cost, appointments, proofs, etc. The fact that the photographer didn't bother to answer her letter cost him more than one customer, since reports of "out" letters are made in class. Another photographer took three weeks to answer, by which time the girl had made other arrangements. Both of these businessmen nullify the elaborate advertising they pay for by not following up on inquiries.

One toothpaste company sent a duplicated letter in answer to a complaint about the product. The letter, which had no salutation or inside address, said in part, "Your comments about our product have caused us some concern. Thank you for calling this matter to our attention. We have referred your comments to our quality control." This brush-off indicates the necessity of printed answers because of a large volume of complaints and is not conducive to repeat business.

Then there is the record company which sends out a duplicated letter printed in all caps directed to "Dear Customer" followed by IN REGARDS: with directions for returning the defective record for replacement. Again, the very necessity of duplicating such a letter indicates many complaints. Then, of course, there should be no "s" on in regard. These poor letters of the no-response reaction are infrequent. It is easy to judge an individual or a company by their responses.

The carbon copy of your "out" letter which your instructor will maintain in her file should carry a notation of the date that the letter is mailed out if it does not coincide with the date on the letter itself. As soon as you receive an answer, record the date of receipt on the copy of the "out" letter. This little survey will be an interesting class project. Try to determine the average length of time required to receive an answer. And if you fail to get an answer the first time, try, try again.

Following are actual examples of answers to "out" letters. I feel that the one from General William Knowlton is especially significant, and this surely exemplifies the fact that big people have time for little people. In granting permission to use his letter in this text, General Knowlton said in part, "I might say in passing in most of the Army staff positions which I have held, I have encountered the conditions which you mention and which are so common in America. Unskilled writers often feel that the longer a letter is, the better it is. It is also a bureaucratic tendency to use jargon of many syllables when simple English would do the job better. Many draft letters which have come to me over the years gave no indication that the author had read the incoming letter to which his word was a response. I hope you are able to persuade people to use simple English in preference to jargon, to answer the points raised by the incoming letter, and to write simply."

You can imagine how grateful I was to receive these words from a general who is now Superintendent of the United States Military Academy at West Point.

Cheryl's letter, which I have copied (with her permission), since I have only the carbon of the letter she sent out, is self-explanatory. The answer, I feel, is classic.

My classes have enjoyed this unit so much, and have been so pleased and surprised with responses that they have written more than the one "out" letter assigned.

February 11, 1972

Lippold, Brenner, & Bingenheimer
275 State St.
Salem, OR 97301

Gentlemen:

Is the computer taking over the accounting profession?
This is a question that I am concerned with, since I am an
accounting student at Merritt Davis School of Commerce.

I am interested in your opinion on this subject.
Specifically, I would like to know whether there is a good
future in the accounting field or is the computer actually
taking over in this profession.

Enclosed is a stamped self-addressed envelope for your
reply. I am looking forward to receiving your answer.

Sincerely yours

Richard C. Clark
Addressxxxxxxxxx
XXXXXXXXXXXXXXX

LIPPOLD, BRENNER & BINGENHEIMER
PUBLIC ACCOUNTANTS

Paul J. Lippold, P.A.
Dennis M. Brenner, C.P.A.
Ivan J. Bingenheimer, C.P.A.
Robert Guthner, C.P.A.
John H. Hancock, C.P.A.
Marvin E. Walpole, C.P.A.
Elba C. Pielstick, C.P.A.

275 STATE STREET
SALEM, OREGON 97301

(503) 585-8414

WOODBURN OFFICE
345 NORTH SECOND

982-9551

February 15, 1972

R. C. Clark
2420 N.E. Laurel
Salem, Oregon 97303

Dear Mr. Clark:

In answer to your letter of February 11, 1972, I will try and give
specific answers to your questions.

The first was, "Is the computer taking over the accounting profession?"
In my judgement this is a definite "no". The computer is taking over
some of the detail work that had been done in the accounting profession
and is supplying additional information which was sometimes not
practical to be done manually. There is still a need for a preparation
of the input work into the computer, which requires accounting knowledge
and judgement exercised, based on the technical knowledge.

Your second question was with respect to if there was a good future in
the accounting field. In my judgement there is a very good future in
the accounting field for the young person who has aptitudes and abilities
that coincide with the demands required for that of an accountant....
namely, he should have good character; be able to communicate well;
have an adequate technical knowledge and possess a reasoning mind.

I hope this has been of some help to you with respect to the questions
you had.

Very truly yours,

Dennis M. Brenner

Dennis M. Brenner, C.P.A.
Partner in the Firm of
LIPPOLD, BRENNER & BINGENHEIMER
Public Accountants

DMB/cmw

Example of "Out" Letter

This "out" letter of Don Ohmart's was a sincere request made to two of Oregon's outstanding leaders.

May 6, 1969

The Honorable Clay Myers   (The Honorable Robert Straub
Secretary of the State of Oregon   Oregon State Treasurer
Salem, Oregon   Salem, Oregon)

              REPUBLICAN. . . . . . . .DEMOCRAT??????????

WHY SHOULD I BE A REPUBLICAN?   (A DEMOCRAT?)

Dear Secretary Myers: (Dear Treasurer Straub)

     I was recently separated from the service after serving two years in the USNR. I have always had a deep interest in the history and politics of the United States of America. Since I have been in the service, my interest has grown much deeper. I am more concerned about how I should vote.

     I have spent a year overseas and have served in many states in America. While overseas, I started taking an interest about my one vote and how important it is to me. It's a privilege that all Americans have and should use. If it were not for our history we wouldn't have the privilege to vote and live in a free country.

     Most young adults usually follow their parents' advice on how to vote and for whom. One of my parents is a Democrat and the other is a Republican, so it is a little hard to decide which one to follow. I usually follow my father's advice and his views on politics, but he happens to be a Republican. I know this isn't a concrete reason to be a Republican, so I am asking you for advice.

     My reason for writing to you is to ask you why I should be a Republican? (to Mr. Straub—why I should be a Democrat) I have not registered to vote as I should like your opinion on this matter first.

     I am sure your answer will clarify a lot of doubts and questions I have on why I should be a Republican. (a Democrat)

                              Very truly yours,

                              Donald Lee Ohmart
                              xxxxxxxxxxxxxxxxx
                              Salem, Oregon

              ELEPHANT......DONKEY?????

Note the fine answers to this inquiry.

CLAY MYERS
SECRETARY OF STATE

GEORGE H. BELL
JACK F. THOMPSON
ASSISTANTS

May 14, 1969

Mr. Donald Lee Ohmart
3840 Cooley Drive NE.
Salem, Oregon 97303

Dear Donald:

I am honored that you should seek my advice about your
political party registration. It is a decision that a young
person should make only after long and careful consideration.

Let me tell you why I am a Republican, and you can perhaps
judge better from my reasons what your own registration
should be.

First let me say that the differences between the two
parties have blurred somewhat in recent times, so that, for
example, a progressive Republican might find he has a great
deal in common on certain issues with some Democrats, and
vice versa.

Basically, I find most of my Republican friends try to
solve their problems on the local level. They resist the
notion that one should automatically look to the federal
government for solutions. Some, frankly, are out-and-out
states righters, almost to the point of believing that
state government should have sovereignty over the federal
government. I do not believe that, but I do think states
need to work harder to attack and solve their own problems.

Secondly, I somehow find that most of my Republican friends
are more fiscally responsible. Perhaps that is because many
of them have had experience in the business world. Money comes
hard for them, and they believe the government should expend
it with care. This does not mean they are tight-fisted about

human programs and needs; quite the contrary. But, their
business training makes them aware of the need for sound
administrative structure and control, which is an absolutely
essential element in good government.

It seems to me, too, that Republicans have a more realistic
concern about the underprivileged in this country. Too
often, the Democrats have been eager to dump billions of
dollars into ill-considered and wasteful War on Poverty
programs, for example, without taking the time and effort
to make certain the projects were properly conceived,
administered, staffed and kept in proper bounds by tight
budget controls. My experience is that Republicans demonstrate
more interest in programs which help people improve themselves,
through education or training, rather than just handing out
monthly doles.

All in all, though, there are fine public-spirited persons
in both parties. While I hope you make the decision to
join the Republican party, the more important thing is that
you continue your interest in politics and government. Our
nation badly needs good people in both areas of activity,
and you appear to be the kind of person whose participation
could be most valuable to society.

                                        Sincerely,

                                        Clay Myers

CM:bw

July 1, 1969

Mr. Donald Lee Ohmart
3840 Cooley Drive, N. E.
Salem, Oregon 97303

Dear Donald:

I am sorry for the delay in answering your letter, but June was an exceptionally busy month for the Straub family and your letter was put aside with others in the midst of a wedding, house guests, cherry picking, etc.

I appreciate your letter and the spirit in which it was written. Your desire to "think through" and develop your personal political philosophy before registering to vote is commendable.

If politics is the art of governing, as Adlai Stevenson often said, then one's political philosophy should not be a static, unchanging thing. The world in which we live is certainly a challenging, changing one, and to wisely govern any part of it requires that a political party be dynamic and flexible enough to meet the needs of the times. Progress cannot come from those who fear change or unpopular stands.

I am a Democrat because I believe the Democratic Party has proved to be closer to this philosophy and because it has shown a deeper concern for the interests of the average citizen.

Whichever party you choose, I hope you will work actively in it, both to make it better and to be well informed yourself. And you can take comfort in one fact -- that whatever your decision today, it is not unchangeable!

Best of luck, and thanks for writing.

Sincerely,

Robert W. Straub
State Treasurer

RWS:b

May 20, 1963

Governor Mark O. Hatfield
State Capitol Building
Salem, Oregon

Dear Governor Hatfield:

Since I am a young lady approaching the voting age, I should
like to know why I should vote the Republican ticket.

As you are one of the more prominent Republicans of this
country, I feel that you are the most qualified to give me the
information I want.

Would you tell me what the difference is between the Democratic
and Republican Party.

                              Yours truly,

                              Ginger Derksen

June 19, 1963

MARK O. HATFIELD
GOVERNOR

Miss Ginger Derksen
Route 4, Box 75-A
Salem, Oregon

Dear Miss Derksen:

Thank you very much for your recent letter. I am frequently asked "What distinguishes Republicans from Democrats?" In brief, here is my answer:

Republicans have a concern for the individual and his rights. It was this great concern that caused people to establish a Republican party. At its inception the Party sponsored, among other things, two important projects - the Homestead Act and defense of minorities - which demonstrate this point in our philosophy. The former Act was predicated on the assumption that man has an obligation to permit his fellow man the full opportunity to develop his talents. The defense of minority groups is but the opposite side of the same coin. We cannot permit government, labor, business or any other group to take away the rights which make a human being a free man. There can be no "second class" citizens.

Republicans know that government is a public trust. We believe in a balanced budget and fiscal stability. Our Party has a continuous faith in a free economy which is unshackled by undue government interference. Government's role should be that of protection of the public interest. The individual must be free to develop to his fullest potential.

Republicans think that it is vitally necessary to make as many decisions as possible at the local and state levels. We reject the notion that government can do all things for people. And regardless of where a governmental program is inaugurated, we must ask ourselves if that program is necessary or if it is merely desirable.

Republicans are committed to assist other peoples in the
world. Our Party sponsored the "Open Door" and "Good
Neighbor" policies. We don't condone waste, but we do
support legitimate assistance to the world's emerging
peoples.

Republicans believe in the future. We realize that two
important things are occurring in this rapidly changing
world: (1) the present is quickly becoming the past; and
(2) the future is rapidly becoming the present. In order
to meet the changes that lie ahead we must be prepared.
Programs which appealed in the 1930's cannot meet the
challenge of the present and future. We must be the
Party of both the present and the future.

I am always pleased to see our young people taking a serious interest
in their privileges of citizenship, and I appreciate having the
opportunity to answer your question.

With every good wish.

                                        Sincerely yours,

                                        Governor

MOH:mg

Copy of "out" letter to General Westmoreland which was answered by General William A. Knowlton, Secretary of the General Staff, now Superintendent of the United States Military Academy at West Point.

XXXXXXXXXXXXXXXXXXXX
Salem, Oregon 97303
February 17, 1970

General W. Westmoreland
Department of Defense
Pentagon
Washington, D.C.

Dear General Westmoreland:

My father served 21 years in the Army, and I am now engaged to a young man who is also serving my country. I am very proud, as you are, of the job they and others have done and are doing to keep us free and safe. But I also have a problem and, although I know you are extremely busy, I hope you will help me.

I want to know what I can say to my friends when they ask me why I am supporting the war. I want to know how I can answer them when they ask why I advocated killing. How can you explain? These ''friends'' all attend college and participate in the demonstrations and moritoriums. I have tried to listen to their point of view, but I cannot understand why they believe this is the true way of insuring peace.

My father's death was caused by a service connected disability, and even this has not turned my thinking against the military. It hurts me deeply to hear people my age talk against our country. I have tried to stand up and tell them this is wrong. But it is so difficult to put into words the pride, trust, and gratefulness I have felt. I should appreciate it if you could tell me your own feelings about this situation with our country.

War is wrong, but it is also necessary in insuring peace. When my father died, I believed he gladly gave his life so our country would continue in freedom. My friends believed he was murdered by America.

They will not listen to the trite explanations given in the newspapers or on television. Perhaps they will not listen to me. But I have to try. Or else my father and all the other fathers, brothers, and husbands have died for no cause at all.

Respectfully,

Miss Cheryl Edgar

DEPARTMENT OF THE ARMY
OFFICE OF THE CHIEF OF STAFF
WASHINGTON, D.C. 20310

6 MAR 1970

Dear Miss Edgar:

This is in response to your letter of 23 February, in which you
requested information to justify your support of US involvement
in Vietnam. I asked General Westmoreland if I could respond to
your letter, because I have a daughter who will enroll in college
this fall and she, too, has encountered a similar problem.

I was very impressed by your letter, particularly by the esteem
in which you regard your late father's military service and by
the pride you have in our country. Since such traits are lightly
regarded by many of our youngsters today, their expression by
you was indeed refreshing.

As you indicated, US involvement in Vietnam continues to be one
of our most controversial national issues. The seemingly endless
debate in our government and news media often confuses many
Americans as to our true, limited objective in Vietnam. Yet, in
simplest terms, this objective from the outset has been to create
an environment in Vietnam wherein the Vietnamese are _free_ to
choose their own course.

Contrary to some opinion, the accomplishment of this objective has
proceeded in a rather logical and orderly fashion. Our national
leadership has exercised unprecedented restraint on the use of our
available military power in Vietnam, and only increased our effort
there in response to the increased aggressiveness from North Vietnam.
Ironically, much of the public frustration is perhaps a manifestation
of our failure in Vietnam to have achieved early the traditional
military victory.

In order to provide you with some substantive background information
supporting US involvement in Vietnam, I am enclosing two pamphlets
which I consider very informative. Neither of these pamphlets is
an official publication of the US Government; however, I think you
may find them quite useful in discussions with your "friends."
Moreover, in tribute to your late father, you might find some
consolation in the following quotation from the British philosopher,
John Stuart Mill (1806-1873):

"War is an ugly thing, but not the ugliest of things: the decayed and degraded state of moral and patriotic feeling which thinks nothing <u>worth</u> a war, is worse. A war to protect other human beings against tyrannical injustice; a war to give victory to their own ideas of right and good, and which is their own war, carried on for an honest purpose by their free choice -- is often the means of their regeneration. A man who has nothing which he is willing to fight for, which he cares more about than his personal safety, is a miserable creature who has no chance of being free, unless made and kept so by the exertions of better men than himself."

General Westmoreland appreciated your letter, and I hope that the inclosed pamphlets will at least serve as a partial solution to your problem.

Sincerely,

WILLIAM A. KNOWLTON
Major General, GS
Secretary of the General Staff

2 Incls
As stated

Miss Cheryl Edgar
4332 40 Court N. E.
Salem, Oregon 97303

P. S. I served 2 years in Vietnam; my second son served a year there as a parachute infantry Sergeant; and my oldest son is a Vietnam volunteer when he graduates from West Point this year. We three believe!

96

It is ridiculous to assume that any person can express himself well in English without knowing the construction of the English sentence. Those Tarzans who claim the "Me Tarzan—you Jane" communication as the limit of expressiveness should go back to their tree swinging. We're thinking about business and social communication now, and this involves precise use and arrangement of words. Clothes, coifs, material possessions, and other status symbols will never hide an inability at oral and written expression. Ideas and ideals will be to no avail unless they can be put across with well-chosen and correctly arranged words.

The construction of the English sentence always involves a subject-verb arrangement—always these two basic parts. There may be other parts—the direct object, the predicate nominative, or the predicate adjective—but there are always the subject and the verb, and they relate to each other. Take the verb lie. I hear this word misused almost every day, and its misuse is not confined to the uneducated. Professional men, college graduates, even those with advanced and impressive degrees are wont to let slip "...the papers that are laying on the desk," or "I think I'll go lay down for a while." Let's clear this up.

1.   lie, lay

The verb lie, meaning to rest or recline, is an intransitive verb. This means that it takes no object—it is not acting upon anything.

Study the following:

Today I lie down.	present tense
She is lying down	present progressive
Yesterday I lay down.	past tense
I was lying down.	past progressive
I have lain down.	perfect tense
I had lain down.	past perfect tense

The verb lay means to put or place, and it is transitive, meaning that this verb does take an object.

Study the following:

She lays the book on the table.	present tense
She is laying the book on the table.	present progressive
She laid the book on the table.	past tense
She was laying the book on the table.	past progressive
She has laid the book on the table.	perfect tense
She had laid the book on the table.	past perfect tense

97

The trouble lies in the fact that the past tense of the verb lie is the same as the present tense of the verb lay. No wonder your dog ignores you when you say, "Go lay down." Lay what? Wrong verb. Try saying, "Go lie down."

So much for lie and lay.

2.   affect and effect

Affect is always a verb. It means to influence, to produce an effect upon.

> The news greatly affected his behavior.

Effect is usually a noun.

> The effect of the pep talk was good.

However, effect may be used as a verb. When it is, it means to bring about.

> The company intends to effect a change in policy.

3.   Don't confuse may and can.

May and its past tense might refer to asking or giving permission or to a possibility.

Can and could mean the ability to do something.

> May I leave early? (asking permission)
>
> > She said I might leave early. (might used with past tense)
>
> He said he might be late. (possibility)
>
> Can he lift that heavy box? (Is he able to lift it?)
>
> When he was younger, he could walk much faster. (He was able to.)
>
> > NOT: Can I borrow your pen?
> > > or
> > He said I could leave early.

4.   The verb agrees with its subject no matter how many words come between the subject and the verb.

> One of the men is to be here by noon.

One is the subject. Men is the object of the preposition of and does not affect the relationship between the subject and verb.

The secretary as well as the bookkeepers is going to attend the meeting.

Secretary is the subject. Words which follow as well as, in addition to or similar expressions do not affect the verb.

However, to make it easier to remember this, you may enclose these expressions in commas. This is correct punctuation, but not necessary.

The secretary, as well as the bookkeepers, is going to attend the meeting.

5.   Even grammarians cannot always agree on collective nouns—whether they should be used with a singular verb or a plural verb. I suggest that the easiest rule of thumb to follow is to ask yourself whether the words it or they may be substituted for the noun.

His family (it) is well known.

His family (they) have many different ideas on the subject.

The jury (it) has not yet made a decision.

The jury (they) are not able to agree on a verdict.

The choir (it) has given its concert.

The choir (they) are ordering their robes.

The one exception with regard to the agreement of subject and verb with intervening prepositional phrases has to do with fractions. The rule is this: When the subject is a fraction, the number of the verb depends on the object of the preposition which intervenes.

One-half of the tax was paid.

One-half of the taxes were paid.

One-fourth of the members were absent.

One-half of a loaf is better than none.

6.   The number is singular; a number is plural.

The number of students in the school has increased.

A number of students have expressed their ideas on the dress code.

7.   If I had the authority, I would repeal the rule regarding the use of shall and will (and should and would). Since we usually speak in contractions (I'll, he'll, etc.), the rule seldom affects oral usage. We seem to resist the rule when we write. Here it is:

Use shall with first person to express simple futurity.
Use will with second and third persons to express simple futurity.

For strong determination turn this rule around: shall with second and third persons, and will with first person. Then some grammarians include promise or compulsion along with determination. The same rules follow for should and would, except when should means ought to.

I shall appreciate it if you will send me the report.

My eye is oriented to this usage, and so I correct violations on assignments; but this does not keep me from thinking the shall-will rule is nit-picking.

8.   In business, amounts of money or periods of time are usually singular.

   Five thousand dollars <u>was</u> too much to pay for the lot.

   Two weeks <u>was</u> too long to wait for the contract.

Assignments

1.   Write an "out" letter, following suggestions outlined in this chapter. Compose it with the idea of getting an answer. As you write it, think of the recipient. How would you like to receive it?

2.   Correct the following sentences:

   a.   He said I could use his pen.

   b.   Her coat was laying on the chair where she put it.

   c.   The personnel director ordered that the transfer be affected at once.

   d.   After lunch, he laid down for half an hour.

   e.   He said four months were too long to wait.

   f.   The number of letters sent out each day were increasing.

   g.   Five hundred dollars were collected for the project.

   h.   The Board of Directors have approved the proposal.

   i.   The faculty was not able to agree on the policy.

   j.   The instructor as well as the students were in favor of a three-day weekend.

chapter seven

people need people
(the biography)

A biography may seem somewhat out of the business writing area, but, surprisingly, it can have a definite significance. I started incorporating this feature in my correspondence classes when my students found, in applying for jobs, that many companies put out an organization news publication (frequently called the "house organ") and that one of the principal items included in this paper is the biography. Companies of any size keep personnel posted on inter- and intra-office news by means of the "company blurb." This publication is the means of introducing new staff members, of covering news items such as promotions, marriages, and honors, and of apprising all personnel of company changes in policy.

Since nearly everyone likes to see his name in print, effort is usually made to include at least one biography in every issue of an organization publication. While everyone likes to read this sort of thing, it seems that no one enjoys writing it, and unless the publication is very large and very professional, finding volunteers for this kind of writing is difficult.

One of my former students reported to me that the determining factor in her being selected for a secretarial position over many other applicants was the fact that her resume indicated that she had been editor of her high school paper. She had an inside track for the job because of her attractive appearance, her interview, and her resume, but the company manager gave her his approval as soon as he found out that she had had experience in writing and that she would be happy to help in this area.

The effectiveness of the biography depends not so much on writing skill as on the interview. If the interview is well planned, the writing flows easily and naturally. Nothing is more boring than a chronological blow-by-blow account of the "interviewee." A good opening question is "What was the most exciting thing that has happened in your life?" The response to this question will set the stage for further questioning. If the person being interviewed lights up like a candle and launches into an exciting experience, the biography should be a breeze. If, however, the person indicates that nothing exciting ever happens to him, further prodding will usually elicit something special that will serve as a better introduction than where he was born and where he attended school.

Other warm-up questions can be, "How did you happen to decide to become an accountant (or a secretary, or whatever)?" "Who, do you feel, has had the most influence in your life?" "What three men, living or dead, do you admire the most—and why." "What is your favorite food?" "What are your favorite colors?" Size up the person. Try to determine what sort of questions turn him on, and then pursue this tack. Then, incidentally, get around to the routine questions of birthplace, schools, training, travels, family, hobbies, etc. Sometimes the discovery that a person has an avocation will expedite both the interview and the writing. This human interest angle will be appealing to the reader, and you, as the writer of biographies, will earn the praise that you are sure to deserve. If this type of writing is a new experience, you will find that it will come easily after you have written the first one or two.

To avoid being amateurish, resist any temptation to include first person in the writing unless the entire biography conveys your personal impression of the person about whom you write. The best approach for a biography is the omniscient one which places the writer in an anonymous situation. Such expressions as "When I asked him....he responded...." are unnecessary; just indicate the response—no need to reveal how you found out. By the same token, a personal wish for good luck is ill advised, such as, "I am sure we will all enjoy having Joe in our office. Best of luck to you, Joe."

Here are three biographies which may serve as examples. Remember, however, that each person about whom you write has a different personality and interest. A format or formula for this kind of writing is impractical.

SID FRANKLYN
A Biography

Sid Franklyn, a six-foot four-inch ex-basketball player, is the newest member of our accounting department, and if his height isn't enough to identify him, you're sure to notice a thatch of bright red hair on top of all that height. Yes, Sid played varsity basketball at the University of Nebraska back in 1964-65, and he resisted opportunities to go pro because he was interested in a pretty dark-haired girl whom he hoped to convince to become his wife. Sid Franklyn and Elaine Marcotte were married exactly five days after they were graduated from the University, and after a honeymoon to Glacier National Park, the young couple visited Elaine's parents in Butte, Montana. Although Sid had intended locating in Oregon or Washington, when he was offered a position with the Wright National Insurance Company as office manager, the opportunity seemed too good to pass up; so Sid and Elaine established their first home in Butte, and it was here two years later that their son, Randy, was born.

Since this couple are the outdoors type, it should come as no surprise to learn that hunting, fishing, and camping are their favorite recreations, and along with these hobbies goes a keen interest in photography. In 1967 Sid won four blue ribbons at the photography division of the Montana State Fair, and Elaine was awarded two blue ribbons and two red ones. Scenic photography is their favorite, but they admit that young Randy has had his fair share as a subject for their picture taking.

A summer vacation to Oregon this year inspired Sid's visit to Ridpath's, with the result that he accepted an offer as head of the Accounting Department.

Both Sid and Elaine are excited about living in Oregon and can hardly wait to get out their cameras to take along on many weekend trips in the Valley.

Elaine hopes to take advantage of art classes in Salem, and although she is a qualified teacher, she plans to be a full-time homemaker until Randy is in school. Then she hopes to serve occasionally as a substitute teacher in the physical education and science areas.

The Franklyns are living at 1345 Trelawn Avenue. Sid has admitted that he and his wife are eager to get acquainted with the Ridpath staff. He says that the cookie jar is always full and the coffee pot is always on at their home. This friendly, outgoing couple promise to be a real asset to the Ridpath family.

NANCY ELLEN SMYTH – GIRL OF THE MONTH

Our March Girl of the Month is a most surprising young lady. Most of her fellow classmates at Clarke Business College picture her as that quiet, refined, intelligent, and, yes, beautiful girl who always has the right answers in class. She seems to do everything right, yet no one would ever think of being jealous of this exemplary young lady. Perhaps this is so because she has a warm smile and a friendly, quiet personality.

Last month she was elected student body secretary—the only office that had a single nominee. Students seemed unanimous in considering her suitable and responsible for the job.

What is she really like? Well, there are many surprises. The most surprising fact is that there are two of her—well, not literally just that, but she does have an identical twin who is at Providence Hospital in Portland studying to be a nurse. This is the first year that the two have been separated, and Nancy Ellen has mixed emotions about this new experience. Her twin, Harriet, and she have seldom worn clothes that are alike, and for several years they have had different hair styles—just so that they could be individuals.

Their grandfather gave them a car for graduation, and this joint ownership poses a small problem because the girls live in different cities. The problem, however, is solved very amicably by the arrangement of taking turns with the car. Harriet has it one week, and Nancy Ellen, the next. This means that they get to see each other every weekend. It also means that one of them will have to make a trip by bus one way each weekend—but neither seems to mind this.

Another interesting fact about Nancy Ellen is that she lived in Hawaii most of her life and attended school from the first grade through her sophomore year in high school at a private school. She attributes her apparent scholarliness to the training and discipline which was part of this school's policy. When Nancy Ellen and Harriet were sophomores in high school, their father, who is a chemical engineer, was transferred to Southern California. The girls and their mother stayed in Honolulu until school was out in May, and then they flew to Portland where their maternal grandparents live. They liked Portland so well that they got permission to live with their grandmother and attend Grant High School. Here both girls became active participants in school affairs, and each was selected as a member of National Honor Society. They have spent their summers and vacations in Southern California with their parents, who live near Escondido.

Nancy Ellen admits that she and her sister have a sort of ESP understanding. They have intuitions about each other—like the time Nancy Ellen was just sure something was wrong with Harriet and felt impelled to call her. When she was unable to get a response, she was really worried. Sure enough, she soon learned that Harriet had been involved in a minor accident and had been taken to the hospital for emergency observation.

Harriet is completely happy with her nurses' training, and Nancy Ellen is sure she will enjoy being a secretary. The girls will always keep in close touch with each other, but they have no plans for pursuing their careers in the same city. Harriet is engaged, with marriage plans set for next year. Nancy Ellen hopes to work for at least three years before marriage. The girls are different in minor ways, too. Harriet's favorite colors are yellow and orange, while her twin prefers blue and green. Our girl loves to snow ski, while Harriet enjoys water skiing. Their handwriting is so similar, however, that a handwriting expert can barely tell the difference.

While Nancy Ellen has an alter ego, she is every bit an individualist, and she can hardly wait to get that first job as a secretary.

* * * *

This is a rather detailed type of biography suitable for a school paper feature. Since the subject was interesting and obviously not the type to talk about herself voluntarily, other students likely enjoyed reading this much information.

While most businesses, even the largest organizations, are becoming more informal all of the time, some more dignified concerns still prefer the formal perfunctory format. Something like this:

MR. S. STEPHENSON SHEPHERD

Lathrop's, Inc. is pleased to announce the appointment of S. Stephenson Shepherd as operations analyst. Mr. Shepherd replaces Gerald Minter, who recently retired.

The new executive received his B.S. degree in business administration from Stanford University in Palo Alto, California, and his M.A. degree in merchandising from Columbia University in New York. He has recently been affiliated with Lawton, Inc., in Dallas, Texas. Mr. Shepherd is married and has two children, Kimberly, 5, and Duane, 3.

An introduction luncheon is planned for officers and department heads to be held Friday, April 21, in the Round Table Room.

- - - -

Other occasions for biographies are retirements, special honors, promotions, and even obituaries. Frequently, family members of personnel provide biographical information for house news sheets. One such biography included in the news of a rather large firm was that of a wife of an official who had just passed the bar examination after having attended law school since her marriage. Another told of a son who was a star player on a well-known football team. One told of the daughter of a member of the firm who had won art honors at a state fair.

People like to read about people, and they like to be recognized and appreciated by members of their own firms.

Usually, I handle the biography assignment in my correspondence classes by simply having the students draw names. Occasionally, they draw names of good friends, but more often they find they must interview someone whom they scarcely know. I always enjoy reading these papers, for I learn a great deal about students that I otherwise might never know. I found out, for instance, that one student had been a professional singer in a night club, that another had been a sky diver, that the favorite hobby of one frail, very feminine young lady was riding a motorcycle, and that another assisted her father in branding cattle. These sidelights of information frequently provide news stories for our school paper.

One girl added a note to her biography thanking me for introducing her (by name drawing) to a young man in whom she had more than a biographical interest. It seems that the interview had resulted in a date. I wrote on her paper as I corrected it, "Just call me Cupid."

Biographies need not be of class members. This assignment could easily involve business men and women. What a great opportunity to meet civic and business leaders! Almost any man or woman is complimented to respond to an interview for a biography, even if it is for a class assignment. A compilation of such biographies could provide enlightening reading for young people who would like to become leaders in their communities. Here again, the interview is frequently an entree to acquaintances or associations which prove invaluable to the interviewer.

Another type of biography which provides more than writing experience is the selection of someone (for a biographical sketch) who has a responsible position or perhaps the kind of job the interviewer would like to attain. This is a fine opportunity to ask pertinent questions about preparing one's self for the ideal job. First-hand information about a position can be more valuable than just reading about it or being told second hand. Interviews of this kind can even lead to job interviews.

A program chairman who has arranged for a speaker could regard this as an opportunity to make a biographical interview to be used for publicity purposes or an introduction of the speaker. If tactfully arranged and tastefully executed, this interview can be a legitimate entree to meet and converse with prominent businessmen or persons of high rank.

People who enjoy their careers like to talk about them, and even big people, remember, have time for little people.

Assignments

1. In the spaces provided rewrite the following sentences taken from actual biographies:

    a. Her previous education was in Silverton where she spent the majority of her life.

    b. With two brothers, Bruce 27 and Peter Jr. 15 and one sister, June 21 who she is very close to she did not lack childhood companionship.

c. Vicky likes to play Tennis and wants to learn to Snow ski, she also likes to raise animals.

d. Her favorite books are one's that "mean something" and movies are romantic and exciting.

e. She went to the state university where she was envolved in atheletics and was on the girl's tennis team.

f. Considering all these facts about John Doe, he will probably go far in his field of business administration and serving the public.

g. Janet would make the perfect one girl office secretary because it would make the challenge which she enjoys so much.

h. Jerry James is very outgoing and friendly both of which are required in public relations.

i. Riding horses, volleyball, and basketball are her favorite activities while cooking fancy dishes and antiques are her hobbies.

j. Some of her interests during high school were participating in Honor Society for two years, she was active in band and won two band scholarships.

chapter eight

position yourself
(the business of getting a job)

The word position is derived from the Latin ponere meaning to place. In business it has come to mean the professional placement of a man or woman. It means, actually, a post of employment, but the word position itself lends dignity to that post. When we speak of a person of position we think of status—this is a complimentary expression. Its colloquial counterpart is job, which covers all work for which pay is received. However, we would never speak of having a position as ditch digger, nor having a job as president of a bank. Ditch digging is a job for which wages are paid, while a bank president receives a salary.

True, we speak colloquially of our jobs as teachers, secretaries, or accountants, but when we start looking for work in business, let's give this work status. We may refer casually to a job, but let's look for a position. In application letters the preferred terminology involves position and salary.

Probably the most important letter you will ever write in your own behalf is the application letter. Since statistics indicate that the average length of time on a job is three and a half years, chances are that in the normal course of your working years you will need to apply for a position several times. You must remember that this statistic takes into consideration those fly-by-nights who flit from one job to another after a few weeks or months; yet it also considers those who stay on the job for forty years or more. Either record is extreme. We'll discuss a little later in this chapter how and when to quit a job, but first let's discuss that all-important application letter which too few know how to write.

I am dismayed that many state schools of higher learning which make swimming a requirement for graduation make no provision for any skill in writing an application letter—or any other kind of letter for that matter. Newspapers have deplored editorially the illiteracy displayed in the application letters of most college graduates—letters that are beset with misspelled words, poor English, and awkward sentence structure.

One of our former Merritt Davis graduates is the executive secretary to the personnel director of a large insurance company. It is up to her to screen application letters. Having had training in written communication, she was, at first, shocked at the number of poor letters that were screened out because of carelessness in typing, spelling, and composition.

THE DON'TS OF THE APPLICATION LETTER

Besides poor construction, what is wrong with most application letters and what should be avoided in them? This is the only chapter in this book which deals first with the don'ts. These are the things to avoid:

1. Don't talk about money. This should be discussed in the interview. We'll point out later just how this should be handled.

2. Don't run down your present position, or make any derogatory remarks about your boss. Remember, if you do this about one job, you will do it about another. Employers are wary of chronic complainers.

3. Don't use the emotional appeal. While there is no need to apologize for applying for a job, don't ever give need as a reason for applying. Don't emphasize the fact that you have school debts or that you have financial responsibilities to meet. Emphasize only your qualifications.

4. Don't be subjective. Don't express opinions about yourself. Let your references do that. Your resume will outline your qualifications.

5. Don't be arrogant. While you may have to use the pronoun "I" more frequently in the application letter than in most other letters, don't presume to tell the employer something that he should already know. Such statements as this are out: "A knowledge of letter composition is necessary in a secretarial job such as the one you have to offer."

USING THE TRI-ASK TECHNIQUE

So much for the don'ts. Now what SHOULD a good application letter contain? Well, let's not forget the TRI-ASK TECHNIQUE:

1. What do I want to accomplish? (The answer to this also answers the following questions: What determines the success of an application letter?)

   I want to get an interview. If you get an interview, you may be sure that your letter was a success. If you get the position, the interview was a success. While the letter and the interview are closely related, they are two different and distinct phases in job getting, and each requires its own technique.

2. How am I going to do this?

   I am going to outline why it would be to this employer's advantage to consider my qualifications. This could be, specifically, education, experience, and possibly special skills (but without subjective opinion). I am going to ask for an interview.

3. How would I feel if I were to receive this letter?

   This may sound a little ridiculous, but, if possible, pretend that you are the one who will read this application letter—the one who would decide whether or not to grant you the interview. Would you be inclined to act favorably? Answer honestly.

THE OLD AND THE NEW

Application letters have changed greatly in the last ten or fifteen years, but some old-timers seem not to be aware of this. It used to be that the application letter itself would open with the personal data of the applicant, including, quite likely, a picture stapled to the first page. This first page would include the height, weight, age, etc. of the applicant, the number of dependents, if any, and details of his school or civic activities and personal interests. Following this was a detailed description of qualifications, with a sprinkling of personal opinion thrown in. Education was described in detail with experience information well padded. All of this would be followed by a list of references, and then the request for an interview. After wading through all this, the employer understandably might feel disinclined to grant an interview during which he might have to listen to a repetition of the applicant's history.

Fortunately for both the employer and the applicant, all this has changed. The application letter, now, is short and to the point, and the resume or data folder is presented as a separate unit for the prospective employer's perusal.

Let's talk about this letter. While the ultimate purpose of the application letter is a job, the immediate purpose is to get an interview. In my research, I have found that employers are dismayed with the tenor of the letters they receive, and most of them agree that about nine-tenths of the letters are thrown out without being considered. Many of these letters violate the "no-no's" already described, and too many of them are handwritten or sloppily typewritten with misspelled words and poor English. They simply do not demonstrate the qualities of a good employee. So remember, if one hundred persons are applying for the position in which you are interested, and you have written a good application letter, you will have, not one chance in a hundred of getting the job, but one chance in ten, since you will be one of the ten who will be interviewed. Your chance will be further enhanced by the resume, which is fully described in this chapter.

THE SPECIFIC FORMULA

Although it has a formula, the application letter need not be stereotyped, for it cites your individual qualifications, and may even exude your personality. Here is the formula:

1. State the qualifications you have that would serve the employer. Use the YOU attitude.

2. Mention a particular skill or accomplishment which you feel would enhance your chances.

3. Ask for the interview.

WHAT TO SAY

Here is one example:

> Dear Mr. Holden:
>
> My training in secretarial science at Tri-County Community College should qualify me as secretary in your firm.

I can type accurately at 60 words a minute, and I can take dictation at 140 words a minute. My training includes experience in the school office, and I have been on the honor roll the last two terms.

I should like to show you my resume which gives a complete background of my qualifications and references. May I have an interview at your convenience? Please write or call me at 641-0875 after 4 p.m.

Sincerely,

Miss Jane Beggs
841 Heather Lane
Salem, Oregon 97302

Remember, always, to include your address on any letter you write in your own behalf. This need not be done, of course, when there is a letterhead. The address is correctly placed either above the date at the top of the letter, or just below the typed name as Jane Beggs has done here. It is the writer's option to use the Ms. title, but this does not indicate the marital status, which could be a factor in the application letter. It is good to repeat here that a woman who is widowed or who is living with her husband should indicate his name or initials in parentheses under her typed name.

This letter is that of a girl who has just graduated or who is about to graduate from a community college where she has majored in secretarial science. If she has had experience in addition to her training, she should, of course, mention this. She might say, "My training at Tri-City Community College and my experience as part time secretary at the ABC Company should qualify me for a position as secretary in your firm."

If this girl is applying for a particular position which she knows is available, she should specify: "My training at the ABC Company should qualify me as secretary to your Vice President." (Note the importance she accords to the vice-president by capitalizing the title and leaving out the hyphen.)

A man may use the same type of application letter, stressing his particular training and experience. "My training in professional accounting at King Business College, and my experience with the Radford Bookkeeping Service should qualify me for the position of accountant with your firm." He might include as special qualifications his courses in cost accounting, tax, municipal accounting or whatever, and then mention, briefly, the specific responsibilities entailed in his experience.

The important thing to remember is to ask specifically for an interview. Few people are employed without an interview; so actually the application letter is asking for consideration as an applicant at the convenience of the employer or the person in charge of employment.

The question has come up in my classes about enclosing a self-addressed stamped envelope. The consensus of many businessmen is this: If the company is large or if the employer is a part of any municipal, county, state, or federal body, a self-addressed envelope is not necessary. A small office, however, is more likely to feel obligated to answer if the self-addressed and stamped envelope is included. So base your decision on this research.

THE NAME BEGINNING

What if someone has told you of a particular opening and has given you permission to use his name in your application letter? When this is the case, always use the name at the beginning of your letter. Never mention the name incidentally somewhere after the first paragraph, and never be vague about where you heard about the vacancy. You would not say, for instance, "I heard that there is to be a vacancy in your personnel department within the next month, and I should like to apply for the position." This is not only too vague to be ethical, but it is entirely possible that those outside the company might have heard through the proverbial grapevine about the vacancy before the departing employee has decided to turn in his (or her) resignation.

Here is an example of a name beginning:

Dear Mr. Weaver:

Mr. Tom Young of our Accounting Department has informed me of a vacancy in your Business Office, and he has suggested that my training should qualify me for the position.

I shall be graduated from Barrett School of Commerce June 22. I am an executive secretarial major, and my training includes, besides the usual typing, shorthand, and secretarial subjects, an intensive course in business machines and three courses in accounting.

I should like to have the opportunity of talking with you and of showing you my resume. May I have an interview at your convenience. Please call me at the school before 4 p.m. at 564-1894 or after 4 p.m. at my home, 564-7862. I shall look forward to hearing from you.

Sincerely,

GIMMICK LETTERS

Employers have indicated that they do not favor gimmick letters—ones that are arrogant, aggressive, or "different." These vary according to the personality of the applicant, but such a letter could be similar to the following:

Dear Mr. Durkin:

How would you like to have a very unusual person as your secretary? I'd like to have the job as your secretary, and here's why I believe I would be your best choice:

1. I have a degree in secretarial science from Midstate University.

2. During my senior year, I was counselor at Belden Hall, a campus dormitory.

3. I have taken an advanced course in Written Communication and I can compose good letters.

4. I like people and have never had any trouble getting acquainted or making friends.

5. I am persuasive, so I could serve as a good buffer for my boss.

6. I think quickly and I am an "idea" person.

7. I think your company is great, and I would consider it a privilege to be in a position to help solve your problems.

When may I see you—at your convenience, of course. I should like to show you my complete resume and answer any questions you might have. Please use the enclosed self-addressed and stamped envelope for your answer, or call me at 365-0962 after 3 p.m.

Sincerely,

Some businessmen who have been shown this type of letter admit that they would be curious. They might like to see what this aggressive young lady looks like, but generally they would be very wary of her aggressiveness. She has expressed a personal opinion about herself, suggesting that she is friendly and aggressive, that she is persuasive, and that she has ideas. These are the very characteristics employers might fear, since they could trigger personality conflicts among other employees who might not be so forward. Self-confidence is one thing, but without a degree of humility, it can become overbearing.

If such a gimmick letter creates enough curiosity to succeed in getting an interview, then the applicant would have to exert the utmost care in presenting herself personally as a desirable employee. One young applicant was successful in getting both an interview and a position with this approach, but she sent out only one such letter to an employer whom she had cased before she applied for the position. She felt sure that he was an aggressive civic leader type who would appreciate a secretary who could assume the "Girl Friday" role. This was a gimmick approach which worked out happily, but this is not the usual outcome. Think twice before you submit this kind of application letter, and know enough about the prospective employer to judge that his response would be favorable to a "different" approach.

THE RESUME

Before an application letter ever goes out, an applicant must have his resume ready to take with him on an interview. Remember that the application letter used to include complete information about the applicant. This policy, very happily, has changed, so that now the application letter itself is very short, but it is backed by a resume. College academicians usually refer to this as a *vita,* but this is really not a correct term, since a vita is a biographical sketch, which is different from a qualification resume. A brief biographical resume of one's career is correctly termed *curriculum vitae,* but this Latin expression is awkward to use, and is not so descriptive as simply resume and data sheet. One fine distributive education instructor has his students label their resumes "Data Folder," and he has his students enclose them in clear plastic folders. This folder is very professional looking, but it is difficult to file; so its use is simply a matter of preference.

Let us here use the term resume to mean the complete information data about an applicant which would be pertinent to qualifications for a position. The precis, on the other hand, is a one-page brief form of the resume which may be enclosed with the application letter.

Usually the resume is not enclosed with the letter of application for two reasons. If an applicant is using the shot-gun method rather than the rifle method in searching for a job, making multiple resumes is a lot of trouble. Second, it is better psychology to be able to hand to the prospective employer the resume, so that he may scan it at the same time he is interviewing the applicant. If his decision is deferred, as it usually is, he makes better connection between the person and the information if they are presented to him simultaneously.

Unless an applicant has his heart set on one particular job, he seldom uses the rifle method—which means he sends out this one application and just waits until he hears. He might, of course, use this method if he already has a job and is sending out a feeler for one he considers more desirable.

Usually, an applicant sends out several applications in order to save time and to have, perhaps, a better selection.

Unemployment statistics float around rather freely; yet the fact is that there is less unemployment in the business world than in either the blue collar field or in the top technical and academic area. In spite of women's lib, women seem to have less trouble getting positions in business, and men get better paying jobs, although it may take the men a little longer to get just what they want. There is, however, relatively little unemployment in business. I have yet to see a well qualified person wait very long for a good job in the business world.

All right, now let's tackle the resume. I am going to present here the format we have evolved after years of experimentation. Many of my students have reported that the resume "did the trick." One former student wrote that when her interviewer looked at her resume he asked her whether she had composed it herself, and when she said she had, he answered, "Anyone who has gone to that much trouble deserves a job." And she got the job. She wrote later that when he found she had had training in composing letters, he was delighted to give her much of that responsibility in order to save his time for more pressing matters.

Included here are two actual resumes, one of a young woman, and one for a person of wider experience. As an introduction to this assignment, I ask my students to submit to me a brief description of the courses they have taken at our business school. These descriptions include not only all of the courses they have taken but also the ones they are taking at the time. A list of subjects to be taken follows on a separate page. These will be described and added to the previous list as soon as they are completed. The reason for this is that it seems important for each student to give his own idea of courses he has taken. If I feel that these descriptions have been copied from our school catalogue, I turn them back to be done over. My only directions for this part of the resume are that the student use nonsentence structure and that he put no periods at the end of the descriptions even though (since they are itemized) each starts with a capital letter. Notice as you scan the examples that descriptions do not make such statements as, "I learned to operate common types of business machines such as the rotary calculator, the ten- and full-key adding machines and posting machine." In no case is there a subject and verb combination to make these descriptions sentences. This form seems to be preferred, but if you do choose sentence structure, be sure that your construction is parallel—that all descriptions use the same form.

In my own classroom situation, I proofread these course descriptions carefully, correcting an incorrect division of words at the end of the line, any misspelled words, or incorrect punctuation. If, as you make your resume, you are not in a classroom situation, it is a good idea to have someone else proofread this for you, since most people are careless in spotting their own errors.

Note that the format of the resume mentions first the information that any employer wants to know—education and experience.

Seldom are employers interested in pre-high school education; therefore, the high school from which the student has been graduated is indicated first under the heading EDUCATION. Dates are placed at the left, with the tab key set to itemize the schools on the right. Mention the high school from which you were graduated and the town in which it is located, with the month and year of graduation next. At this point list any business courses completed in high school or any courses that might be pertinent to the job for which you are applying.

If you did not graduate from high school but did pass the equivalency tests, usually referred to as G.E.D. tests (General Education Development), indicate this in place of the high school, or immediately after the last high school attended, like this:

1968-1969   Central High School
                                             Springdale, Idaho

June, 1972   G.E.D.
                                             Mid-State Community College
                                             Springdale, Idaho

If you attended no high school, then list simply the equivalency information.

If, after high school, you attended a technical school, a college or university, or any other school, or even if you received some sort of education in the Service or took USAFI courses in the Service, list these in chronological order under education with the dates at the left and the school or courses at the right. Use your judgment on this. If the courses you took in a community college or in the Service are in no way applicable to the position for which you are applying, merely list them or mention the general category or your major. If they are pertinent to a forthcoming job, list the courses or even describe them fully. If you have a degree from a college or university, indicate your major and describe only the pertinent courses. This is wherein your resume will be yours—it cannot possibly be stereotyped.

As you apply for a position, if you are in school, if you will complete your schooling soon, or if you are a recent graduate, list the courses and their descriptions at this point. Since this is a continuation of EDUCATION, this information is placed on your first page, and continued, if necessary, to page 2. This is copied from your proof-read course description assignment and is followed on a separate page by a list of courses not completed, if this applies. So much for education.

The next thing that an employer is interested in is your experience. Those of you who have had business experience are fortunate. This is listed in <u>reverse</u> chronological order under the general heading EXPERIENCE. This begins a new section in your resume. Dates should be at the left with experience listed at the right, something like this:

1971 to present

Security National Bank
Springdale, Idaho
L. J. Granger, Supervisor
Posting Department
(Part time)

June, 1970 to Sept. 1970
and December, 1970

Meyer Dept. Store
Springdale, Idaho
Mrs. Marian Jenks,
  Dept. Head
(Sales)

Notice the format and arrangement of the examples. Here, again the information is personal, and you may adapt the wording to suit your preference, but be sure that experience is listed in <u>reverse</u> chronological order and that you indicate specifically where you worked and what you did, giving, if possible, the name of your immediate superior.

Now, what if you have had no experience? What if all you have done is baby sit? What if you have worked on a farm, in a cannery, or in a factory? This type of work is listed separately under: JOBS HELD TO HELP DEFRAY SCHOOL AND PERSONAL EXPENSES.

If this sort of work is all you have done, then the page normally devoted to EXPERIENCE would have to imply this. If you have had some experience but also have held nonbusiness type jobs previously, then this page in your resume would have two separate headings.

If you have had a great deal of experience and are older than most school graduates, just forget this JOBS HELD section. However, if you are recently out of school, most employers are interested to see that you have had seriousness of purpose in helping to pay for part of your own expenses. Besides this, some of the people for whom you worked might serve as good references.

If you have done the same type of work every summer, simply indicate this by your date designations and not by repeating the same type of work. For instance:

Summers of 1968-1971

Picking beans,
strawberries, etc.

1968-1972
After school and weekends

Baby-sitting

This may seem silly, as perhaps it would be for a person in his mid-twenties or older, but many application blanks have questions which cover this type of work. This simply indicates to the employer habits of industriousness which he realizes are formed early in life.

It is important to mention here that those who have had extensive experience, particularly men, should be careful to include all of it. Questions might be raised if there are gaps. With girls and women it is different, since they frequently take time out for marriage and family responsibilities. One student admitted that he had "goofed off" a year after his stint in the Service. His tour of duty had been in the Far East; he had saved his money, and so he spent the year after his discharge traveling over the United States. He asked what he could say. As always, he was told to tell the truth—to indicate that this year was devoted to travel. Gaps in employment or education might occasionally be explained better during the interview. Decisions of this kind rest with the applicant, but he should be aware that the question might come up.

The next section of the resume is devoted to personal data, and this is the part that can be strictly individual. The usual information concerning age, height, weight, marital status, dependents, health, etc. should be indicated first. This should be followed by an enumeration of activities, honors, interests, and hobbies. While this part should not be padded, neither should it omit any phase of a person's interest or experience which might add to his attractiveness as an employee. If he (or she) is a recent graduate, then high school or college activities should be included—all the kinds of things that are usually listed in a high school annual or college yearbook: clubs, honors, offices, scholarships, athletic activities, etc.

Out-of-school activities and interests should come next. It is interesting to note that many current application forms include questions about Boy Scouts, Girl Scouts, Campfire Girls—affiliations of various sorts which go rather far back in any person's life. Scout ranks should be indicated as well as special honors in Scouting or in any other organization. You see, leadership qualities sometimes begin to show very early in a person's life. On the other hand, there is the late bloomer who will have to indicate that his interests and activities started much later in life. This is not unusual.

Arrange this page as attractively as possible, and don't hesitate to use two pages if necessary. In other words, don't try to crowd it all on one page.

The question has come up about nationality and church affiliation. Most businessmen would prefer that these be omitted. No person should be employed or denied employment because of either of these; so, the best bet is to forget them at this point. However, if you are active in a church, such as teaching church school or acting as lay assistant, there is no reason to withhold this information. It might, in fact, indicate leadership qualities.

Older applicants should always list civic interests and affiliations. Service club memberships, such as Jaycees or Rotary, and any specific offices or responsibilities are important phases of activities and interests. Toastmasters and Toastmistress clubs might indicate articulate speaking ability that an employer is looking for in an applicant. The rule of thumb is, "Don't pad, but don't hide your light under a bushel."

So much for the PERSONAL DATA part of the resume. Now for the final part. This is the list of references. The page should simply be listed REFERENCES and *(With Permission)* should be below it in parentheses.

Three references are the minimum, with as many as six or seven if you have an impressive list. These should include, if possible, at least one business or professional person who could be a former employer, an attorney, a doctor, a store or department manager, or

someone well known in government. If you happen to have a more than bowing acquaintance with a governor, a legislator, or some other person in state or even municipal government *and* you get his permission, by all means use his name as a reference.

One year several of the girls in my classes worked for two weeks on a volunteer basis for the State Legislature when the state budget didn't allow for expenses of a called session. Although the girls received no pay, they gained a fortune in experience, and many of the legislators and state officials offered to lend their names to the girls as references. This two weeks became part of the girls' experience on their resumes, although it was indicated that the work was done on a volunteer basis.

References should never be minors, even if the applicant is under 21. There should be at least one character reference, usually a teacher or a clergyman who can vouch for the applicant's character even though he may not be familiar with working habits or abilities. One reference may be simply a friend, but his word will count little unless he is a person known in his own field. References cannot afford to jeopardize their own credibility; so while they may accentuate the positive, they will tell the truth. Always get permission to use a person's name as reference. Renew this permission if more than a year has elapsed since the original request.

As an instructor I am glad to permit students to use my name as reference. I make it quite plain to them that I will accentuate the positive but that I will never stretch the truth. Otherwise my word would be worth nothing. I will answer honestly any questions that are put to me. On one occasion, I received a call from a company about a girl who had applied for a position and had used my name as reference. I answered questions truthfully and positively about her letter-writing ability, her typing, and her spelling—all of which were good. However, when I was asked specifically about her attendance record, I

117

referred to my grade book and reported that she had had six absences during one three-month term, and these absences were usually on Monday or Friday. She simply liked long weekends. In spite of good reports on her ability, this poor attendance record brought the blunt response, "We are not interested in her." I mention this in passing, since so many employers place this question among their first, "What is the attendance record?" They ask about this before they ever inquire about grades.

So there you have it, an outline for your resume. Refer to the examples and adapt yours to the format, but be quite sure that the context is your own. If you are a student or a recent graduate soon to be looking for a job, describing briefly the courses you have completed is a good idea. If it has been some time since you completed your education, list the schools with your major and go more into detail about your experience.

After you have completed a rough draft of your resume, ask yourself this question: How would I feel if I were to look at this resume? Answer this as objectively as you can.

Now, how do you use this resume? Do you ever send it with an application letter? Experience and research show that it is advisable to take the resume with you on the interview unless you are applying for a position which is out of town. Since duplicated copies of resumes should never be used, typing a number of copies for several out-of-town applications could mean a lot of work. You should, of course, resign yourself to the idea that landing a good job is worth a lot of work. One of my former students obtained three interviews and the job of her choice by sending three data resumes to a city in another state. She wrote later that her employer had said that he had decided in her favor before the interview—on the basis of her "beautiful" resume.

AN OUT-OF-TOWN INTERVIEW

How do you get an interview in another city? This requires just a little different technique in writing the application letter. Since most companies are reluctant to commit themselves by having an applicant incur the expense of making a long trip for an interview, the letter should state a possible visit to the city at a designated time. Something like this: "I plan to be in Seattle from March 20 to 25. May I have an interview at your convenience during that time? I enclose a self-addressed and stamped envelope for your answer."

While the trip made to another town, at possibly a great distance, may be with the specific purpose of trying to find a job, no company is obligating itself if you indicate that you plan to be there anyway. Several days could be set aside for this purpose and several application letters could request interviews. The trip is a small investment for going after a position in the city of your choice.

THE PRECIS

Suppose you would like to give an employer enough of your background without sending him a complete resume. This situation calls for a precis, a short version of the resume summarized on one sheet. This includes usually a brief outline of education, experience, and personal data, and possibly a reference or two. Note the example of this, but compose your own version accentuating the highlights of your qualifications.

Some applicants regard this one-page summary as a resume, but as far as I know, the use of the precis backed by a complete resume is original with my students and me. It came about because one of our students planned to apply for a legal secretarial position in a nearby city of her choice. She wanted to put out five "feelers," but she didn't want to make five copies of her resume. She said, "Why can't I just make an outline of my qualifications and then take the complete resume with me when I get an interview?" The precis evolved from this, and although she was the first to use it, it has proved to be an effective technique for many of our students.

This girl found a telephone directory of the city of her choice, and, turning to the yellow pages, she closed her eyes and put her finger down on the list of attorneys. She noted this particular firm's name and address. She did this five times, and sent an application letter with a precis to each of the attorneys selected at random. She sent these all out on a Monday. On Wednesday she received a telephone call at the school from one of the attorneys asking her to make the 75-mile trip that afternoon for an interview. She complied, had the interview, and was asked to return again on Friday to meet other members of the firm. She agreed to this. Then on Thursday she received a call from another one of the attorneys to whom she had sent her application. He asked her to make the trip for an interview that afternoon. She asked if she might change this to Friday since she would be in the town that day, but he insisted that she come that very afternoon, Thursday; so she did.

She had the interview, and the attorney seemed favorable, but he asked her to return the next day for an answer. Since she was making the trip to see attorney No. 1, this would not be too inconvenient, and she agreed. Somehow each attorney found out that she had been interviewed by the other, and the outcome was that they were actually vying for her services. She had her choice, accepting the offer of the one who had interviewed her first. She heard from all five attorneys, actually. One told her that he could see no vacancies in his firm in the foreseeable future; another wrote that he likely would have a vacancy within the next two months and asked her to inquire again, and the last one of the five suggested that she come in at her convenience to talk with him. He made no commitment.

The interesting fact is that five letters brought five responses, which included two firm job offers and possibly another offer. These were "cold" applications. This young lady was quite sure that her good application letter with the precis and the resume, which she presented at the time of her interviews, had much to do with the favorable responses. As a matter of fact, the attorney for whom she chose to work admitted that he had never seen anything so complete and impressive as her resume.

DISCUSSING SALARY

In connection with job application, I should like to mention something here that I always discuss with my students, something that is of particular interest to the girls. This has to do with salary. Remember, one of the don'ts at the first of this chapter is, "Don't talk about money." This had to do with the application letter itself. Now, how about the interview? What are you going to say if the prospective employer says, point blank, "What pay do you expect?"

This question puts an applicant at an unfair disadvantage. If she states an amount which is high, she will price herself out of a job. If the amount is too low, she isn't worth anything. I would counter this question with, "I am sure you know more about salaries than I do." or "What is the usual beginning salary that you pay?" This answers an unfair question with a question.

It is wise to be familiar with the going salary so that you can react intelligently to the discussion of money. Some firms have salary scales with periodic increments, but there are always those who depend on a discussion in determining the beginning pay. If you are aware of the customary salary for the kind of job for which you are applying, then you will know how to react when a figure is mentioned. If the figure is lower than you expect—and this applies more to girls than to men—indicate that you had expected more, but that you might be willing to accept this amount if you could feel sure that you would have a chance to advance. Indicate that you would like to be paid what you are worth. If the salary mentioned is higher than you expected, this is great. Just make up your mind that you will put forth every effort to be worth it.

Men are usually more familiar than women with prevalent salaries, and more frequently men have an absolute minimum which they can accept. However, if a man is willing to start with a salary lower than he would like but is assured a chance for advancement, he may prefer this arrangement. Everyone has to set his own standards with regard to salary, but neither a man nor a woman should go into an interview without having first considered how the question of salary will be answered.

THE FOLLOW-UP LETTER

Not later than 24 hours after the interview, the applicant should mail the follow-up letter. This is a very simple letter expressing appreciation for the interview. Usually, it has three parts, although it might vary with circumstances of the interview. Here is the formula:

1.   Express appreciation for the interview.

2.   Refer to something discussed during the interview which would specifically identify you in the mind of the interviewer.

3.   Express hope that your qualifications are being considered favorably.

This is a very short letter, and only the second part (or paragraph) keeps it from being somewhat stereotyped. Let's talk about this second paragraph, for which the groundwork is laid during the interview.

Although it is advisable to remember to let the interviewer lead the discussion and ask the questions, it is important not only to assume an attitude of interest but to ask some question or make some comment that would stimulate an answer or a discussion that would set you apart from the other applicants.

This could be a question about the filing system, about the correspondence policy, or about some other procedure or policy of the company. Try to be alert in your response to the explanation, and perhaps pursue the question further. This then, can serve as the basis for your second paragraph in the follow-up letter. After you have mentioned your appreciation for the interview in the first paragraph, slip into a reference to your discussion. If you use this ploy wisely, it will set you apart from other applicants and will refresh the memory of the interviewer of you in particular.

Here is an example of such a letter:

Dear Mr. Blount:

I should like to express my appreciation to you for the interview that you granted me yesterday. After talking with you, I feel that it would be a great privilege to be a part of the XYZ Company.

I especially appreciated the explanation of your new filing system, and I can certainly understand how its use can mean more efficiency in your office. Besides being easily accessible, the stacks of color-coded files add greatly to the attractiveness of the business office. Thank you for taking the time to show them to me.

I hope you are considering my application favorably. I look forward to hearing from you.

Sincerely,

Any admonition to avoid using the pronoun "I" at the beginning of each paragraph does not apply to application letters. How much more natural this sounds than referring to yourself as the writer or the undersigned or some other circumlocution. Worse than using the pronoun "I" is awkward passive voice. "Your interview yesterday was appreciated by me." This is not the way people talk, and it sounds stilted and unfriendly. Stick with active voice.

REFUSING AN OFFER

If your applications for positions have earned several interviews and you have written your follow-up letters, then it would seem that all there is to do is to sit back and wait. However, chances are quite likely that your beautiful resume, your poise during the interview, and your follow-up letter have resulted in more than one offer—then what?

You should, of course, consider thoughtfully which job you will accept. Income in itself is not always the criterion of your choice. Consider personnel, working conditions, chance for advancement, and most especially the sheer joy of challenge and work that will prove rewarding. After this choice is made, your answer will be made either by letter or by phone, unless, of course, the job of your dreams has been offered, and you have answered a phoned offer with a quick acceptance.

Ethics and courtesy demand that you give an answer to the positions which have been offered but which you must refuse in favor of your choice. Even if it were not common courtesy, there could be an outside chance that sometime you might have future dealings with the company which has offered you the position you feel you must refuse. Here we rely again on the TRI-ASK TECHNIQUE. What do I want to accomplish? The answer is, "I want to say 'no' in such a way that goodwill is not damaged." How can I do this? I soften the blow, explain, and specifically complete the refusal with a sign-off of goodwill. You do not, in this letter, offer an alternative. It would be out of order to suggest someone else for the job. Here is an example, but do remember that your own situation would dictate the specifics of the letter.

Dear Mr. Knapp:

I feel greatly complimented that your company has offered me the position of secretary to the Business Manager. Yours is a fine organization and I am sure that I would enjoy this opportunity.

I have, however, decided to accept an offer from the Carlson Company as secretary to the General Manager. The determining factor in this decision is greater responsibility and an opportunity for a two-month training course in management techniques. I am sure you understand my desire to take advantage of this education.

I shall always remember the courtesy you extended to me during my interview.

Sincerely,

Note that the opening is complimentary, that the boom is lowered gently without any negative words—nothing like, "I regret to inform you that I must refuse your offer." By saying that she has decided to accept another offer, the writer clearly implies a refusal, but does not spell it out in a negative way. Since this writer has made a decision, it is quite ethical to mention the name of the company where she will be employed. The explanation for her decision is reasonable—more responsibility and an educational opportunity, and she has placed the recipient of the letter on an intellectual level by telling him she is sure that he will understand. Her reason might have been higher salary, and it is quite all right to explain this. Her sign-off is more or less perfunctory—it could have been the fact that since they are in the same line of business, they will chance to see each other at a convention or meeting.

This type of letter should not in any way compare unfavorably one company with the company for which she has chosen to work. The writer should be honestly grateful for the offer, but not overbearing about having received a better offer. Most important, this letter should always be written. Too many applicants forget the courtesy of a refusal when a better offer comes along.

REQUESTING A DECISION

What if you have made several applications, have written your follow-up letters, and are now in that hopeful and uncertain state of simply waiting for an answer? Then suppose that the job you least want is offered to you first and you have a limited time in which to give your decision. Suppose that one particular job for which you have applied, the one you really want, has not materialized. Suppose that although an answer has been promised within a week, ten days have gone by without an answer. Is it ethical to ask for a decision in this case, and is it all right to mention the fact that you have another offer? The answer to both of these questions is, "Yes, indeed." Go ahead and try to get an answer one way or another. This, of course, requires finesse and diplomacy. Remember that the following is only an example, and that such a letter would have to reflect very clearly your own particular situation. Here it is:

Dear Mr. Owens:

The more I have thought about my recent interview with you, the more I feel I can fulfill the responsibilities of the position that you outlined.

I have, however, been given another offer, and I must give my answer within the next week. I would prefer working in your office, but I am sure you understand that I must make a decision.

I should certainly like to know what your decision is. May I hear from you?

Sincerely,

Be sure that what you say in this letter is true. Don't claim to have another offer unless you actually have, although you could give another reason for wanting an answer. Plans for a trip or an opportunity for an educational workshop, both of which you would be willing to forego if the job of your choice materializes, would be logical reasons for requesting a decision.

Since you would not mention the name of the company which has made you the offer, it would be quite all right to indicate that you would prefer the position you are mentioning.

This type of letter almost always brings an answer, and it just could be the determining factor in getting the results that you want. If the employer has given the job to someone else and has not let you know, he has been remiss in his obligation if he told you that you would hear from him. At least your letter should bring forth an answer, and you will know where to go from there.

Going after a job is quite a process. It is far more than just writing a letter or getting an interview. It begins, of course, with your training or your education and with any experience you might have had. From there the resume and possibly the precis must be carefully made; next comes the application letter itself, followed by the interview, then the follow-up letter, and then possibly a letter turning down an offer or one asking for an answer.

Most people just starting out in the business world know what kind of job they want, but do not have their hearts set on any particular one. But there are exceptions. Let me tell you about one girl who wanted a good job with a particular company—a very large organization. She had an appointment set up with the personnel director on the basis of her application letter, but before this took place she wanted to familiarize herself with the company. She went to the company and asked whether it would be possible to take a tour through the offices. This took a lot of nerve, but it paid off. She was conducted through the many departments of the organization, and she asked questions all the way. She took notes, and when it came time for her interview, she not only answered questions intelligently but gave evidence of knowing a great deal about the company. Furthermore, she knew exactly what kind of job in the company she wanted, and she had no trouble getting it.

Another example is that of a high school junior who went to a large law firm and offered to work for just the experience. She was turned down because of her youth and inexperience, but, after she had completed her junior year, she again asked if she could work without pay, explaining that she could type, that she had had one year of shorthand, and that she had had some training in the high school office. She explained that her goal in life was to be a legal secretary and that she wanted very much to learn all she could. One attorney in the firm was so impressed with her determination that he gave his consent for her to work without pay as a trainee. She was a good student, and her work was so accurate and she was so willing to accept responsibility that before long she was presented with a pay check. She worked part time during her senior year and then stepped into a full-time job after she was graduated.

The firm sent her to a business school for special training that she had not been able to get in high school, and she returned as a career girl fixture in that law firm. This true story ended on an especially happy note, for this girl subsequently married a young attorney who became the junior member of the firm. This romantic ending was not part of this girl's original goal. I guess you might call this serendipity—in her zeal at reaching her professional goal, she found something better that she was not even expecting. I am certainly not suggesting that the way to find a husband is to be conscientious in pursuing a professional goal, but the rewards of going after a goal with determination can bring many kinds of pleasant surprises.

I have cited these examples to show that anyone who zealously pursues a job can get one. The employment field is wide open for responsible persons of any age who are not afraid of work. Remember, that nearly all personnel directors or employers who interview applicants ask during the interview, "Why do you want to work for our company?" You'd better have an answer that reflects your interest or knowledge of the company.

INTERVIEWS

It is perfectly natural to have butterflies in your stomach during the first interview or two, but remember that a really big person will put you at ease. If you come across a boss who seems to get some sadistic pleasure out of scaring you (this is rare), it is good to find this out before you commit yourself to being around such a character every day. Some employers will put you at ease but will ask questions to test your mettle. If you are asked about some particular type of training which you haven't had—for instance, if you are asked whether you can operate a certain kind of machine and you have never seen the machine before—you will have to answer truthfully; but instead of panicking, simply respond, "No, I have never operated that particular kind of machine, but I have learned how to operate others; so I am sure I could learn." No boss wants a secretary who will panic at a new experience. Two of the most valuable traits of any good employee—man or woman—are adaptability and versatility.

Is it ethical to apply for a job when you have heard of no vacancy? Of course. Vacancies occur frequently, and applications are usually kept on file. One of my students greatly admired an office where her family did business. Her dream was to work in this office; so, shortly before her graduation, she took her resume in her hand and went in cold to apply for a job. Not only did she get a job, but the employer could hardly wait for her to complete the final three weeks of her classes. He just happened to have a vacancy, and he admitted later that two factors turned the trick in granting this job—the "beautiful" resume and the very complimentary fact that the girl was quite frank in admitting that this was the office of her dreams.

APPLICATION FORMS

How about filling in application blanks? You will find that your complete resume may preclude having to fill in such a form, but many companies require these to be completed for uniform filing on applicants and employees. A representative of the State Employment Service who spoke to my classes suggested that applicants ask for two copies of application forms and for permission to take them home for leisurely and more accurate completion. One copy, filled in for practice, could remain in the applicant's files. My students have followed this advice and have not met with any objections on the part of employers.

If you have not filled in an application form recently, you may be surprised at the nature of the questions which seem, in many cases, to be an invasion of privacy. The types of questions asked emphasize the importance of a good employment record. All forms request information about previous employment; therefore, it seems advisable to leave any job under favorable circumstances rather than to quit in a fit of temper. I have heard former employees brag about how they "told off" their bosses when they quit because of personality conflicts or disagreements. This may seem to have temporary therapeutic value—from "getting off the chest" standpoint, but frequently former employers are asked for information whether or not their names are given as references.

Most state and federal civil service employment application forms require similar information which includes personal data, marital status, and information about education and employment. It is a good idea to know dates—the month and year of starting and of leaving—both for education and employment. There should be nothing nebulous in this area, no stating that you have a college education if all you have had is two years and one

term. Each month and year must be recorded together with the exact number of term or semester hours. Starting salary and last salary are to be listed and usually the reason for leaving the job.

Too many times, when people start out on their occupational careers, they have trouble locating the spot where they feel they will be happy, and frequently the grass looks greener on the other side of the fence. It is wise to remember that a record of your work experience follows you wherever you go and that if there is indication of too frequent changing, you may be identified as a job hopper, and your chances of further employment will be jeopardized.

Questions on employment forms vary somewhat, and some are much more detailed than others. I have in my files one questionnaire designed for executive applicants of a large company, and this constitutes the most flagrant case of privacy invasion I have ever seen. I wonder that the company ever gets any applicants. Besides the usual questions involving personal data, education, and experience, the applicant must spell out what he liked or disliked about his previous jobs, and he is asked to give his opinion about the companies' policies. Specific questions cover how the applicant has spent his spare time, records of arrest, his net worth, what debts he owes, the payments on his house, and the occupations of his wife, his father, and his mother, with ages and earnings of each. Then other questions cover the applicant's relationships with his father and mother and which had more influence in his life. He is asked when he last had a drink of intoxicating liquor, how he spends his leisure time, whether or not he goes to church, to what extent he and his wife entertain, and the extent of arguments with his wife. If he is divorced, he is asked to explain the nature of the difficulty. His health is covered in detail by questions about any specific illnesses, when he last visited a doctor and why, and whether he was ever hospitalized.

The reason I have this in my files is that one of my former students asked permission to take the questionnaire home, but when he got to the question about how he gets along with his wife, he refused to let his privacy be invaded to this extent, and so he gave one copy of the form to me. I have never seen any other so extensive as this; however, many ask questions about debts, arrests, relatives, and living quarters. Quite a number of questionnaires require the applicant to indicate whether or not he has ever applied for unemployment compensation. Some employers are inclined to look upon this type of record with disfavor. In spite of the prevalent feeling against any kind of discrimination, employers cannot help discriminating when it comes to selecting employees. If an employer chooses not to select an employee who has received compensation for unemployment, one who smokes, or even one who chews gum, this is his privilege. Nearly everyone has prejudices. Remember, Thomas Edison would not hire anyone in his laboratory who salted his food before he tasted it—a silly prejudice of a great genius.

Most employers do not carry prejudices this far, but in applying for a position everyone should make every effort to present himself as a desirable employee. When a person asks for a job, he is scrutinized carefully; he is examined and prodded, but he doesn't have a reciprocal privilege. He cannot say, "Just a minute, if I take this job, what am I getting into? Are the people with whom I'll be expected to work easy to get along with? Please don't put me near any gum chewers, and by the way, do you have air conditioning?" He can size up the situation and the employer. He can take a cursory look at the surroundings and guess at the working conditions, but he must take a certain calculated risk in accepting employment, and then it is up to him to do the adapting.

The person who learns early in his business career to adapt his personality to those with whom he works will find that personality conflicts may be avoided. He should submit his applications carefully and somewhat widely; he should choose carefully—going after the job that appeals to him most with an eye to a chance for professional advancement. Many top men in business started at the bottom, and many women in executive positions started as file clerks or stenographers. The secretarial route can lead to exciting top careers—possibly even to marriage.

QUITTING A JOB

How about quitting a job? Please refer to Chapter 13 for the report on How to Quit a Job. This report submitted by one of my students indicates that a letter of resignation should be written when a person decides of his own volition to terminate his employment. Anyone should be careful about keeping such a decision to himself until after he has submitted a letter of resignation to his immediate superior. Nothing could be more unethical than for the news of his quitting to reach the employer before the word comes from the departing employee himself. It has been known for the employer to beat the resigning employee to the punch by firing him. Perhaps he doesn't like the idea of "his" employee going to a competitor. Perhaps he might feel that the resignation is a reflection on him, so all right, he'll make it appear that the decision was his. In the event that a former employer reports that the separation was his decision, a copy of the letter of resignation would be proof of the contrary.

THE LETTER OF RESIGNATION

Even if the boss is aware of an employee's quitting, the resignation letter should be written, simply as a matter of record. Here is a simple example:

Dear Mr. Kean:

I want you to know how very much I have appreciated my association with your firm these last two and a half years. I have especially enjoyed the rapport that has existed in our department.

For this reason I am sorry to submit my resignation effective March 15. My husband has been transferred to Denver, and he must report to his new assignment April 1. While I am pleased with his promotion, I reluctantly leave this fine company.

I shall seek employment in Denver, but I know I'll never find a situation which is as pleasant as my job here. Thank you for everything.

Sincerely,

This is directed to her immediate supervisor, and this particular letter presupposes a very pleasant situation. Her reference to seeking employment at the new location may prompt a To Whom It May Concern letter without her having to ask for it.

What if the situation has not been so pleasant and the change of jobs is the result of looking for and finding a job that offers more opportunity and better pay—a legitimate reason, certainly, for making a change? Such a letter could be something like this:

Dear Mr. O'Connor:

This is to notify you of my resignation to be effective November 1. I have accepted a position with the Bronson Company as office manager.

I have appreciated my associations here at Clifford's and the opportunity to improve my skills. However, I am sure you understand my desire to accept an opportunity that offers more responsibility and better pay.

I shall be happy to do whatever I can to assist my replacement to become oriented with the responsibilities of my position here.

Sincerely,

Resist any temptation to be resentful of your associations or overbearing about getting a better job. No matter what, try to leave on a happy note. If possible, coordinate the time element with your pay check. If you are paid twice a month, two weeks' notice is enough, but a monthly pay check indicates a month's notice.

THE *TO WHOM IT MAY CONCERN* LETTER

A thoughtful employer or department head will present to a good employee a "To Whom It May Concern" letter without solicitation. It is, however, quite within reason to ask for such a letter of recommendation, particularly if the relationships have been pleasant. This letter is especially helpful if the person is applying for an out-of-town job. Asking references to make several such letters would be an imposition, so duplicating such originals is accepted practice. Following is the context of an actual letter I wrote in behalf of a student whom I felt I could recommend. This was typed on the school letterhead.

TO WHOM IT MAY CONCERN:

Mary Doe has been a student in my classes for the last year at Merritt Davis School of Commerce, and I consider her an exemplary student. Her attendance record has been excellent; her work has been completed on time, and her grades have been high. She has been on the honor roll each term since she has been here.

Besides doing proficient work in all of her classes, she is capable of assuming responsibility. She has shown especial proficiency in her ability to compose and write a good business letter.

I feel that Mary would make a good employee, and I am happy to recommend her.

Virginia Lee Hallock
Academic Department
Merritt Davis School of Commerce

This letter recommended an outstanding student, but here is an example of a letter that may be written about a student of lesser qualities.

TO WHOM IT MAY CONCERN:

John Jenkins will soon complete his course in Junior Accounting at Merritt Davis School of Commerce and will be ready for employment. He was a student in two of my classes, and I found him to be most responsible.

His attendance was good, and his assignments were turned in on time. His response was satisfactory, he contributed well to the class, and he seemed to be liked by the other students.

He was a member of the Student Council, and was always ready to do his part in any school activity. I feel that as an employee he would assume responsibility, and that he would make every effort to do his best.

Virginia Lee Hallock
Academic Department
Merritt Davis School of Commerce

Note that this letter did not say anything about grades, which could have been average. In answering questions about this student, I would, of course, tell the truth. If he had been a C student, I would say this if I were asked, and I would never recommend him for a specific job that I felt he could not handle, but I would make every effort to accentuate the positive.

An employer of a departing employee might point out specific skills or aptitudes, but he would, of course, stick to facts. This type of letter is written on a business letterhead and is dated.

As a member of a professional personnel and guidance organization, I attended the planning session for a state Job Fair. This session was attended by personnel representatives of large companies and by employers of smaller businesses. When we teachers and counselors asked what we could tell our students to encourage them to prepare themselves as good employees, these people who were responsible for personnel selection stated that the first question they ask a prospective employee is about his attendance. It seems that they prefer an average student with good attendance and a record of responsibility to one whose exclusive record is high scholarship. Not that grades are unimportant, but high grades do not insure responsible, steadfast, loyal employees. In my classes good attendance and prompt assignments are important factors in computing grades. Assignments are late if they are not turned in on the due date regardless of the reason for their being late. Students sometimes say, "What if a person is ill?" I remind them that personnel managers say, "We don't want sick people." These executives avoid applicants who have records of illness, and while this may seem hard-hearted, we really can't blame businesses for wanting to employ those who are healthy, especially since physicians and psychologists now agree that most illness is psychosomatic and much absenteeism is unnecessary. So—you'll have one foot in the door if you are a healthy applicant with an impressive data sheet and a good attendance record.

While this text stresses written communication which, in this chapter, encompasses the application letter and related communications pertinent to obtaining a position, these would be nullified if they were not based on a foundation of job readiness and followed with an inventory of impressive personality characteristics. The many personnel managers and employers whom I have consulted and those who have spoken to my students have provided me with an impressive list of suggestions for the job hunter. These suggestions are neither provincial nor Western, for my research has been nationwide. Employers from North to the South, from the East to the West, in city or small town agree on standards for employees.

EVALUATE YOURSELF

The consensus of experienced personnel managers and employers includes the following characteristics as being the most important for prospective employees. It behooves each job hunter to evaluate himself on these points:

Knowledge of English usage — Can you express yourself correctly?
Can you write a good sentence?
Is your pronunciation accurate?
Are you willing to expand your vocabulary?

Good health — Have you had a good attendance record at school or at work?

Enthusiasm	— Are you alert and interested in the work for which you have prepared yourself? Are you eager to learn more?
Courtesy	— Are you thoughtful? Do you show deference to the feelings of others?
Pleasant voice	— Is your voice adaptable to telephone usage? Does your voice reflect optimism and courtesy?
Attractive appearance	— Are you well groomed? Do you use good taste in dress? Are your nails well manicured and clean? Do you avoid extreme dress or hair styles?
Dependability	— Do you have emotional stability and the ability to assume responsibility?
Honesty	— Do you have integrity? Can you be diplomatic without being blunt? Can you avoid exaggeration and gossip?
Poise	— Can you keep your composure even under pressure? Are you patient?
Good memory	— Can you remember customers, clients, deadlines, dates, appointments? Can you remember to remind the boss?
Social acceptability	— Can the boss be proud of your out-of-office behavior? Are you a positive reflection of the company for which you work?
Punctuality	— Are you aware that punctuality is more important for checking in than for checking out?
Sense of humor	— Are you mature enough to know the appropriateness of the right kind of humor? Do you avoid sarcasm, practical jokes, and off-color jokes?
Initiative	— Are you resourceful? Can you take over in a pinch? Can you assume responsibility when necessary without being told?
Reliability	— Can you be depended upon?

| Diplomacy | — | Can you handle awkward situations and avoid being tempted to resort to sarcasm? |
| Loyalty | — | Are you prepared to be loyal to the company for which you work? Can you keep any complaints within the company? Can you keep company secrets confidential? |

If you find yourself lacking in any of these areas, try using Benjamin Franklin's method of self-improvement. Determine which is your weakest area and work on eliminating this deficiency. Evaluate yourself in this area until you are satisfied with your improvement, then start working on another. In helping my students evaluate themselves, I ask them to list their negative characteristics on the left side of a sheet of paper, then list their positive traits on the right. Since no one else will see these lists, I encourage them to be as honest as they can. I suggest, then, that they use the technique of accentuating the positive by stressing good points to the extent of crowding out the negative ones. They think more about what they are working for than what they are trying to eliminate. For instance, if you work at being dependable, you will gradually learn to assume responsibility. If you work at being poised—keeping yourself under control—you will automatically overcome that temper that is on the negative side. And so it goes. It always works.

Anyone who aspires to be an employee in business can aspire to the top if he (or she) wants to. Most young men are serious about finding their niches in the business world, but too frequently girls regard business training as a stop-gap until they find a husband. Marriage is the goal of most young women. However, statistics show that the average woman has employment outside the home for 20 years. Helping the husband complete his education, boredom with domesticity, and helping children get their education are a few of the reasons that women are employed. Business is actually smiling on the mature woman with business training and experience because she is less likely to quit than the girl who interrupts her career for marriage and children.

All this is by way of pointing out that employment should be more than a stop-gap. A good record of employment can enhance a person's chance of getting a better job whenever that person seeks employment. Recent articles in reliable magazines have described secretarial positions which pay salaries from $10,000 to $25,000.

While starting salaries for inexperienced secretaries may be low, businessmen have indicated to me that the "sky is the limit." This is especially true with top executives, attorneys, and managers. An attorney told one of our graduates when he employed her, "If your efficiency can save me time, this is money in my pocket, and this will be reflected in the money you can have in your pocket—the sky is the limit." He followed through on this promise by giving this girl raises commensurate with the responsibility she assumed.

Remember, there is very little office unemployment. In most areas there are actually more jobs than applicants, and employers sometimes despair at not being able to get employees—men and women—who can spell and write a coherent sentence and who can be mature enough to assume responsibility with a minimum of supervision. Among the occupations now in the largest demand are secretaries and general office employees.

One bit of advice I like to give the young men in my classes is to take some form of shorthand, preferably a simplified form based on the use of the alphabet. Men seem to shy away from shorthand because they consider this secretarial subject feminine; yet many successful men have made their way into the top echelon of business through the "executive assistant" route, and this is a glorified term connoting male secretary. One of our accounting majors attributed his quick rise to an assistant directorship of a state commission to the fact that he had a knowledge of an alphabet shorthand. His responsibilities, for one thing, entailed taking minutes at the board meetings, and while he composed most of the letters he wrote, there were times when it was necessary for him to take dictation from the director.

Degree of education does not seem to enhance a person's ability to know how to go about seeking employment. An editorial in a metropolitan newspaper quoted actual application letters of college graduates which abounded in errors in punctuation, grammar, and spelling. Many college graduates are deficient in this area, and they have little opportunity to learn the art of writing unless, as undergraduates, they stumble into an elective on written communication. One engineering senior at a large university did elect such a course, simply because he needed an extra three hours credit and he was looking for an easy elective. After the term was over, he told his instructor that this was one of the most valuable courses he had taken and that he felt that it should be a required course for every student in every department. After a student has completed his college career, how often does he have the responsibility of writing a composition? Seldom. Yet letter writing is something which he will use, not only vocationally, but personally, for the rest of his life.

One business administration graduate who had a good background in English and spelling and who elected a course in written communication as a lower classman admitted to me that he attributed his 3.7 cumulative average directly to his knowledge of written expression.

One would imagine that teachers would know how to go about preparing a letter of application and a personal resume, but even this prestigious profession falls sadly short in this area.

I have in my files the application letters and personal records of two men and one woman who applied for teaching positions in a business school. They were handed to me as examples of how this important chore should not be handled. Let's take the application of the young woman first. Her husband was a college professor, and she appeared in person to apply for an English teaching position. The school director was favorably impressed with her, and, since she had no written information with her, he asked her to submit a data sheet. Although this young woman had a Bachelor of Arts degree from a large state university, she not only had never prepared a resume, she didn't even know what one is. When she submitted one, all information was crowded on one sheet, and, to put it bluntly, it was a mess. She must have received advice on making one from an old-timer, since this data sheet opened with personal information and activities. The experience, which was of far more importance than her high school and college activities, was tucked in at the bottom of the sheet.

Here was a college graduate with teaching experience on the college level, qualified to teach English and economics, who had never received any kind of training in writing an application letter or making a personal record. Neither her data sheet nor her letter of submittal did justice to her training and experience.

Following is the context of an application letter which is more or less self-explanatory, except that the original version, typed in an indifferent format, contained erasures and strikeovers.

Dear Mr. Drager:

At age 56 I am in a position to take minimum retirement under our Texas system and seek part to full time employment in a more favorable climate. I am attracted to your town since my father lives in retirement there with my sister and husband. I also have numerous other relatives and friends scattered between there and Portland.

I am enclosing a detailed resume of my entire background of training and experience in order that you may be the judge as to whether or not I could fit into your organization. You will please note that by training and experience I would be able to teach: Business English, Salesmanship, Business Organization and Management, Economics and Business Law.

Please let me know as to whether or not you may have an opening in the foreseeable future. In the meantime, please keep the enclosed resume in your application file and hold in abeyance in the event of a future vacancy.

Sincerely yours,

This man's description of his resume as detailed was not an understatement. To put it quite bluntly, it was padded with all manner of information that was not relevant to his qualifications. The resume, which was mimeographed, contained eight pages of single spaced typewritten material. It was entitled "COMPLETE EDUCATION, ADMINISTRATIVE AND INDUSTRIAL RECORD OF JAMES STEPHENSON JENKINS (not his real name, of course), along with the COMPLETE SUPPLEMENTARY DATA.

His personal data came first: height, weight, age, marital status, even the color of his complexion, hair, and eyes. He listed every course he had even taken anywhere whether it pertained to teaching or not.

He included detailed information on a visual aid program in which he had been involved. Two pages were required to describe his educational philosophy, and one page was dedicated to a list of every job he had ever held including custodial work, chauffeuring, and icing refrigerators. Another whole page described one job which he felt would qualify his instruction in business.

He gave a descriptive list of his visitations to "places of scenic, historic and industrial importance." I am sure that a prospective employer would be delighted to know that he has visited the House of Magic at Mela Park or the Winkley Artificial Limb Plant, the Missouri Ozarks, etc. ad infinitum.

Since this man is far removed from Oregon, I describe this data sheet to my students as a horrible example. I suppose that, comparing his resume with the brief data sheet of the young lady, we could say these examples run from the "sublime to the ridiculous," although each is ridiculous in its own way, and neither is effective.

Another "horrible example" came from an applicant who boasted a Ph.D. degree. His duplicated application letter was redundant with errors. The inside address was not even aligned with the body of the letter, and the applicant forgot to type in a salutation. His duplicated data sheet was crowded on one sheet of paper, single-spaced, with a picture of the applicant and personal data at the top of the page. He used essay format with no paragraphing, although wading through this crowded, ill-prepared resume proved him to be academically qualified (with his summa cum laude, his Ph.D., and his authorship of several textbooks in economics and education). An employer would be justified in wondering at this man's utter lack of training in writing an application letter or preparing an effective resume.

Contrast these poor letters from presumably qualified applicants with the following letter from one of our students which resulted in an interview and subsequently a position in the home office of an Oregon Senator.

2243 Morgan St. SE
Salem, OR 97302
May 24, 1968

Senator Wayne Morse
Federal Court Building
Portland, OR 97207

Dear Senator Morse:

After spending the last fifteen months in the best business college in Oregon, I will be graduating from Merritt Davis School of Commerce on the 21st of June. I feel that my previous experience and the fine schooling I have received here qualify me for a position on your staff.

As secretary of the Greater Salem Young Democrats, I have been in contact with many of your people, relating to the campaign for renomination as our Senator from Oregon. I have been working very hard for your renomination and I am confident that you have more than the majority of the people behind you.

When would it be possible for me to have an interview with you? I realize that you spend most of your time in Washington, D.C., and that when you are in Oregon, your time is budgeted trying to cover as much ground as possible during your campaign. Maybe you could suggest someone I could see who would be in a position to inform me of your schedule and any spare time you might have. You can write to me at the above address, or phone me at 474-9756.

I have enjoyed working on your campaign and hope to be able to see you soon.

Yours truly,

Kathy- - - - - - -

Enclosure

Kathy didn't hesitate to mention her political interest, but she told the truth, and she certainly had qualifications to back up her desire for an important position. She got the job and had a never-to-be-forgotten experience. She was a devoted and loyal employee.

Students who have taken my course in correspondence become aware of good letters and critical of poor letters; they frequently bring to me samples of each. One such letter which I have in my files was written by a mortician applying for a position in a funeral home in the Willamette Valley. This applicant obviously had never heard of the "you" attitude, and he seemed to imagine that his desire for a change of scene was adequate reason for consideration of his application.

Here is his letter written on the top half of a letterhead:

GENTLEMEN
WILLIAMS, OREGON

DEAR SIR:

I AM DESIROUS IN A CHANGE OF CLIMATE SUCH AS THE
WILLAMETTE VALLEY. RECENTLY I HAD A VISITE WITH A RETIRED
MINISTER WHO WAS VISITING SOME OF HIS OLD PERISHINERS IN
THIS DISTRICT. HE WAS TELLING ME WHAT A NICE CLIMATE THEY
HAVE IN THE WILLAMETTE VALLEY AND SHOULD COME DOWN
THAT WAY TO LIVE, SO I SAW YOUR ADD FOR AN EMBALMER &
FUNERAL DIRECTOR IN THE MORTUARY MANAGEMENT AND
DECIDED I WOULD LIKE TO LIVE IN THE WILLAMETTE VALLY.

I AM WELL EXPERIENCED IN THE MORTUARY BUSINESS AND HAVE
OWNED AND OPERATED TWO FUNERAL HOMES. I AM MARRIED AND
HAVE THREE CHILDREN. ONE IN COLLEDGE THE OTHER TWO IN
HIGH SCHOOL.

                                              Yours very truly,

Until I read the complimentary close I assumed that he had an upper case
typewriter. This sad application demonstrates how important it is for anyone, in any kind
of business, to have some idea of how to compose a letter, particularly an application
letter.

Several years ago the *Reader's Digest* published a story about a young man who
carried a pigeon in a cage into the offices of the National Broadcasting Company and
asked that it be delivered to the local station's manager. The homing pigeon had a message
on its leg which instructed the reader to release it with one of two items checked. One
indicated a time for an interview, and the other indicated that the applicant was
presumptuous and that an interview would not be given under any circumstances. The
curiosity of the executive resulted in an interview and subsequently a job for the ingenious
applicant.

Irvin S. Cobb, after a fruitless search for a job, early in his career wrote the
following letter to the leading newspaper editors:

"Here I am, the liveliest reporter, the best writer, and the ablest
editor that has ever come to New York. Yet nobody has jumped at the
unparalleled opportunity of hiring me.

"Now this is positively your last chance. I'm weary of waiting in
your anterooms, and a modest appreciation of my own worth forbids my
doing business with your head office boy any longer. Unless you grab me
right away I will go elsewhere and leave your paper flat on its back, and
your whole life hereafter will be one vast, surging regret."

I do not suggest in my classes any such drastic gimmick approach, but I do suggest
originality, enthusiasm, interest, and just plain good sense—anything to lift you out of the
"blah" category.

SUMMARY

Getting the just-right job is worth the effort. Reread this chapter again and again. Profit by the examples and the experiences of others. Consider carefully each step.

1.   Prepare your resume carefully.

     Allow yourself time enough to get permission to use names as references.

2.   Decide where to submit applications.

     a.   Use the employment service of your school.
     b.   Accept suggestions from friends or acquaintances. (Can you use a name in your application letter?)
     c.   Consider employment agencies.
     d.   Avail yourself of the classified ads, but use care in sending applications to "blind" ads.
     e.   Consider sending out "cold" application letters.

3.   Write several letters asking for interviews.

4.   After each interview write a follow-up letter.

5.   Submit letters of appreciation and explanation for any job offer you decide not to accept.

6.   Request an answer when time is of essence.

7.   Submit a letter of resignation when you decide to quit a job.

8.   Don't hesitate to ask for a letter of reference—a To Whom It May Concern letter—if you feel you deserve it.

9.   Keep a careful record of employment, dates, salary, supervisors' names, etc. to keep your resume up to date and to be able to answer accurately questions on application forms.

10. Do your very best on every job to establish a record of responsibility. Avoid personality conflicts.

Trouble? Of course. Getting the right job is serious business. For a man, finding his occupational niche is probably the most important step in his life. For a woman, a job may be a career or it may provide that necessary experience insurance for the future.

Following are words that are frequently misspelled in application-related letters. Write each one twice, dividing the word into syllables. Then, without looking at the syllabicated word, write the word correctly once. Look at it. Pronounce it.

1. con ven' i ent

This most frequently misspelled word is actually pronounced con ven' yent, but by separating the "i" and exaggerating its pronunciation, the word can never come out "convient."

2. prin' ci pal

Since students usually connect this word with a principal of a school, they imagine that all other "principals" are spelled differently. This word means the MAIN thing—whether it refers to a school principal, the principal on which interest is figured, or the principal (main) reason.

3. prin' ci ple

This means an underlying truth or rule. The PRINCIPLE on which this business is founded is honesty.

4. per son nel'

Remember two n's and one l. The accent is on the last syllable. The word is usually a noun, meaning a body of persons employed in a service. You may, however, refer to the PERSONNEL manager. Here the word is an adjective.

5. per' son al

The accent is on the first syllable. The word is an adjective—PERSONAL characteristics—PERSONAL habits. The remark was PERSONAL. (predicate adjective)

6. all right

Always two words. ("Alright" may be found in most dictionaries with the explanation that this spelling is not considered good taste. You wouldn't write "alwrong.")

7. ful fill'

One "l" in the first syllable; two in the second

8. su per sede'

The only sede-cede-ceed word spelled with "sede."

9. sim' i lar

There is no "liar" in similar.

10. priv' i lege

There is no "d" in PRIVILEGE.

COMMENTS ON THE TWO RESUMES

While the format of these resumes is similar, note that each adapts itself to the person to whom it pertains. These are, in a way, composites, but each is patterned after an actual resume. The first one is that of a young lady who has one more term of business school and is now working part time for the attorney for whom she may have a full time position after her graduation. Her fiance, whom she plans to marry during the coming summer, has been tentatively accepted at a law school located in the city where his fiancee is working. If this acceptance materializes, she will keep the position with the attorney. If he finds he must attend another school, where he has already been accepted, then a move is in the picture for the couple, and she has her resume ready to use in her search for a position in the different college town.

Since the man whose resume is illustrated was born in 1937, he has had enough experience, both professional and civic, so that he need not go back to his high school activities or youthful responsibilities. Note the difference in the description of school courses on these two resumes, although some of them are the same courses.

The man prepared his resume as part of his school training in Correspondence, and while he plans to continue working with insurance, his ambition is to become a C.P.A.; so his resume will be ready to use when he completes his training. The pages are not numbered since he will pull the COURSES TO BE COMPLETED page and replace it with the description of these courses as he completes them.

These resumes are merely suggestions. They are arranged in the order of importance, but they should include all information which would accentuate the positive in an honest and straightforward way.

RESUME

JANE DOE

School Address:

2460 Green Place
Salem, Oregon
Ph. 561-1862

Home Address:
870 Archway Drive
Eugene, Oregon
Ph. 620-9008

Prepared expressly for:

The XYZ Company

EDUCATION

1966 - 1969	North Salem High School Salem, Oregon Graduated June, 1969
1969 - 1971	University of Oregon Eugene, Oregon Major: English
1971 - 1972	Merritt Davis School of Commerce Salem, Oregon Major: Legal Secretarial Program

COURSE DESCRIPTIONS

Typing II	Review of basics; stress on speed and accuracy; building of net speed to 50 words a minute
Typing III	Further attention given to speed and accuracy; building of net speed to 60 words a minute
Typing IV	Typing of various letters and business forms; tabulation practice; typing problems; setting up graphs and tables
Basic Bookkeeping	Basics of accounting; accounting for merchandise, cash, and payrolls; periodic summary and adjusting entries
Intermediate Bookkeeping	Accounting for notes and drafts; accounting for purchases and sales; monthly and yearly statements
Accounting Principles I	Deeper study into accounting; accounting for service and merchandising enterprises; various accounting systems and concepts

Payroll Records	Computation of all payroll taxes; payment of such taxes; filing reports with State and Federal governments
Business English	Practical use of English in business; parts of speech, capitalization and punctuation
Spelling and Vocabulary	Rules for spelling difficult words; vocabulary building and accuracy in spelling; proofreading
Office Machines	Training in common types of office machines; key-driven calculator, rotary calculator, ten-key and full-key adding machines
Transcribing Machines	Practice in use of dictaphone; transcribing neat and accurate letters
Business Psychology	Study in human relations; personal efficiency, personality, emotional health, leadership, and group cooperation
Personal Improvement	Self-improvement and personality development; social and business etiquette; conversation and speech
Penmanship	Improvement of writing and printing for legibility; writing and printing numbers and filling in forms
Filing and Indexing	Practice with rules of filing and records control; alphabetic, numeric, geographic, and subject filing
Business Mathematics	Practice with all common types of business math; banking, depreciation, discounts, interest, and payrolls
Shorthand Theory	Theory for rules and brief forms; practice for speed and accuracy in taking dictation and transcribing
Dictation	Speed building in dictation and transcription; accuracy

Correspondence	Effective composition of business letters; claim, adjustment, inquiry, sales, credit, and collection letters
Secretarial Procedures	Learning and practicing various duties of a secretary; receiving callers and making appointments; travel arrangements; preparing manuscripts, arranging for meetings and conferences
Economics	General understanding of macro-economics; concepts of wealth, output, savings, investment, and employment

COURSES TO BE COMPLETED

Transcription

Business Organization

Business Law

Accounting Principles II

Federal and State Taxes

Legal Office Practice

EXPERIENCE

Summer, 1970
Part time, 1970-71
Full time, 1971---

Walters and Blake
Attorneys at Law
918 Knight St.
Salem, Oregon

Duties: General Secretary
Typing letters and legal papers, taking
dictation, answering the phone and
greeting clientele

Summer, 1969
Part time 1969-70

John Farnum Investment Co.
Commercial St.
Salem, Oregon

Duties: Typing, answering the telephone,
clerical responsibilities

JOBS HELD TO HELP DEFRAY PERSONAL EXPENSES

Summers, 1967-1968

United Packing Co.
(Cannery)
Salem, Oregon

Duties: sorting beans
weighing cartons

Summers, 1963-1967

Field work, picking beans and berries

1966 - 1969
(part time, during school year)

Baby-sitting

Jane Doe

PERSONAL DATA

Name	Jane Ann Doe	Weight	115 pounds
Address	4578 Ash Street Salem, Oregon	Health	Excellent
Age	20	Marital Status	Single (Engaged, but plan to work after marriage to help future husband through law school)
Height	5' 4"		

ACTIVITIES AND INTERESTS

HIGH SCHOOL

    Clubs

International Relations League

German Club

Future Business Leaders of America

    Activities

Orchestra

American Field Service Representative

    Honors

Junior Prom Queen

Girls State Representative

National Honor Society
(3.64 GPA)

CURRENT

    Business School

Girl of the Month Club
  Club Secretary
Member of Student Council

YWCA

    Interests

Mountain climbing and hiking
Skiing
Tennis
Music
Reading

REFERENCES
(with permission)

Mr. John Walters
Attorney
Walters and Blake
918 Knight St.
Salem, Oregon 97301
Phone 365-0974

Mrs. Juanita Kauffman
Head, Secretarial Dept.
Merritt Davis School of Commerce
Salem, Oregon 97301
Phone 581-1476

The Rev. Joseph Doakes
Salem Community Church
1652 Arbor Lane
Salem, Oregon 97304
Phone 392-3481

PERSONAL DATA SHEET

JOHN J. DOE

920 Hale Avenue N.E.

Salem, Oregon

Ph.   368-0927

EDUCATION

1950-1954	Central High School Portland, Oregon Graduated June, 1954
1955-56	U. S. Air Force School Scott Air Force Base Illinois (graduated with honors)
1957	Bell & Howell Gun Camera School (factory) Air Force training
1958	Foster Air Force Base Victoria, Texas (Advanced Electronics)
1970 - 1972	Merritt Davis School of Commerce 210 Liberty Street SE Salem, Oregon 97301 (Phone 581-1476) Professional Accounting

DESCRIPTION OF COURSES COMPLETED

Business English	Efficient use of business English in today's office
Correspondence	Complete in-depth study of all forms of business communication and composition of reports, credit letters, collection letters, memos and handling of complaints
Spelling and Vocabulary	Emphasis on spelling accuracy and vocabulary building
Filing and Indexing	Comprehensive study of methods used in modern offices for the filing of important information including: alphabetical, numerical, geographic, and subject
Penmanship	Rapid, legible writing and printing for business
Business Law	Understanding that portion of law that most affects business, such as contracts, sales, bailments, negotiable instruments, and formation and authority of corporations, partnerships and sole proprietorships

(DESCRIPTION OF COURSES COMPLETED - continued)

Typing I	Mastery of the keyboard
Typing II	Review of techniques and the building of speed to a net rate of 50 words a minute
Office Machines	The operation of common types of business machines, including rotary calculator, ten- and full-key machines and posting machines
Bookkeeping Machines	Using machines to record simple bookkeeping transactions such as accounts receivable and payables and control uses
Transcribing Machines	Transcription of letters and documents in correct and mailable form
Basic Bookkeeping	Modern procedures and application of principles of accounting in the business world
Intermediate Bookkeeping	Principles applied to partnerships and changing from partnerships to the corporation
Payroll Records	Computation of payrolls and their payment, filing reports to Federal and State agencies
Federal and State Tax	Income taxes for individuals, partnerships, corporations, fiduciaries, estates and inheritance
Personal Improvement for the Businessman	Personality development, proper business dress and grooming, speech power and creative thinking

COURSES TO BE COMPLETED

Cost Accounting

Typewriting IV

Salesmanship

Business Organization

Economics

Intermediate Accounting I

Intermediate Accounting II

Advanced Accounting I

Advanced Accounting II

Municipal Accounting

Auditing

Finance

Automation Accounting

CPA Review

Business Mathematics

John Doe

EXPERIENCE

1967 - present	Hobard Insurance Agency Salem, Oregon (Insurance salesman full time to 1970, part time while I am attending school)
1965 - 1967	People's Food Service Portland, Oregon Wholesale food distributorship Self employed
1961-1965	U. S. Postoffice Portland, Oregon clerk and mail carrier
1958 - 1961	Doe Sign Company Russett, Oregon (Business owned by father) painted and installed signs kept books, public relations, etc. etc.

PERSONAL DATA

Birth date	April 26, 1937
Height	6 ft.
Weight	180 lbs.
Health	Excellent
Marital Status	Married
Dependents	Wife, three sons

CIVIC ACTIVITIES AND INTERESTS

Boy Scouts of America	Troop leader
Toastmasters	Speech club
Knife and Fork	Lecture club
United Good Neighbors	
PTA	Hoover School
Church School Superintendent	(1 year)

REFERENCES

(with permission)

Joseph Hobard
Hobard Insurance Agency
1470 Green Street S.
Salem, Oregon 97304
Phone 564-1980

The Rev. Loy Brown
Salem Community Church
Salem, Oregon 97302
Phone 564-7235

Robert Youngman
Attorney
Youngman and Bridges
Castle Bldg. 97301
Salem, Oregon
Phone 564-9075

PRECIS OF RESUME

of

JANE DOE

2460 Green Place, Salem, Oregon

Age 20   Height 5' 4"   Weight 115   Health Excellent
Marital Status   Single   Plan to continue working after June marriage

1972 graduate Merritt Davis School of Commerce
Legal Secretarial Major

Courses completed include:

Typing	Shorthand
Bookkeeping	Business Machines
Accounting	Spelling
Filing	Payroll
Psychology	Correspondence
English	Penmanship
Economics	Mathematics

Secretarial Procedures

Experience:

Walters and Blake   John Farnum Investment Co.
Attorneys at Law   Salem, Oregon
Salem, Oregon   (Secretarial duties)
(Secretarial duties)

References:

Mr. John Walters   Mrs. Juanita Kauffman   The Rev. J. Doakes
Attorney   Head, Sec. Dept.   Woodland Chapel
Walters and Blake   Merritt Davis School of Commerce   Salem, Oregon
Salem, Oregon   Salem, Oregon   Phone 392-3481
Phone 365-0974   Phone 581-1476

1. Write an application letter for the kind of position you would like to have. You may mention your resume at this point without including it with this assignment.

2. Assume that you have had an interview for the position above. Write a follow-up letter.

3. Make a description of courses sheet to be incorporated in your resume. List the course at the left and, by using your tab key, itemize the description of each course in the column at the right opposite the course name.

4. Write a letter refusing an offer for employment. Determine your legitimate reason for the refusal—a chance for further study, more responsibility, a better salary, etc.

5. Write a letter asking for a decision on the position for which you have had an interview. Determine your own reason for rushing an answer. This could be another position offer, an opportunity for a trip, a decision to go to college, etc.

6. Make your own resume. Incorporate in this your proof-read copy of description of courses.

7. Make a precis of your resume (not longer than one page).

chapter nine

personal selling
(the sales letter)

The sales letter has the edge over other advertising media since it is by far the most selective, it is less expensive, and it can be more personal. Furthermore, this type of selling makes its presentation without the competition of other advertisers such as there is on radio, on television, or in magazines or newspapers. While most of us object to junk mail, the very proliferation of this type of selling indicates its effectiveness. The sales agencies and advertising specialists who formulate these extensive projects appear to be highly successful.

But let's leave the mass selling to the pros. The type of letter we'll discuss here is what I call the PERSONAL sales letter. If you have occasion to compose a sales letter for yourself or for your employer, bear in mind that the first consideration is the desire to serve. The sincerity of this desire measures selling success. It is the little man or woman with the big-shot complex who is too busy to be concerned with little people. His goal in life is profit and hang the service.

Actually, every letter you write is a sales letter. It sells you or it doesn't. The simple friendly letter, which makes the person who receives it feel as if a living human being is communicating with him, is the ultimate in sales letters. This is where the YOU attitude comes in.

The reason the words "selling" and "salesman" have come to be regarded with such suspicion is that there has been, in our society, entirely too much wheeling and dealing. There has been too much hard sell, too many sales letters from companies that fall short of promises—too much concern for profit. Not that there is anything wrong with profit—it is, after all, the backbone of our free enterprise system; but unless the seller is himself sold on the object of his selling, his presentation becomes empty, and he—the salesman—is a hypocrite. Selling is the highest paid profession in the world, and it is completely honorable if the seller believes what he says and if, in selling, he is performing a service.

If he has his fingers crossed when he is writing a sales letter, and if he regards his customer as a sucker for falling for his line, he will likely fail in spite of initial or temporary success.

The first thing, then, to consider in writing any sales letter is being sincere about the product or service. Know the service backward and forward, and when you honestly

157

believe what you say about it, your sincerity will come through loud and clear in your letter. This philosophy, of course, would sound naive to some dyed-in-the-wool wheeler-dealers; nevertheless, sincerity has proved itself time and time again.

The reason so many of the letters, in what we are wont to call "junk" mail, sound canned is that they were ground out of the promotion hopper by pseudo-pros who frequently have only a cursory interest in the thing about which they write. The best advertising experts will thoroughly familiarize themselves with the service, accentuating, of course, the positive before they attempt to create written promotion.

The structure of the conventional sales letter has become so standardized that it is well to mention it here. Its four parts are:

1. Attract attention.

2. Create desire.

3. Convince.

4. Motivate action.

Just remember four words: attention, desire, conviction, action.

Sales letters vary as to format and style, but these four parts are easy to spot. Attention may be anything from size, pictures, color, questions, split beginnings, explanations, and gimmicks.

Desire has two basic appeals, depending on the product or service. Necessities, money makers, and money savers appeal to reason. Luxuries appeal to emotion.

Conviction is accomplished by statistics, testimonials of well-known people, experiences of satisfied customers, and logic. It sometimes entails money-back guarantees.

The final part points out the advantage of taking action, and this is made easy by enclosing addressed and stamped cards or envelopes. Extra bonuses for acting NOW are promised, and some advertisers even include a small ball point pen to use in placing an X in the YES box. (You don't even have to be literate.)

See an example of this kind of letter at the end of this chapter.

Hundreds of books and pamphlets have been written about this type of sales letter, and many of them are excellent. This pattern is good for mass mailing, and it may do a good job.

It is unlikely, unless you decide to go into the professional advertising business, that you, as either an employer or employee, will be responsible for composing a mass mailing sales letter.

The kind of letter, however, which I should like to encourage is the PERSONAL sales letter. This is the one-human-being-to-another communication.

Suppose someone were to confront you and ask about the service or product your firm represents. What if he should say, "Why should I buy your insurance policy?" (or your tires, your car, your business cards, your camping equipment, your advertising service). Would you have any trouble answering this question? Of course not, and that is what I propose that you do by letter. Describe in your own words your service or your product, and tell how it can be of advantage to the recipient of that letter. Don't worry too much about the conventional formula, but do be aware of the YOU attitude. This letter needs no subformula as such. Use the TRI-ASK TECHNIQUE—always use this.

What do I want to accomplish?

I want to sell my service (or my product).

How can I do this most effectively?

Here we have, not a formula, but a four part attitude:

1. Sincerity

2. Enthusiasm

3. Knowledge (of your service or product)

4. YOU attitude

The last item actually is the answer to your third question, the one you ask <u>after</u> you have written the letter.

How would I feel if I were to receive this letter?

Remember that you answer this as if you were the one receiving the letter—not the one writing it. Here is an example of such a letter sent to a very selective list:

Dear Professor Flaubert:

As a music instructor you have, I know, a keen appreciation of fine musical instruments; so I feel that you should be the first to know about our plans for expansion.

Next month, the 15th of May to be exact, we are moving to our new studio on Ashwood Drive. There we shall have room to display our fine instruments, and our customers will be assured of plenty of parking space.

I am sure you will be especially interested to hear that from April 15 to the 25th we are having a pre-advertising sale of all our present stock. This sale is planned especially for those who, like you, are in the music field. It will include all our stock at drastically cut prices.

As an instrumental instructor, you will appreciate the wonderful buys, not only on organs and pianos but also on fine brass and woodwind instruments. Our store will be closed except to those few of you to whom we are issuing invitations so that you and your students will have the opportunity to see and try out these instruments at your leisure.

I enclose ten cards for you to distribute to selected students who, you think, may want to see our stock. Your name is on each card. We'd appreciate your writing the student's name on each one and asking him to present the card when he attends the presale.

After April 25, this sale will be advertised and will be open to the public. I feel sure you would be interested in a more leisurely examination of our instruments.

We at Page Music Center Studio will look forward to seeing you during our sale and after May 15 at our new store, where we will be more conveniently situated to serve music lovers like you.

Sincerely,

An insurance agent might send a periodical PERSONAL type of sales letter to his policyholders. This COULD be mass produced, but how much better to have his secretary type the letter from a guide to be sent over his signature. (He is fortunate if he has an electronic tape typewriter which gives the effect of a personally typed letter.) A handwritten postscript always adds extra appeal. Something like this:

LETTERHEAD HERE

ADDRESS

Dear Mr. and Mrs. Tracey:

I have just been checking your homeowner policy, and it occurred to me that you might want to have more coverage. With rising property values and the high cost of duplicating home furnishings, your present insurance might not be adequate.

I am enclosing an inventory booklet for your convenience. I suggest that you enter in this the appraised value of your home and an estimate of the furnishings of each room.

When you figure the total, based on today's values, call me so we can go over your present coverage and see that it is brought up to date. If it is inconvenient for you to visit my office, I'll be happy to call on you at your home whenever you say. Just call me at 521-4897.

Sincerely,

P.S. Don't forget to update an appraisal of your coin collection.

Whether you are an employer or an employee, it is likely that any mass mailing programs will be handled by professionals. This is not the type of sales letter to be discussed here. The small-scale selective personal-type duplicated letter is frequently very effective, but even it should sound like a letter written by one interested human being to another.

Personal sales letters take time, but the benefits will usually pay off by establishing a reputation for friendliness and service. A car dealer for instance, might be aware of returning veterans. Realizing that transportation could be among the vet's first interests on returning home, this dealer might send out a personally typed letter something like the following:

Dear Joe,

Welcome home! I'll bet it seems good to be back, and I know your family and friends are glad to see you.

If you are like most other returning vets, the first thing you'll want, now that you're back, is good transportation.

Will you give me the privilege of showing you what we have on our lot? We have good buys in any price range, and the special feature of both our new and used cars is that every single one goes through a diagnostic center before it is sold. The dyno check is followed by a full correction of any defects that show up, and every car is sold with a service warranty. You simply can't get a better car offer than this.

I'd like personally to show you around our lot and give you some demonstrations. We at Blaine's Motors give an extra special service to our vets. My card is enclosed. Call me soon. I'll look forward to hearing from you.

Sincerely,

This kind of letter may take a little more time, but its results in sales will be great—besides giving the writer a feeling of service in personal interest. Such a letter could be typed from a guide letter, but above all, it should sound like the person who signs it.

The first job one secretary had was for a construction company. The first two weeks of each month her various duties of sending out statements, paying bills, making out payroll, etc. consumed every minute of her time on the job. The last of the month, however, she found that she had time on her hands. So in addition to familiarizing herself with the vernacular of the trade and with the filing system, she decided to send out sales letters—with the lukewarm approval of her boss. This contractor's main type of construction at that time was laminated rib farm buildings—in the $10,000 to $30,000 price range.

She was able to obtain names of members of a cattlemen's association, and, as a starter, she composed a sales letter as a guide, and whenever time allowed, she typed out letters to these ranchers. One day a long distance call came in for her boss. Fortunately, he was there, and when she heard him say, "What letter?" she felt sure this must be an answer to her brain child. She whipped out the guide so her boss could understand and act intelligently. He caught on quickly and soon she heard him say, "Yes, Mr. X, I'll be happy to explain what we build." This telephone call was followed by the sale of not one, but two farm buildings to one of the most prominent cattlemen in the West. Needless to say, that contractor's lukewarm attitude toward sales letters changed.

No company is too small or too large for the PERSONAL type of sales letter. Other types of letters along this line are described in Chapter 15, the Over-and-Above-and-Beyond-the-Call-of-Duty Letter.

Anyone can be wooed by sales letters. Young people spend money; so do "senior citizens." No matter what business you are in, make a study of the people whom you feel you could serve; make a selective list and direct the presentation in their terms. Use the YOU attitude. Be able to say frankly and personally, "My service or product will benefit you." If your list is directed to young people, use empathy, the art of putting yourself in others' shoes. Talk to young people—read about them—research.

If it's a car you are selling, what are young people interested in? A car to many of them is a status symbol as well as transportation. Maybe they are impressed with appearance, color, bucket seats, power. Talk to young people; find out.

A travel agency would do well to direct its efforts toward retired people. Visit a senior citizen group. Find out what they like. Do they want short trips? Long ones? How much do they want to spend? How do they like to travel? Bus? Air? What accommodations do they prefer?

Perhaps you are promoting a condominium. Determine what features appeal to them most. Is it privacy? Is it recreational facilities? Location? How many rooms does the average retired couple require? How much do they want to pay? Answer these questions. Determine the selling point of your letter. National statistics which you find in many business and news publications are fine, and they could well provide a basis for service, but personal research will be more nearly accurate for local preferences.

The mass mail that nearly everyone receives daily is so full of promises, bonuses, pictures, coupons, and flashy brochures that we become satiated with such blatancy and discount these super offers. The volume of such mailings has to be enormous to bring results, and it is this very enormity and impersonality which turn people off.

Professional men, prevented by business ethics from using a direct selling approach, can attract clientele very effectively in more subtle ways. For instance, I appreciate the six months' reminder for a checkup that my dentist's assistant sends me. Some medical doctors will send reminders, but too many are afraid of compromising their professional dignity. They don't seem to realize that patients appreciate this small indication of personal interest and that this sort of attention might help to dispel the too prevalent feeling of being rushed through a doctor's office like one of so many sheep through a chute. It might even make patients more willing to pay their bills. I know one doctor who sends letters of appreciation to patients who recommend him to his friends. Can this be construed as unethical? It's a switch, certainly, from the doctor who, in limiting his practice, makes his patients feel that they are lucky, indeed, that he has agreed to serve them.

One kind of effective personal sales letter is what I call the Good Joe letter. This one, in short, says, "We didn't get your business this time—but you'll get good service from our competitor. Don't forget us, though—how about next time?

Here is what I mean:

We're sorry, Mr. Bracken

that we lost out this
year. I understand that your
Northwest Building Association
is holding its convention at
the Sheraton. That is good.
You will get top treatment
there.

But how about next year?
Will you consider the beautiful Crestview Inn? I'll be
happy to save the same dates.
Shall I put a "tentative hold"
on them for you? Do let me
hear from you.

P.S. I've enclosed a stamped
addressed envelope for your
convenience. Just use the
other half of this letter
for your answer.

There is no use pretending you are not disappointed when you lose a client, but sour grapes attitude will never regain him. Show him you can take it on the chin and spring right back. He'll admire you for it.

If you have time—and who doesn't for a good customer?—create a gimmick letter—one, for instance with a real hole burned in it which starts this way, "We're burned up, Mr. Wilson (at ourselves, of course), for letting you get away. But do think of us next time you need a good printing job. ."

In their effort to woo back previous customers, many businesses use the statement gimmick: sending a statement form with the amount due listed at $0.00 with WE MISS YOU either printed or handwritten conspicuously. One merchant, who gave me permission to describe this, uses a statement form with a bright new penny glued in the balance due column. Printed across the face of the statement is: YOU DON'T OWE US A CENT—WE WISH YOU DID.

Any employee who realizes the value of selling and who has enough initiative to suggest a PERSONAL type of sales letter and the willingness to follow through on it is worth his (frequently, her) weight in gold (possibly in the form of a share of the profits).

If any businessman feels that his organization hasn't had the breaks, he can make them. He can boost his business with the effort of a PERSONAL sales letter.

Recent Associated Press stories have apprised the public on ways of spotting misleading advertisements and sales letters, with the admonition that it is not possible to apply logic to advertisements to get the truth. Twisted words and exaggerated claims have had their day. People are more impressed with simplicity, sincerity, and honesty; these are the characteristics of the PERSONAL sales letter. Chapter 14 recounts the story of a man who built an independent bank with 8000 accounts and assets of $15 million in a town with a population of 514. How did he do it? By writing personal letters, that's how.

Here is an example of a guide sales letter to be adapted to each specific prospect.

Dear Mr. Knowles:

As one of the state's top dairy farmers, you know the meaning of the word QUALITY. Your dairy herds and your milk products have a fine reputation far and wide.

When it comes to farm buildings, we feel quite free to use the word "quality." Our custom-built Lam-Rib farm buildings are the last word in durability, efficiency, and sheer good looks. A fine building constructed with our laminated trusses will make any rural land owner proud and secure.

Don't let the word "custom" scare you. Our prices belie this great service. We have many designs and dimensions from which to select the buildings best suited to your particular need. If you want changes here and there—no problem. We'll give you exactly what you want at prices no more than ordinary run-of-the-mill buildings.

Our representative, Joe Caldwell, will be in your area the week of February 2. Use the enclosed card to let us know just when it will be convenient for him to answer your questions and to discuss your particular needs. You will be under absolutely no obligation, and Joe will not twist your arm or give you any hard sell. He will simply show you illustrations and describe the buildings we have to offer. You'll be surprised at the prices that he will quote.

If you feel that you want a building by summer, our spring crews are ready to go and we have a good supply of Lam-Rib trusses. If your needs are "sometime in the future" this is fine with us. We would still like to tell you about Lam-Rib buildings.

Don't forget to mail the card we are enclosing.

Sincerely,

This type of letter may be the guide letter to send out to top dairy farmers, but it should not be duplicated. It may vary with the type of farm or crop, and it should be adapted to the individual. Lists may be obtained from any rural paper. These publications are full of names of prominent farmers. Lists of memberships in cattlemen's associations, potato growers' organizations, etc. are not too difficult to obtain, and could be excellent sources for farm building customers or customers of any type of equipment customarily sold to farmers.

Remember, if the item to be sold represents a substantial investment on the part of the buyer, as little as a 3 percent return on letters sent out would be well worth the time and effort of sending the PERSONAL sales letter.

EXAMPLE OF A MASS MAILED SALES LETTER WHICH IS USUALLY ACCOMPANIED WITH BROCHURES, PICTURES, GIMMICKS, AND RETURN CARD OR ENVELOPE

Dear Music Lover—

attention   REMEMBER WHEN MUSIC WAS SOOTHING AND SENTIMENTAL? Tired of noise? Wouldn't you enjoy some really lovely dinner or background music?

desire   You are invited to listen to the timeless music of great composers played by top contemporary artists. We offer you a two-record album of beautiful performances in the finest miracle stereo sound.

desire— conviction   These are not one-era selections but everything from The Blue Danube to Yesterday. You'll simply have to hear this beautiful instrumental sound to appreciate it.

conviction   Don't take our word. Send no money. Listen to these records for ten days, and if you don't agree that they are soothing, soul satisfying, and absolutely indispensable to your peace of mind—return them. You are under no obligation to buy.

action   Just sign the enclosed card so there will be no delay in experiencing this musical treat.

Cordially,

Louis Colby

LC:sd

P.S. If you have an 8-track cartridge player or tape cassette, check the appropriate box on the card.

(This, actually, is a condensed version, since most sales letters of this type are four pages—much too long.)

As I have checked with instructors from other areas of the country, I have found that their students make the same kinds of errors in grammar, punctuation, sentence structure, spelling, and word usage that mine have made. So we cry on each others' shoulders and resolve to try to correct all we can and to stress to our students that trial and error is a learning process. Again, I stress that this text does not attempt to cover all areas of English grammar and word usage, but only those specific areas that seem to be repeat errors among my students. If you make an error and your instructor calls attention to it (with a trusty red pen), then make every effort not to repeat that error.

I call this study Nots and Buts (or Not's and But's—either is correct). This means: Not this—But this. The Nots are those errors I have found repeatedly in students' writing. You'll recognize some of them, I'm sure.

NOTS AND BUTS

NOT: She had <u>less</u> students in her class this term than last.

BUT: She has <u>fewer</u> students in her class this term than last.

Use the word <u>less</u> with quantity; <u>fewer</u> with number. If you can count them, use fewer—chairs, tables, reports, rooms.

Use <u>less</u> with nouns that cannot be counted—less time, less money, less noise, less corn.

NOT: Jane <u>inferred</u> that she did not approve.

BUT: Jane <u>implied</u> that she did not improve.

When it is said, it is <u>implied</u>; when it is heard it is <u>inferred</u>. Simple, isn't it; yet this is such a common error.

NOT: She went <u>further</u> than she planned.

BUT: She went <u>farther</u> than she planned.

<u>Farther</u> means distance; <u>further</u> refers to time or quantity.

In his research, he went further into the subject.

NOT: I do not approve of <u>him</u> cutting class.

BUT: I do not approve of <u>his</u> cutting class.

I may approve of him, but it is what he does that I do not like.

Ordinarily when a gerund is preceded by a noun or pronoun, that noun or pronoun should be in the possessive case.

There was little prospect of the <u>Senate's</u> voting on the measure.

NOT: Most all of the money had been raised.   (WATCH THIS)

BUT: Most of the money had been raised.

Almost all of the money had been raised.

Most is not used as an adjective to mean nearly.

Most is a superlative word meaning greatest in amount or degree or number.

Susan was the most efficient.

NOT: She is the most.   (Except colloquially)

Most may be a noun: Most of the girls are secretaries.

NOT: In a recent survey it showed an increase in teen-age credit.

BUT: A recent survey showed an increase in teen-age credit.

NOT: Donna writes well like a secretary should.

BUT: Donna writes well as a secretary should.

Like is a preposition; it is not correctly used as a conjunction.

As may be used as a preposition, but it is usually a conjunction.

(In spite of the popular cigarette commercial "..like a cigarette should," a new sequence was presented in answer to objections.)

ASSIGNMENTS

1.   Revise the following letter:

Dear Mr. Tackett:

We are disappointed at your failure to respond to our two previous letters about the Art Fair to be held at Crystal Gardens, August 10 and 11.

We feel sure that our letters reached you since they were not returned.

We are making up our programs and these are going to press July 10. We'll have to hear from you by July 5 in order for your name to be included.

Your former customers and your many friends will certainly be disappointed if you fail to show up with your crafts at the Fair.

If we don't hear from you, we'll just conclude that you are not interested.

Very sincerely yours,

2. As a professional photographer, write a sales letter promoting a special price on photographs for Father's Day.

3. Select an advertisement from a magazine or newspaper and write a sales letter based on the advertising material. Use illustrations or pictures cut from the ad if you feel they would make the letter more effective.

4. Write an original sales letter on some service, product, or merchandise, real or imaginary, which would particularly appeal to you or which you feel might have a good potential.

5. Make a critique of an actual sales letter, pointing out how attention, desire, conviction, and action are developed, and tell whether or not you would respond favorably to the letter. Attach to your critique the actual letter with the four parts of the conventional letter clearly marked or designated.

6. Rewrite the following letter:

Dear Mr. Phillips:

We have on hand hundreds of yards of beautiful fabrics which we must dispose of before we move to our new location September 1.

These fabrics are top quality at 40% to 50% off the regular prices.

We'd like to get rid of this merchandise so we won't have to move it and so we may start our new shop with fresh new fabrics.

Stop by. Surely you'll find something you can use at drastically reduced prices.

Sincerely,

7. Write a sales letter to be used as your general guide to promote your resort hotel for conventions. This letter, to be sent to convention chairmen, will stress accommodations, cuisine, local recreational and cultural points of interest, as well as convention facilities.

chapter ten

where credit is due

Since credit is such an integral part of any business, it behooves anyone who is in business or who plans a career in this area to acquaint himself thoroughly with credit and how it works. Those involved in credit are most cooperative in sharing information. Since my original research was confined to the Northwest area, I felt this willing response could be simply an exemplification of Western friendliness. However, in my research over the years, I have found that those involved in credit, regardless of geographical location, seem eager to contribute to the credit education of the general public.

Find out all you can about credit while you are a student. This knowledge will serve you well both for yourself as an individual and as a part of the business world in which you find yourself later. Familiarize yourself with the operation of the Credit Bureau. Realize that it is an office where credit records of all persons in your community are recorded. If you have ever charged anything anywhere, your paying habits are a matter of record at the area credit bureau. If possible, become familiar with your Credit Association, which is composed of those men and women in business who have to do with credit and collection. If your area has a Credit Counseling Service, find out how it works.

If your instructor arranges for speakers, don't hesitate to ask questions about credit. I have been grateful for the pertinent questions asked by students, the answers to which have clarified for both the class and me the many-faceted structure of credit operations. To be knowledgeable, even sophisticated, in the area of credit will enhance anyone's value as a business employee. When I think of all of the graduates of our school who have assumed responsible positions in business, many of them in the credit area, I like to think that their knowledge of credit was stimulated and enhanced by what they learned in my class of business communication. It is unreasonable to assume that it is possible to compose letters on credit without a foundation for its operation.

Although the unit on credit has followed the "out" letter unit in my classes, several students have been so curious about credit that they have voluntarily written letters for further information.

A bank manager, in speaking to our class on credit, explained briefly about Dun and Bradstreet. He brought with him the D and B "bible," a 24-pound reference of more than three million businesses in the United States and Canada. He explained that while credit bureaus record the credit information of individuals, Dun and Bradstreet is its counterpart for businesses. He explained also how pertinent credit information is recorded by code in this huge volume, which is published every two months. New business, for instance, is coded "A". When a rating changes, a "C" precedes the listing. In answer to a question about what happens to outdated references, he said that these large volumes are destroyed because the information may no longer be up to date.

One student, who had never heard of Dun and Bradstreet, was so curious about its operation that she wrote a letter to the Portland, Oregon, office. She was delighted to receive a six-page hand-written reply plus a world of information about this prestigious corporation from a Manifold Supervisor.

She imagined that business would be reluctant to impart freely information about assets and liabilities, and she asked whether D. and B. representatives had trouble in getting this information. I have permission from the Portland, Oregon, office to use here the answer that this girl received to her questions. (Remember, this came in the form of a hand-written letter.) Here it is:

Dear Carol:

Enclosed you will find one of our D & B forms and I hope it will be of assistance to you in your current studies. Dun and Bradstreet has numerous forms but the enclosed is the type we mail direct to the new business when we want to learn the entire story. By this I mean we want to know who the owners are, their background, when the business started, the type of operation, financial details, references, etc.

Dun and Bradstreet maintains a permanent staff of fulltime employees known as country travelers. These men are experienced employees and operate on a revision schedule whereby they visit each and every business listed in the D & B reference book once a year. Each traveler has an area of responsibility, usually comprising several counties. Dun and Bradstreet maintains a complete office in some 140 major U.S. cities. Each office has a complete staff of reporters, service personnel and sales people. For example, Portland has a staff of approximately 75. All offices throughout the nation are tied together by our private wire network, which incidentally is the largest in the U.S.

Now to answer your question regarding the reaction of businessmen to our request for information. I can truthfully state that in 80% plus it is favorable. Most business people, regardless of their education or experience, realize the importance of credit, and the free flow of goods from manufacturer to wholesaler, to retailer to the consumer. Recent studies have shown that 95% of business transacted is on a credit basis. And what is credit? Credit is nothing more and in the same light nothing less than man's confidence in man. Before confidence can be established, there must be certain factors brought to focus and analyzed. For example: Are the owners respectable; are they experienced; do they have adequate funds with which to do business. The average businessman, in order to do business, has to have an inventory. And like most average businessmen, he does not have adequate finances to pay cash for everything. Therefore, to continue in operation, it behooves the businessman to prove to his suppliers that he can and will pay for merchandise at a later date. To do this, he must provide certain information and that is where Dun and Bradstreet comes into the picture.

I hope the foregoing information is of some help to you. If I can be of further assistance, please write.

Sincerely,

From the information included with the letter, Carol learned that Dun and Bradstreet not only puts out the six large reference books each year but that pocket-size editions of this book for each state are published for local reference. In her report to the class, Carol also included many other items of interest based on material which was part of the answer to her letter. For example, Dun and Bradstreet publishes a monthly magazine which covers business, finance, and industrial topics. Specialized D and B reference books include those on manufacturers, transportation, lumber and wood products, metal-working, corporate management, and others. In addition, besides regular trend and outlook services (apparel, for instance) D and B offers extensive educational services by means of correspondence courses in such fields as financial analysis, personal investment, sales training, management for small business, etc. Furthermore, its specialized library in New York City is open for public use.

See Chapter 13 for specific reports on credit. All of this may seem like an extensive background on one subject in a class on business communication; however, business entails many letters written in the area of credit, and a knowledge of the subject certainly enables you to send out letters backed by understanding.

Since more than 90 percent of American business is transacted on a credit basis, it stands to reason that communication dealing with credit rates prime consideration.

One hundred million credit records maintained by the Associated Credit Bureaus of America give instantaneous answers daily to thousands of inquiries on credit. The proliferation of electronic data computer installations is setting up a world-wide credit network communication system capable of providing information on the bill-paying habits of anyone who has ever charged anything anywhere.

Computer credit technology, as efficient as it is, will never take the place of person-to-person written communication involving the many phases of this area. While computer intercommunication on credit data has materially decreased, the number of routine credit letters and the need for clientele interpersonal relationships have increased. The very efficiency of computer communication has created suspicion and resentment among customers because the "personal touch" seems to have been lost. People dislike being numbers; they resent losing their identity and individuality—they want to feel important. This is exactly where personal typewritten communication can fill the gap in credit. Computers do not win friends and influence people. Effective letters do.

Credit involves several types of letters:

1. Acknowledging request for credit

2. Requesting credit information

3. Giving credit information

4. Granting credit

5. Refusing credit

Each of these has a specific technique and three of them have definite formulas. Let's take them in order.

First, the letter acknowledging a request for credit does have a formula. Business is always eager to increase its clientele, so the first response to a request for credit would be one of appreciation—a welcome to the prospective new customer. Next would come a request for credit information or references and a promise to keep such information confidential. Individual company policy would dictate this part of the letter. In spite of the accuracy of central credit information, forms are still provided for the applicant to complete, and references are still requested. Computers cannot pass judgment on character or moral risks. Data processing might reject credit for an individual or business that is quite capable of recouping.

Finally, action would be encouraged by stressing the expediency of completing this routine. Referring to this process as being routine prevents the customer's feeling any discrimination. So here we have it:

1. A welcome or appreciation

2. Request for credit information or reference

3. An incentive to action

Many businesses make the mistake of explaining in this letter (the answer to a request for credit) the firm's policy with regard to credit and payment of bills. This, obviously, need not be mentioned until after credit is granted—and then only as a matter of routine.

A model letter, as such, would be impossible, for each circumstance would be individual, but here is an example of such a letter from a wholesaler to a retailer:

Dear Mr. Doyle:

We certainly appreciate your interest in our company and your request for credit, and we shall make every effort to give you good service and provide the best in plumbing supplies. Your clientele will appreciate Morris Brothers quality merchandise.

Will you please complete the enclosed form from our credit department—or if you prefer, just send a copy of your financial statement. Any information you send will, of course, be kept absolutely confidential.

Your account will be opened just as soon as we receive favorable information. We'll do our best to make our relationship a profitable one.

Sincerely,

Arnold Morris

Frequently, an order will accompany a request for credit, and the policy of the company would have to determine the response to this kind of letter. Some companies would make a quick check with a credit bureau and, on the basis of a favorable report, send out the order before competition steps in.

In the case of response to a new business, a check of individuals involved could be such that filling an order along with credit information request might warrant a gamble. Here again, the willingness to take something of a chance depends on the desire for new business. This action, which implies trust, could be the basis of such appreciation that a lasting business relationship might result. It is quite natural to be grateful to a company willing to take a chance on you when you are getting started.

A letter requesting credit information follows the pattern of the letter of inquiry discussed in Chapter 3. Above all else, it should be easy to answer, and this is usually assured by providing a form along with the request. This easy-to-answer form would depend on the credit policy of the business. See an example at the end of this chapter.

Letters giving credit information will, naturally, have to be adapted to the subject of the inquiry. A favorable response would be fairly simple, but the inquirer expects more than an OK answer. If the subject of the inquiry has a top record with your company, the answer could be similar to this:

Dear Mr. Robinson:

John H. Nagle, about whom you inquired June 10, has a good credit record with us. Our business relations have been excellent.

He has always paid his bill before the tenth of each month, entitling him to our 3 percent discount. We feel he is a good credit risk.

Sincerely,

Circumstances of your experience must qualify your answer. Remember, your word will be worth nothing unless you stick to facts. Here is an example of a good reference which is qualified by a specific circumstance:

Dear Mr. Richards:

Jules Robinson, about whom you inquired June 10, has a good credit record with us. We feel he is a good credit risk. He has been owner-manager of the Robinson Sand and Gravel Company for about 15 years, and our business relations with him have been most satisfactory.

About six years ago, however, illness forced him to turn the management of his company over to someone else, and during that time, payments fell somewhat behind. Just as soon as Mr. Robinson resumed control, payments to us were made on time, and they have been made promptly since then.

I hope this answers your question satisfactorily. If we may help you in any other way, don't hesitate to let us know.

Sincerely,

With credit, the important thing is to be objective and honest. A response to an inquiry should involve facts and not opinions—either favorable or unfavorable. You would not favorably color a report on a close friend nor disparage a person or company against whom you have a personal or professional grudge. Note that in the preceding letter ethics were not violated by naming the person who was Mr. Robinson's substitute manager. You would not offer the opinion that someone is a "Good Joe," nor would you recount the basis of your personal dislike for someone else. The only acceptable opinionated comment that is frequently used in credit and banking circles is "moral risk." The word moral here does not imply a person's out-of-office social habits; it simply refers to his credit reputation. If he is a good moral risk, even though he has met reverses, his intent to fulfill his credit obligations is presumed to be good. Even this term is based on credit history and facts.

The letter granting credit should be a pleasure to write and to receive. Granting credit means that the credit report is satisfactory and references have spoken favorably—and now there is a new customer.

Since you are granting credit, you want it to be used; therefore, this letter becomes more than a routine notification—it becomes a sales letter. It is necessary here to mention the policy with regard to payment of accounts. Thus, the answer to the first question of the TRI-ASK TECHNIQUE, *What do I want to accomplish?*, is: I want to welcome this person as a new credit customer. I want to encourage him to use his credit, and I want to apprise him of our payment policy. Next, how can I do this? And here is the formula:

1. Welcome the new customer expressing appreciation for interest in our service.

2. Encourage him to start using his credit by convincing him, in some way, that our service can be to his advantage.

3. Make an explanation of credit terms and payment policies.

4. Make a goodwill sign-off.

Observe the difference in the two following letters:

Dear Mr. Higgins:

In answer to your request for credit, this is to advise you that we are granting you credit with a top limit of $500. Our bills are sent out on the 25th of each month and are payable by the 10th of the following month. We hope you enjoy shopping at our store.

Sincerely,

This letter (an adaptation of an actual letter) seems to say, "OK, you have credit with us now, but be careful not to charge too much, and be sure you pay your bills on time. We aren't sure, but perhaps you might enjoy shopping in our store."

175

Now notice the personal type of letter:

Dear Mr. Higgins:

   We're happy to grant your request for credit with us, and we shall make every effort to serve you in any way we can.

   Our service to credit customers includes advance notice of all sales which are later advertised for the general public. You have the privilege of ordering by phone, and delivery service is yours for the asking.

   We enclose credit cards for the convenience of you and your wife. These are good for charges up to $500. Bills are payable on the 10th of each month and are mailed out on the 25th.

   Enclosed is our advance notice sheet of special buys for August which will save you time and money. We look forward to seeing you and Mrs. Higgins in our store soon.

                                          Sincerely,

Suppose a man's credit record seems to be poor and you find it necessary to refuse credit. The line of least resistance is to send out a curt duplicated letter apprising him of this fact. Research shows that this type of letter is frequently tactless. Some even state, "Your credit references spoke poorly of your paying habits. . ." If a person is a notorious deadbeat, perhaps he could be cut off at the pockets. The thing to bear in mind, however, is that there are few individuals or businesses that do not have their ups and downs—their statistical curves of growth and recession—and that the possibility of their having recouped or being able to do so in the future is wholly reasonable. Even if it is necessary to refuse credit temporarily, a courteous, diplomatic refusal would prevent the resentment that might preclude business in the future. This refusal of credit has a specific formula.

The answer to the question, "What do I want to accomplish?" is, "I want to turn down this request for credit without losing goodwill."

Here is the formula which answers the question, "How can I accomplish this?"

1. Soften the blow before you lower the boom.

2. Refuse.

3. Explain.

4. Give an alternative of cash basis.

The blow can always be softened by an expression of appreciation for the credit request. It is quite true that anyone can feel complimented that his business or service has been solicited.

This paves the way for the refusal which is accompanied by an explanation. Now, this is the one area of the business letter in which the writer can temporize. He will not use such statements as "We dare not risk credit losses" or "Your credit references were unsatisfactory" or "You are a poor credit risk." While the truth is not to be compromised in this letter, the explanation may circumvent the cold facts. Something like this: "The information we have is such that we cannot at this time grant the credit that you requested. I am sure you understand." This last sentence is appropriate in many letters since it places the recipient of the letter on an intellectual basis with the writer. From this point, the writer slips easily into the alternative of a cash basis. This is a perfectly sound suggestion, since cash buying usually has the advantage of two or three percent discount. Buying smaller quantities for cash over a period of time, usually six months, will establish a reputation that may warrant the granting of credit in the future. Smaller orders, more frequently made, usually mean more up-to-date stock.

Notice how tactless is the following typical letter of credit refusal:

Dear Mr. Wiley:

We regret to state that our investigation of your credit record shows that your present standing is not good. We operate on such a small margin of profit that we can't take any chance on credit losses.

We think you should order on a cash basis until you can establish your credit.

If you still want to place your order on this basis, we'll be glad to fill it. We do have the best prices in town.

Yours very truly,

This typical letter breaks every rule of good letter writing. It starts with a negative expression, "We regret," and it continues in a negative vein. It violates credit ethics by giving personal business reasons for not granting credit or for collecting a debt. "We think" is definitely not the YOU attitude. The recipient at this point couldn't care less what "we think."

"If you want to place your order" implies that the recipient likely would not, after all the preceding gloom. An "if" always implies doubt, a poor technique to use in business. Tucked away at the very end of the letter is a very insignificant sales sentence, but it is much too late for this now. Let's re-do this, using the formula.

Dear Mr. Wiley:

We certainly appreciate your thinking of us for your paint and hardware supplies. We feel we carry the very best line in town at prices that are always competitive.

The information we have at present is such, however, that we cannot grant the credit you request. We know you understand.

We suggest the alternative of making frequent orders on a cash or COD basis. This gives you the privilege of taking the three percent discount and the advantage of getting fresh stock. After a period of six months' buying on a cash basis, we'll be happy to reconsider your request for credit.

Enclosed is an order blank for your convenience in placing your prepaid or COD order. We'll give you rush service.

Sincerely,

The style of this letter could be adapted to almost any type of business. A refusal of credit for a service should offer, if possible, an alternative, although it might not be for cash. In the case of a plumbing, electrical, or building service, for example, it could be an offer of installment payments. A bank might suggest a smaller loan than one requested, or it might offer an alternative plan for collateral.

Nothing is more discouraging to receive than a duplicated credit refusal. Who of us hasn't heard someone say, "I'll never do business with X Company or Z Bank. They really cut me off short when I asked for credit."

By the same token, we've heard the comment, "I've given my business to Bank A. They helped me through a rough spot when I needed it most." As I write this, I have just heard from a student that she went into a bank to borrow enough money to pay a doctor bill. Money had not come through from her father, and the doctor seemed insistent. She was turned down because of her age (she is 19), but the bank manager had overheard her request—and the refusal, and he made a personal loan to her. I learned of this incident when she showed me her letter of appreciation to be sure that it was appropriate. The girls in the dormitory heard about it, and you may be certain that this bank manager gained a reputation for being "human." He did this, I'm sure, to be kind and helpful, but he certainly cast his bread upon the waters.

When a person's credit is known to be good, credit business can be solicited and, in this event, should be offered with a minimum of red tape.

Suppose an alert men's furnishing store's salesman has apprised your credit manager of a large cash sale to a Mr. John Ballew who mentioned that he is new in town, having been appointed general manager of a large furniture factory. A quick check with the local Credit Bureau could confirm his credit rating, and a personal type of letter with an offer of credit could be sent to him before competition gets around to sending out its customary credit forms. See the end of the chapter for an example of a letter of this type.

If a company is interested in keeping credit customers, its credit manager or customer relations executive will follow up on those who have not used their credit for some time. Although these letters are fundamentally sales letters, they are closely related to credit. A personal type of letter is more effective than simply a "We miss you" printed on a blank statement, a form used by so many companies.

Another personal letter related to credit is the one of appreciation for paying a bill or paying off a contract promptly. If a company gives a present to an individual or business for long-term patronage, the presentation should avoid, above all, indicating that this is a matter of policy. The gift should be accompanied by a very specific and personal letter of appreciation. People appreciate the personal contact—the individual interest.

If credit makes the business world go around, the credit letter is the current that provides the power.

EXAMPLE OF A ROUTINE FORM USED IN SEEKING CREDIT INFORMATION

(Form letter with name and address to be filled in.)

Mr. Philip Grey, Credit Manager
Powell and Stradley, Inc.
827 Yardley Ave.
Clinton, PA   15026

Dear Mr. Grey:

_____ of _____

has given the name of your company as a credit reference. We shall appreciate your answering the following questions, the answers to which we shall keep confidential. Please use the enclosed stamped addressed envelope for your reply.

How long have you done business with this company?

_____

Have you set a top limit for credit?   Yes_____   No _____

    If so, at what figure? _____

What terms have you extended? _____

Have payments been prompt? _____

    If not, please explain _____

_____

What was the date of the last transaction? _____

Remarks _____

_____

_____

        Signed _____

        Date _____

        From: Louis Gillespy, Credit Manager
              Meier, Berkman, and Williams, Inc.

Mr. Douglas Ballew, Manager
Panella Furniture Manufacturing Co.
Donald Way NE
Gaylord, MN 55334

Dear Mr. Ballew:

Welcome to Gaylord, and congratulations on your position as manager of the Panella Company. I know that you and your family will enjoy our beautiful and friendly city.

I am enclosing two credit cards for the convenience of you and Mrs. Ballew to be used in any department of Eden's. There will be, undoubtedly, many items that you need in getting settled in your new home. Please check our store for all your needs from furniture to kitchen items to hardware. Our friendly sales people will be happy to help you find just what you want, and we have a daily delivery service at your disposal.

Feel free, too, to use your phone in placing orders. Just give your name and mention the number of your credit card.

If other members of your family, besides you and your wife, are authorized by you to use your account, just let us know, and we'll be happy to issue duplicate cards.

Thursday of this week marks the beginning of our annual ramp sale with drastic reductions on quality merchandise from nearly every department in our store.

I feel sure you will be happy with our service. If you ever have any questions, don't hesitate to call me. Our number is 728-9087, and my extension is 102.

Sincerely,

Maurice W. Eden
Eden's, Inc.

This is old stuff from the standpoint of grammar, but I still find errors on assignment papers, and I frequently hear wrong usage. Remember that with English usage you cannot depend on "how it sounds." Students sometimes tell me that they know nothing about English rules but they know correct English by the sound. I don't believe this.

1. Use singular verbs with nouns modified by each, every, either, and neither.

   Neither secretary minds working overtime.

   Either girl is willing to help.

2. Use singular verbs with indefinite pronouns such as either, neither, each, everybody, everyone, and anyone (regardless of words that come between the subject and the verb).

   Each of the secretaries is willing to do her part.

   (Notice the use of her rather than their. Her refers to each not to secretaries.

3. Use a plural verb with a compound subject.

   A green and a black book were left on her desk.   (two books)

4. Use a singular verb when the subject consists of two singular words joined by either—or, neither—nor.

   Neither the secretary nor her employer was in the office.

5. Use a plural verb when the subject consists of two plural words joined by either—or, neither—nor.

   Neither the secretaries nor the employers approve of the proposal.

6. Use a plural verb when the subject consists of a singular noun and a plural noun joined by either—or, neither—nor.

   (Technically the verb is determined by the noun closer to it, but good writing dictates that the plural noun should be closer to the verb.)

   Either the secretary or the girls in the typing pool are expected to proofread the letters.

1. Mr. Fred Coburn has requested credit from your store. Write a letter to Mr. Len Sealy, one of the references furnished by Mr. Coburn, inquiring about his credit record.

2. Mr. Monte Ponder has placed a first order with your firm for $378 worth of merchandise. Your investigation through the Credit Bureau shows that he has an excellent rating. Write indicating that you are sending the order, and tell Mr. Ponder that his credit has been established with a top limit of $500.

3. Revise the following letter:

    Dear Mr. Craven:

    We regret to inform you that we cannot grant the credit you asked for March 4 since the reports from your references were not favorable.

    In view of this, we cannot send the merchandise you ordered. We think it would be a good idea to cut the order and pay cash.

    We have had a great deal of trouble with collections; so you understand that we can't afford to take any chances, especially when credit reports are poor.

    If you send cash, we will be glad to get your order out within one day.

    Yours truly,

4. The Naylor Plumbing Supply Company has written to you asking for credit information about Mr. Gordon Gilbert. Mr. Gilbert owes you at present $415; he has been slow with his payments, and you consider him to be a poor credit risk. Write a suitable answer to the plumbing company.

5. Eight months ago when Mr. Roger Everett started a specialty gift shop, you refused him credit since his business was new. Since that time he has purchased merchandise from you on a cash basis. Write, commending him for his business growth, and offer him credit up to $500.

chapter eleven

collection magic

It stands to reason that if credit is granted, collection will follow. Buy now and pay later is a matter of convenience. Frequently, buying on credit, is far more convenient than paying. Collection, then, quite often becomes a challenge, if not a downright problem.

The reason for granting credit is to make more profit. Credit selling means more customers who will buy more things more regularly. There are, of course, disadvantages in selling on credit. The cost of doing business is greater, capital is tied up, and inevitably there is some loss through bad accounts.

The success of collection depends largely on the wise granting of credit. Credit cannot be granted to everyone who asks for it. The success of any business depends largely on the collection letter, and like all other letters in business, this one is more effective if it is personal. The purpose of the collection letter is twofold: obviously, the first purpose is to collect the money which is due, but equally important is preserving goodwill. The salesman, the underwriter, the field representative—each has exerted all his efforts through expertly planned sales techniques and good human relations to convince the client to buy. Then, when paying time comes, the collection department too frequently nullifies the goodwill which has been established.

Actually, the second specific reason for wanting to collect an account is that no one wants to lose the customer. If he is antagonized through thoughtless collection letters, he will simply take his business somewhere else.

Often the collection letter takes a rough, offensive tone which is a marked contrast to the "winning friends and influencing customers" letters sent by the sales department. The ideal situation exists only when the sales and credit departments cooperate to the mutual advantage of the organization they represent.

Salesmen should accept the fact that credit extension must be selective enough to minimize bad debt loss. The collection department should realize that the customer's goodwill and willingness to make every effort to pay is sacrificed by a letter which annoys or antagonizes. The inclination for urgency in collection frequently must give way to patience.

Most businesses have their own series of collection letters which follow a general pattern—running from the "We just want to remind you" to the "Pay or else. ." letter.

Sending out at regular intervals duplicated letters seems to be the general collection policy of most companies, especially large ones. For the most part these are letters adapted from a guide manual of business correspondence. As such, they are stereotyped and frequently ineffective. The psychological effect of duplicated letters is always poor. People are disinclined to show much interest in a letter that is sent to hundreds of other people. The recipient of a duplicated collection letter is likely to feel that if there are enough people, like him, who are slow in paying their bills, the situation is general and, therefore, not urgent. You know, the "everyone is doing it" rationale.

So, in planning a collection series, two things should be kept in mind, and these answer the question, "What do I want to accomplish?" First, collecting the debt is important, but second, and equally important, is keeping the customer's goodwill. How I am going to do this is specific and personal, with each letter being adapted to the situation. Keeping copies of your own collection letters to use as future guides will make each letter you write that much easier. (I urge you to keep all of your corrected assignments. Many of my former students have told me that they have used them over and over as their guides. Some say that they "couldn't have made it" without them.)

Collection letters run the gamut from reminder to urgency, and herein lies the effective technique.

If a customer has not paid on the basis of a routine statement, the most effective reminder is simply another statement. At this point, most businesses use stickers which presumably serve as reminders. These stickers carry various messages such as "Our accounts are payable on the 10th of the month following purchase," or "Have you forgotten us?" or something facetious like "Doggone it, we didn't get your check last month" with a picture of a sad-eyed dog.

If a client has neglected paying his bill for one month or perhaps two, a duplicate statement is fine, but on this statement a short handwritten notation, perhaps one signed or initialed, is far more effective than the impersonal sticker. Actually, this is not much more time consuming than attaching a sticker. The personal touch of a few handwritten words on statements subsequent to the original one will convey the impression that the credit manager himself or some other top executive is aware of the unpaid bill. This lifts the situation from the routine. These duplicate statements—perhaps two or three of them sent at two-week intervals—are actually more effective than the first two or three letters in the collections series, and they are much less trouble.

The notation may be only the word "Please" written across the statement over a signature. Other suggestions are "Did you forget this?" or "We'd appreciate this payment before July 10th." Also effective is the use of a red pencil on the part of those statements which indicate "Payment due on the 10th of the month following purchase. Interest will be charged on overdue accounts."

If the debtor ignores these several annotated statements, then it is time to start the collection series. Even though at this point the creditor becomes a little uneasy and his prime interest seems to be success in collecting what is due—even then, his collection letter incorporates the YOU attitude. After two or three months, a note of urgency is to be expected, but along with this is the suggestion that it is to the debtor's advantage to pay, since taking care of his indebtedness will reduce the chance of jeopardizing his credit reputation. Here is an example:

Dear Mr. Seufert:

We have appreciated your business in the past, and we look forward to serving you in the future.

However, we have not heard from you recently, nor have we received payment for $79 for office supplies which has been due us since last June. We don't want to lose you as a customer, and we feel sure you wouldn't want to jeopardize your credit standing for such a small amount.

If there is some reason that you cannot pay now, please let us know. Perhaps we can make arrangements to divide your indebtedness into several payments for your convenience.

If we don't hear from you by the tenth, we shall have to report your account to the Credit Bureau. We dislike doing this as much as you dislike having us do it. Do let us hear from you.

Sincerely,

Annoyance and resentment frequently result in sarcasm or bitterness in the collection letter. This negative emphasis succeeds only in compromising the dignity of the writer and the recipient and has never been known to induce positive results. Words to avoid in collection letters are "Your failure," "ignore," "wrong," "cannot understand," and "unsatisfactory."

Experience has proved that the best way to collect money is to keep doggedly after delinquent accounts with insistence that payment be made.

It is well to reiterate that duplicated collection letters are less effective than initialed statements or typed letters, personally signed. However, while each individual and each indebtedness may be different, this does not mean that guide letters cannot be used to simplify the process of sending out collection communications to many people. Remember that multiple letters may seem efficient but that the very fact that they are duplicated makes them lose their effectiveness. Particularly ineffective are the letters with poorly matched typing of dates, inside addresses, and salutations. I have seen some collection letters on which some of these details were omitted entirely.

One letter which protects the creditor is that one which says, in effect, "Is something wrong? Is this the reason you are not paying?" This letter asks for a frank explanation. If the customer does not respond to this question, he cannot, in good faith, say later that his reason for not paying was unsatisfactory service.

Even if the customer responds that something _is_ wrong, the silence barrier has been broken, and the problem, if any, can be resolved. Here's a simple example:

Dear Mr. Mason:

Since we haven't heard from you since August, we wonder whether you are having any trouble with the typewriters we supplied for your office. Payments, you remember, were to have been made in September and October, and you haven't responded to our reminders.

We dislike seeing a good customer like you jeopardize his credit rating for such relatively small monthly payments, and we really don't want you to be subject to the additional service and interest charges if you do not pay regularly as you agreed to.

We service the office equipment we sell, and if you are having any trouble with the typewriters, we'll be only too happy to give you prompt and efficient service.

If you do have a problem, please let us know. If not, we shall expect your check for the last two months' payments or some explanation as to why we haven't heard from you.

Sincerely,

If the debtor points out something that could be wrong, this should be resolved, if possible, to avoid a disputed account. Usually, a reputation of good service will preclude any trouble here.

If any complaints have been handled satisfactorily, it is time for a simple notice saying in effect, "Now that we have done our part, may we expect you to do yours. We shall expect your payment by Friday, November 10."

If, however, the "Is there anything wrong" letter brings no response, there is full reason for urgency. This urgency should be specific. Too many collection letters at this point threaten something like this: "If you don't pay your bill in the amount of $48.50 by July 10, your account will be subject to secondary process." Just what is this secondary process? This bluff will usually be ignored.

Although overdue accounts are usually automatically reported to local credit bureaus, a letter indicating this intent may have the necessary "teeth" to bring action. "Unless we receive your check for $49.50 for your past due account by July 10, we shall report this delinquency to the Credit Bureau."

Next on the urgency agenda is a real threat. "Unless your account in the amount of $85 is cleared by July 15, we shall turn this matter over to our attorney for legal action." Don't bluff at this point. If the account is not paid by the specified date, turn it over to your attorney and let him take it from there. Word of your collection policy, whether you bluff or mean what you say, will get around. Your debtors will learn whether or not you are bluffing. Collection agencies can be relentless, but they are also effective collectors. Use them first as your threat and then as your collection agents.

186

One of my most extensive files is that of credit and collection. I have, indeed, learned much from my students, and I am grateful to graduates and students who have part time jobs for giving me samples of credit and collection letters (with permission of their employers, of course). A hospital, for instance, sends out periodic envelope-statements in different colors to be returned with payment enclosed. The first, a green envelope, is a "Friendly Reminder." The yellow is a "Past Due Notice," and the red is a "Notice of Impending Action." This last appeal indicates the date after which the account will be turned over to a collection agency.

One student, who has had his own business, showed me notices that he sent out that were purely bluff. He bought a book full of notices with varying urgencies as if they were sent out by a national credit association. This series ran from the past due notice to NOTICE OF LEGAL OR STATUTORY ACTION to GARNISHEE NOTICE TO EMPLOYER. They had no legal backing whatever, but they surely looked official, and he said they were most effective. I am not in favor of such unofficial scare tactics.

Another student reported receiving a series of urgent notices such as this, and he paid no attention to them since he actually owed nothing. It seems that a relative had subscribed to a service in his behalf, making the down payment as a gift. He and his wife decided they could not afford to follow through on the service; so they wrote for a refund of the down payment. The request was ignored, but they did receive letter after letter indicating that their bill was past due. Then finally he started receiving these statutory and garnishee notices; so he took the whole file of letters to the credit bureau for advice. He was told to forget it and he did. He heard nothing from all the threats. His experience made him wiser about such bluffs, and I appreciated his sharing his experience with the class.

An effective way of having collection appeals noticed is to send them by registered mail, with a request for return receipt. This may break the silence barrier. Another shocker is a telegram—a straight day wire: "Will take action unless remittance is received by July 10." The signature of the president or the top executive makes registered letters and telegrams more effective.

Urgency would be expressed sooner with a poor risk than with a good one, but patience and understanding may avoid the loss of business.

Although humor is seldom used in the business letter, the sales letter and the collection letter are the exceptions. All commercial manuals on collection letters are well supplied with gimmick and humorous models. The letter with a string attached to it directs that the string should be tied around a finger to remind the debtor of his obligation. Then there's the magic pin to be used to attach the check to the letter—a process which will work magic for the debtor's credit.

Research has shown that while this kind of letter may seem clever, it tends to compromise the dignity of the recipient. Before you send such a letter, ask yourself how you would feel if you were to receive it. Would it prompt you to pay a bill? If you feel it would be effective with someone else but not you—come down off your pedestal and be realistic.

One example of subtle sarcasm states simply, "I'd appreciate your sending me the name of a good attorney in your community. I may have to sue you."

One of the most undignified and ineffective collection letters is the "I need the money" approach. While the need may be real, this is never a reason for expecting an account to be paid. A debtor has a legal and moral obligation to pay as he agreed, and appeal to sympathy has no place here. To admit that you operate on a small margin indicates poor management. To reveal details of expenses puts any business in a questionable light. An exception might be a credit transaction between businessmen of very close personal relationship.

Anyone in business should be thoroughly familiar with both the area credit bureau and with Dun and Bradstreet; the former records paying habits of individuals, and the latter, of businesses.

Collection problems can frequently be prevented or solved by the judicious help of a credit service. Credit information obtained from this source can frequently dictate the type of collection letter which would be most effective. Debtors might be grateful to creditors for suggesting free credit counseling services which are available in most areas. These services are designed to help people help themselves in debt problems and in avoiding bankruptcy.

Any businessman would find affiliation with a local retail credit association to his advantage. This is an association of professional credit executives from all types and sizes of businesses. Members are the men and women whose professions deal with credit. The exchange of information and ideas promotes the intelligent handling of credit problems, one of which includes the writing of collection letters.

The Credit Bureau, not to be confused with the Credit Association, includes among its services the role of collection agency. When a series of statements and collection letters fails, turning an account over to the Credit Bureau or to some other collection agency is the next logical step. Frequently, a letter from the Bureau or from the agency's attorney is official and urgent enough to be successful in collecting a debt. (One of my former students became the secretary to the Credit Bureau attorney, and with her employer's permission, she gave me copies of letters sent out to debtors. While I am not privileged to quote any of these *in toto,* I can assure you that there is no question about the urgency implied in them. One reminds the debtor that, unless he pays, the "normal procedure" would be for him and perhaps his employer to appear in court. The very fact that such a collection letter is written on the letterhead of an attorney implies urgency.)

Anyone who writes collection letters obviously deals in credit, and in this capacity, he should know the details of Chapter XIII of the National Bankruptcy Act, known as the Wage Earner's Plan. Under this plan, the insolvent wage earner can avoid bankruptcy by turning his income over to a trustee in bankruptcy who returns a portion to the wage earner for living expenses and then prorates the balance to his creditors until the debts are cleared. Payments are slower, of course, under this plan, but they are eventually paid and need not be written off as a loss. The wage earner's income cannot be garnisheed while this plan is in effect, and he cannot be sued for nonpayment, but creditors may repossess merchandise that has not been paid for by applying to the bankruptcy court.

Too few businessmen know about this plan; yet a letter suggesting it to a debtor could result in an eventual payment rather than a loss. The procedure simply involves obtaining the proper form and consulting an attorney for help in filling it out correctly. A trustee is then appointed by the court to establish an account at an appointed bank and make disbursements regularly. The debts are eventually paid, and the debtor need not suffer the stigma of bankruptcy.

When collection letters are considered, the inclination is to be concerned with bringing in money which is due. Consequently, creditors often do not think of expressing appreciation to those steady customers who pay their bills promptly and regularly. These are the ones who keep the credit wheels well oiled. A personal expression of appreciation, whether it is a note on a receipt, a letter, or a gift, will do wonders for building clientele loyalty. Be quite sure, however, that this appreciation is personally directed and expressed. A duplicated letter would nullify the intent.

Credit and collection are big business, including many ramifications with which all businessmen and women must be familiar. Collection runs the gamut from dunning statements to the urgency of threats to the carrying out of threats; occasionally it even includes advice. The letter must fit both the debtor and the occasion. The key to collection, however, is persistence with a personal touch without loss of dignity. Since paying habits and personalities of debtors differ so greatly, and since amounts of debts and conditions of urgency are so varied, the collection letter is much too individual to follow a formula.

In summary, however, these are prime considerations:

1. Avoid duplicated collection letters if possible.

2. Use handwritten initials or signatures of executives on duplicate statements or collection letters.

3. Point out to the debtor that meeting an obligation protects his credit rating—the YOU attitude.

4. Don't compromise your dignity by using negative or accusing words.

5. Give the debtor a chance to say whether something is wrong (if this is the reason he is not paying).

6. Don't bluff—carry out your threats.

7. Don't give your need as a reason for his paying.

8. Cooperate with the debtor who communicates his intent to pay in spite of reverses.

9. Familiarize yourself with all aspects of credit.

10. Be persistent.

All of these add up to collection success.

1.   <u>party</u>

    Avoid using this word to indicate person.

    NO: He was with another party.

    YES: He was with someone else. He was with another person.

    Attorneys use the expressions "party of the first part" and "party of the second part" to indicate two different persons or groups in order to differentiate them in contracts and other legal papers. Telephone operators use the expression "party" to mean person. "I have your party now." Let's leave this word <u>party</u> to the telephone operators and the attorneys.

2.   <u>folks</u>

    This is a colloquialism; avoid it. The dictionary indicates that even without the "s" it is archaic.

3.   <u>got</u>

    This is an awkward word which can almost always be replaced by a more suitable one.

    NO: I've <u>got</u> the answer.

    YES: I <u>have</u> the answer.

              He got married.   (Does one get dead?)

4.   <u>kind of</u>, <u>sort of</u>

        He is <u>kind of</u> afraid to ask for a raise.

        She is <u>sort of</u> nice.

    Use <u>somewhat</u> or <u>rather</u>. (<u>kind of</u> comes out "kinda" in oral expression.)

5.   <u>true facts</u>

        All facts are true; there are no false facts.

        This is a redundancy.

190

6.   proposition

This word is not a verb even though it is frequently used that way in business.

NO: The accused man had _propositioned_ the clerk to provide his alibi.

YES: The meeting resulted in a _proposition_ for merger.

(_Proposal_ could be substituted here.)

7.   Drive slow

This expression is accepted now—probably because of traffic signs.

(As an English instructor, I appreciated the signs in the beautiful Crater Lake National Park which said, "Proceed cautiously.")

Also accepted are other adjectives used as adverbs.

For instance: It came through _loud_ and _clear_.
(_Loudly_ has always been an awkward sounding word.)

Ship Direct is good usage (and it doesn't have to be by water).

8.   accept

I shall be happy to _accept_ your invitation.   (Not _except_)

9.   except

This word is usually a preposition.

Everyone went to the meeting _except_ John.

Except may be a verb. As such it means to leave out or take out.

The company cannot _except_ anyone from the ruling.

10.   don't

This is a contraction of _do not_.

NO: It _don't_ matter.
Would you say, "It do matter?"

YES: It _doesn't_ matter. He _doesn't_ want to go.

191

1. Revise the following letter:

   Gentlemen:

   We have sent you statements for the last three months for $180 worth of electrical supplies. We cannot understand why we have not heard from you.

   How would you like it if we had taken three months to fill your order?

   Our expenses are continuing and frankly, we need the money. Why don't you send us a check by return mail and save trouble for both of us.

   Hopefully,

2. Write a letter to Harry Ellis reminding him of $100 which he borrowed from the Employees' Emergency Loan Fund. Point out that prompt repayment means that money will be available to others who have emergencies. Also point out that after 30 days, 7% interest is charged and will be added to the amount due.

3. You have sent two statements and a reminder collection letter to Mr. Art Stace and have received no reply. Write to Mr. Stace giving him an opportunity to explain whether anything is wrong with the office supplies for which he owes you $85.

4. Revise the following collection letter:

   Dear Mr. Oakley:

   I cannot understand your failure to respond to our two statements and two letters concerning the charges for landscaping your grounds. What would your customers think if they knew that all those plants, trees, and flowers are not even paid for? What would they think if I put up a sign beside the entrance to your office which read, "Since this landscaping has not been paid for, it is the property of Powell's Nursery."

   Our expenses go on and I make it a habit to meet my obligations promptly. What if everyone were as negligent as you?

   Now, I'll give you until August 10 to pay this bill or make some kind of explanation. If I don't hear from you by that time, I just might turn you over to my attorney.

   Respectfully,

   Joe Powell
   POWELL'S NURSERY

5. Write a "last resort" letter to Mr. Felix Raynor of Raynor's Variety for merchandise amounting to $315 delivered six months ago. You have heard that since that time he has made purchases from one of your competitors, although you have no way of knowing whether or not he has paid this obligation.

chapter twelve

up and down and across

(the memorandum)

Businesses come in all shapes and sizes. Maybe that is why memorandums are so different. Memorandum forms literally come in all shapes and sizes and even colors. Each business has its own policy for the memorandum, and this policy frequently depends on the type of business. Some memos are simply three-inch squares to be ripped from a pad and used to make notations of incoming calls and callers. Others, while small, have "FROM:" "TO:" "TIME:" and "MESSAGE:" neatly printed as reminders. Still others are the full 8½ by 11-inch size with self-attached carbons and full directions for their use.

Anyone with average intelligence can easily pick up the memorandum policy of his company, whether it is simple or elaborate. Memos, in themselves, are not very difficult. Simply get the directions and follow them.

The thing to remember is that, like charity, communication begins at home. Businesses which expend great effort to maintain a smooth and effective flow of communication with clients to the sacrifice of the home front are like scrapping families who put on a big show to impress the neighbors—the shoemaker's children syndrome. Neglect within is reflected in confusion and loss of face without.

"The right hand should know what the left hand is doing" is a policy which creates within an organization the rapport which is so important for success.

This intra-organization communication flows up and down and across. When an employee writes a memo to his superior, his message is going up. When the vice-president announces a change in policy via memo to his department heads, the flow of communication goes down. The memorandum from one department to another sends information across.

One characteristic of a top executive is his ability to write clear concise memos and to encourage the same from his employees. Such a communication by no means suggests the shirking of eyeball-to-eyeball confrontations. Personal contact to encourage intra-organization rapport is necessary. But written memorandums save time and preclude forgetting. The successful businessman would no more attempt to remember his appointments and agenda than a houswife would try to remember her grocery list. The businessman or the housewife who tries to impress by remembering such trivia is an incurable show-off.

An appointment calendar is a chronological memorandum kept up to date and referred to by that office gem, the Girl Friday secretary.

Some businessmen, who dislike writing memos almost as much as they do composing letters, rationalize that memorandums tend to be authoritarian—an order-from-the-boss type of thing. Not so, unless the boss actually is an authoritarian. An equalitarian boss encourages his employees to have a part in the planning policies and to have a voice in intra- and inter-office communication. His attitude is, "I want to know what's going on, and I want you to know what's going on. We can't sacrifice office time in having a lot of meetings."

The executive sets a pattern for the memo. While it should be concise, it need not be curt. It could easily reflect a feeling, a friendliness, something like that shown in these memos from a top executive:

From:	Fred Langley, Manager
To:	The Shipping Department
Date:	March 27

For the next month I should like you to keep a tally of all shipments to any destination east of the Mississippi. Please record each shipment by date, weight, and specific destination. Results of this will help me decide whether or not to switch to rail. (The more we can save, the more profit sharing for you.)

From:	Fred Langley, Manager
To:	Joe (Shipping Dept.)
Date:	March 27

Joe, will you see that tally sheets are handed to each man and oversee this check. Please collect these sheets on the last day of April and figure the daily weights and destinations, and then a total for the month. I'd like to see you in my office at 10 a.m., May 2, with the results. I know I can depend on you as always.   Fred L.

These are simply examples of friendly "down" memos, and although they are "down," they are in no way authoritarian. Note the word "Please" in each one and the YOU attitude reminder of profit sharing; also note the expression of confidence in Joe. The good executive will delegate authority. An efficient way to do this is by memorandums. Carbon copies of memos will preclude the alibi of losing or misplacing them.

Many guides and so-called authorities on internal correspondence maintain that all memos should be written with the same high standards and good style as external communication. The theory behind this is that a telegraphic style might corrupt a correspondent's writing habits so that he would revert to this staccato policy with clientele. Any businessman who would entertain such an idea is saying, in effect, that his employees are robot-like in their inability to adapt.

Two top traits of an effective businessman, employer OR employee, are versatility and adaptability. Any employee who could not adapt his personality or his writing style to a client or a co-worker has no place in the business world.

Types of communication are so versatile that models are impossible. But the TRI-ASK TECHNIQUE is still appropriate here with a formula of sorts:

What do I want to accomplish?

> I want to communicate a message effectively in such a friendly manner that it will be accepted and acted upon willingly.

How can I do this?

> 1. Consider the person or department who will receive the message.
>
> 2. Make the message clear and concise.
>
> 3. Make it friendly.
>
> If the writer puts himself in the place of the recipient and the message seems clear and friendly, then it should be delivered.

What about the upward memo? Too frequently, here, employees are more interested in impressing than imparting. The employer sets the tenor for messages; so an "up" memo responds in kind. An employee writing a memo to the boss wants to be clear and concise, and he accomplishes this by asking himself these questions:

What do I want to accomplish?

> Do I want to impart information?
> Do I want information?

How am I going to accomplish what I want?

> The answer to this question involves no matter of softening the blow, for no "up" memo should lower any booms. (Emergencies or bad news requires personal contact.) It does, however, involve being respectful and friendly in addition to being concise and clear.

After the memo has been written, ask the third question of the TRI-ASK TECHNIQUE: How would I feel if I were to receive this memo?

If there is any indication of disrespect or arrogance or desire to impress, try again.

This procedure may seem complicated for a mere memo, but repetitive practice makes this process automatic.

How are memos delivered? That depends on the company. Some businesses deliver memorandums by messenger, some tack them on bulletin boards, and some spindle them. Many are placed in intra-company boxes allotted for mail and messages. However they are sent, they make any company or office more effective. Wise executives will send memos of appreciation for jobs well done, for sincere praise nourishes rapport in any organization. The word memorandum is really the Latin *memorandum*, to be remembered. It is directly related to *memor*, which means mindful; thus, praise and appreciation, which show that the executive is mindful of the employee's value, are indeed suitable subjects for a memorandum. The infinitive form *memorare*, means to mention or to remind.

We like to think of the memorandum as being a constructive policy of an organization, but, like all good things, it may be perverted. The kind of memo which is most resented by employees is the periodic intra-office message announcing autocratic orders for the day and pointing out rule infractions. Something like this:

> FROM THE MANAGER
>
> TO: ALL DEPARTMENT HEADS
>
> ALL DEPARTMENT HEADS WILL MEET IN MY OFFICE AT 10 A.M. TODAY. BRING INVENTORY REPORTS AND STOCK ORDERS. COFFEE AND LUNCH BREAKS ARE BEING ABUSED. REMIND THOSE IN YOUR DEPARTMENT TO CHECK WITH YOU OR YOUR REPLACEMENT ON DEPARTURE AND RETURN. KEEP CAREFUL RECORDS OF THESE TIMES AND REPORT ANY INFRACTIONS.
>
> RUSSELL T. BLOOM

This typical memo will never win employees and influence department heads. It indicates the impersonal communication of a little man with a big-shot complex who must order people around and pick nits to boost his ego. Mr. Bloom neglected two things: friendliness and the YOU attitude.

The "across" memos keep the communication wheels well oiled among the different departments. Misunderstandings and lack of rapport between departments are generally caused by lack of efficient communication. Business will be increased and hierarchy pleased if departments compliment each other and if scapegoating is eliminated. Periodic routine memos for up-to-date information are frequently necessary, but these would be supplemented by sporadic, informal, friendly memos to ease tensions and facilitate efficiency. Following are examples of "down" memos which have an "across" effect:

> From: The Office of the Manager   Date: Sept. 12
>
> To: Hank, Shipping Dept.
>
> Orders have increased, which means business is good, but this is going to put an extra load on your department for the next 3 or 4 weeks. Will you be prepared to run two eight-hour shifts for one month. Check with personnel if you need extra men. Watson Bros. is a new big account we've been after for a long time. Will you give this order your personal attention. Don't hesitate to check with me if you have any questions. I know I can count on you.   Bob

From: The Office of the Manager   Date: Sept. 12

To: Dave, Personnel

Hank in Shipping may call on you for extra men for the month of October. Will you screen carefully the men you send him. We don't want any boo-boos on these new orders the Sales Dept. has been working so hard to get. By the way, the secretary in production is great. I know you had many applicants, but you chose the right girl. Thanks, Bob

From: Office of the Manager   Date: Sept. 12

To: Walter, Production

Wade and his crew have outdone themselves with orders this month. This may put a load on your department. Repeats on these orders will be important; so we won't want any delays. Give your crews a little pep talk, will you? Point out profit sharing benefits. If you need any help, yell. I'm counting on you.   Bob

From: Office of the Manager   Date: Sept. 12

To: Wade, Sales

Congratulations to you and your crew for a fantastic job this month! Production and Shipping have been alerted to follow through. Let's plan a celebration, shall we? How about a golf tournament some Saturday or Sunday? If you like the idea, check with your men for the best time and let me know. Bob

P.S. Don't relax too much!!

Memos like these create a feeling of camaraderie which promotes cooperation among departments. The man who wrote these was neither overly friendly nor pompous. He made it clear that he expected his requests to be fulfilled, yet he expressed confidence in his men and appreciation for jobs well done. His warning to the shipping department prevented a surprise last-minute panic which could easily have resulted in careless mistakes. Thoughtful preplanned communication can insure smooth dovetailing which results in unharried, cooperative inter-department operation.

"Across" memos in the situation just described would be from Hank in Shipping and, possibly, Walter in Production to Dave in Personnel requesting employment needs. Wade in Sales likely would communicate special shipping requests of customers, and Walter in Production would point out special handling.

With these types of friendly "across" or interdepartment memos, the right hand will know what the left hand is doing.

In speaking to a group of businessmen on written communication, I suggested leaving memo directives in secretaries' typewriters and always adding to the memo some complimentary remark such as "That was a great job you did on the Jones contract forms yesterday." One businessman spoke with me after the meeting, and he said that it would never have occurred to him to pay a compliment in this way. He added that he was one who really didn't know how to pay a compliment. Within a few days, I received a note from him. All it said was, "I tried it. It works. Thanks." I knew exactly what he meant.

THE BLANK COMPANY
MEMORANDUM

To: Mr. Thompson, President   **Date:**   December 1, 19___

From: Linda Radcliff, Office Supervisor

Subject: Improvements in our correspondence

This memorandum summarizes my recommendations for improvements in our correspondence. I have carefully studied the carbon copies of our outgoing letters for one week, and, as you said, most of our letters, in general, look pretty good. However, effective correspondence is a very important factor in business relations and can always be improved, as we are striving for perfection.

After my analysis of our correspondence, I have concluded that it has only these four major flaws:

1. Excessive wordiness

2. A large number of trite expressions

3. Crowded margins and careless spelling

4. A variety of letter forms

If we could correct these four areas, our letters should be excellent.

CONCLUSION:

Our main purpose is to make improvements in our correspondence so that letters will be not only more effective but also more attractive. My suggestion to bring about these results is that we establish a training program for our typists and dictators. This would familiarize everyone in our company with the proper and standard procedures and make correspondence policies consistent throughout the company. I feel we need this training program.

Although our letterhead is informative, I believe its appearance would be improved by including only our name, address, phone number and slogan. This simplification would avoid the cluttered look of our letters. Also, I feel that we should adopt a standard format for all of our letters. This would avoid any question of what style to use and would help to increase the efficiency in the office.

THE BLANK COMPANY
MEMORANDUM

TO: Employees of Blank Company   Date: December 5, 19___

FROM: Eldon Lane, Manager

SUBJECT: One-half tuitions for beneficial business courses

As you know, our company is offering to pay for one-half of the tuition of courses taken in any local evening schools so long as these courses are of direct benefit to your work and to the company.

The original intent of this policy was to make it possible for the employees of our company to have an opportunity to better themselves in their fields of business and to give them a better chance for advancement. At the same time, it was the intent that these improvements would be of benefit to the company.

Recently, some of you have asked about the tuition for courses in dancing, painting, and music. While these courses in cultural development are good and beneficial personally, you can see that they do not apply to business or to our company. Using company money for these courses would mean an expense that would not directly apply to the best interest of the company.

However, I do encourage you to enroll in these cultural courses on your own. You would, I'm sure, realize a great deal of pleasure and enjoyment from them.

I have listed here some of the courses that would be excellent for the employee and also for the company. The one-half tuition would definitely apply to the following:

1. Business law
2. Business letter writing
3. Business spelling
4. Typing and shorthand
5. Office and secretarial procedures
6. Speed reading
7. Dictaphone
8. Transcription
9. Bookkeeping
10. Office machines

These are some of the most valuable courses to which one-half tuition applies. Of course, there are likely other beneficial courses. If you have any question about some specific course, please see me, and I shall be happy to discuss it with you.

Standard outline format utilizes Roman numerals and capital letters as follows:

I.

    A.

       1.

          a.

These may be used with or without periods. Format on outlining has become more flexible. The modern trend, especially for reports and letters is to stick with Arabic numerals (1, 2, 3, etc.) and lower case letters.

Each topic in any outline which is in sentence format starts with a capital letter and is followed by a period. For example:

1. The method was found to be practicable.

    a. It encourages honesty.

    b. It saves time.

    c. It is economical.

The nonsentence format uses no periods. For example:

1. A practicable method

    a. for honesty

    b. time-saving

    c. economical

(First letters here may or may not be capitalized. I prefer lower case for subtopics.)

The sentence structure of the main topic may be followed by nonsentence structure in the subtopics.

Proved, proven

> While most dictionaries designate both of these words as verbs, preferred usage shows proved as a verb and proven as an adjective.

>> He has proved his point.
>> It was a proven fact.

Drank, drunk

> Drank is the past tense of drink.

> Drunk used with an auxiliary is the perfect tense of drink.

>> I drank my Coke.
>> He has drunk his milk.

Too many avoid the verb drunk because they equate this verb with the noun drunk, meaning an inebriate. (As a verb, drunk is just as appropriate with milk as it is with booze.)

Experts notwithstanding, infinitives may be split. The rule prohibiting the splitting of infinitives is not inviolable.

> Avoid: She tried to carefully write the letter.

> Better: She tried to write the letter carefully.

> But: They seemed to perfectly understand the directions.

If the modifier is very closely related to the infinitive, don't hesitate to split that infinitive.

However

> There is nothing wrong (as some grammarians feel) with using this word at the beginning of a sentence. It is particularly useful in business letters as a transition word to introduce lowering the boom after the blow has been softened. As such, it would introduce the second paragraph. However is followed by a comma when it is used as an introductory transition word:

>> However, we cannot grant your request because. . . .

A comma precedes and follows however when it occurs parenthetically within a sentence:

>> He felt, however, that he could not comply with the request.

However is preceded by a semicolon and followed by a comma when it introduces the second part of a compound sentence.

>> He knew he could not complete the assignment; however, he completed as much as he could.

1. Write a memorandum from Don Prentice, Manager, to all supervisors apprising them of the fact that the company's insurance premiums have gone up because of the high incidence of accidents. Ask for cooperation of each in doing whatever he can to cut down on the number of accidents. Request a report due in two weeks telling exactly what has been done.

2. As head of the Sales Department (Arthur Laird) write a memo to the head of the Production Department asking for information on changes and innovations in hospital supplies and request suggestions for promotion and sales. (The purpose of this intra-organization memo is to provide hospital supply salesmen with complete and late information.)

3. Suggest three situations within a business which might be handled effectively through memorandums.

4. As an answer to Assignment 2 above, write a memorandum to the manager explaining just how the matter of reducing accidents has been handled by your department.

5.   Rewrite the following memorandum:

To: John Ross, Supervisor   Date: Sept. 12

From: Martin Carswell, Sales Rep.

Re: Northwest Hardware Suppliers Convention

Traveled by United from Portland to Seattle. Plane on time, but delayed in reaching hotel from airport. Failed to contact limousine, so took taxi ($4.75). Reservations at the Fontaine o.k., and was able to make it to opening meeting. Ken Byers presided and he introduced national president and other big wheels.

I attended seminar on innovations since I thought this would help me in sales. I suggest you look into Hampton's new door hardware line which seems to be priced right and is attractive. This line has good promotional material which will make my work in selling easier (ha ha).

On Monday afternoon I heard talks on display and on newspaper advertising. These were o.k. and I took notes on everything in case you need further information.

Tuesday morning I went to a seminar on salesmen's incentives. I think the ideas I heard here would be good for our company to consider. Of course, I'm prejudiced, but I like the idea of escalating profit sharing—and also the relaxed method of reporting expenses.

Tuesday night was the social hour (great!!) and the banquet. I met a lot of fellow salesmen here and we exchanged ideas. By the way, Paul Nolan is pretty unhappy with his job and could be induced, I think to work for our company. He's well known in the Spokane area.

The trip back to Portland was uneventful and I was glad my own car was waiting for me there in the parking area.

If you want more details, check with me. I appreciate being given the opportunity to attend this meet. I had a great time and came back with a lot of ideas.

chapter thirteen

up! occasionally across
(the report)

The ability to write a technical report is a rare talent which requires specific technical knowledge and a skill for clear, concise writing. When I say rare, I mean just that. I once saw an executive of the Bureau of Mines literally shake his finger at a group of college instructors and I heard him say, "Your colleges are turning out skilled technicians in the areas of engineering, electronics, chemistry, physics, etc., but YOU ARE NOT TEACHING THEM TO WRITE." He was shaking his finger at the wrong group, for these were members of the former American Business Writing Association. The members of this national organization, who teach business writing, are aware of the situation, and they deplore the fact that more writing is not required in most schools of business on the college level. Few technical graduates, including engineers, geologists, chemists, physicists, etc., know how to write an application letter or prepare a resume, let alone know how to go about writing a report. Many technical corporations find it necessary to employ secretaries to rewrite and proofread reports made by these technicians. For all their technical education, their writing borders on the illiterate.

The TRI-ASK TECHNIQUE still applies to report writing, and its use will make any report more valid and reliable. What do I want to accomplish? How can I do this? How would I feel if I were to receive this report? To these questions we should add three more:

1. Who wants this report?

2. What, specifically, does he want?

3. Why does he want it?

Let's take these in order. First who wants it? By keeping in mind constantly the person who has asked for this report, the writer can gear his efforts to the specific personality. This is simply a matter of adaptation. What does he want, and why does he want it? Determine the answer to these specifically by asking the one who has requested the report. Does he want to find out something or to prove something? Obviously, making recommendations without being expected to would be presumptuous.

Any employee responsible for reports should know something about logic. He should know the difference between deductive and inductive reasoning, which, very briefly, is as follows:

In inductive reasoning, the researcher is looking for an answer to a question. He proceeds from evidence to a conclusion. For instance, a contractor might want to know whether it will pay his company to build package-unit bomb shelters. Research in this instance is carefully plotted and is followed by a summary of results and recommendations.

A great deal of preplanning goes into this type of research report. If this entails interviews, questions will have to be carefully designed before the research itself is launched.

For instance, several years ago when bomb shelters were prime conversation topics, a contractor considering production of package-unit bomb shelters might have asked a number of employees to interview selected individuals to determine whether this venture would be practical. Such questions as these would have been used:

1.   Do you have any desire for a bomb shelter?

2.   Would you spend $1000 for a bomb shelter if it could be paid for by monthly payment of, say, $25?

3.   Do you think the government should subsidize bomb shelters, and if it did would you consider paying half the cost of having one built on your property?

This survey was actually made by a group of business students, with results tallied and recommendations made. Interviewed were some 240 persons in various income brackets. Findings indicated that the average person would not put out money for a bomb shelter, and the research group reported that mass production would not be profitable. It was proposed, however, that plans for custom-made bomb shelters be made since there were enough upper income individuals interested to make this worthwhile. It seems they considered bomb shelters to be as much status symbols as emergency refuges.

A research program of this type may seem somewhat provincial in view of the masses of national and international statistics. However, by its very nature such a project is more effective on a local level than are more sophisticated types of research on a larger scale.

Deductive reasoning in report writing proceeds from an assumption or a known answer to the supporting or determining of it by proof and research. This starts with the conclusion and then seeks or gives the reasons for this conclusion. This type of report usually starts with a summary and then proceeds to prove the point logically. An executive in the case of business usually provides the summary, which he turns over to his research staff to develop for promotion purposes. For instance, an office equipment company executive, in an effort to promote a new type of filing system, proceeds from the conclusion (or assumption) that his files are the most attractive and most efficient on the market. He wants reasons, examples, and testimonies to use for promotional purposes. Proof of his conclusion is what he is after. This is deductive reasoning.

Executives appreciate employees whom they can depend on to bring back reports of conventions, seminars, and lectures. To be effective, this type of report must be prepared with these questions in mind:

Who wants this report?
What does he want—and why?
How can I present this report most effectively?

Neophytes in the reporting field are too much inclined to include trivia by way of impressing and padding. No executive wants to wade through an account of a rough air flight or a mix-up in reservations before he gets to the nitty gritty. Different sessions of a convention should be presented chronologically and labeled by topic and participants. This report is most readable if it is outlined and then summarized, then followed by conclusions and possible recommendations. It should not be considered presumptuous to make the following conclusion: "In view of these lectures and brainstorming sessions, I suggest that the following policies be considered for adoption by our company:"

Notes of appreciation tacked on to memos and reports tend to create good rapport. Such notations could be something like the following:

> to Mr. Webber:
>
> Thanks for the privilege of selecting me to represent the company at the Northwest Builders Association Convention. I was proud to hear our company spoken of so highly. I feel the convention was well worth our being represented, and I hope this report is what you expect. If you want more details, I can supply them, for I have filed all my notes.
>
> Carl

> Miss Dotson:
>
> You did a beautiful job on that Haynes report. Thanks.
>
> Loren

Employers are usually delighted to know that their employees have had experience and training in report writing. Over the groans and gripes of my students, I give them this "opportunity." They have made survey reports, reports or summaries on articles, reports on talks and lectures, and interview reports. I ask the students to assume that they are in an actual situation in which their employers simply do not have the time to cover the pertinent interview, conferences, lectures, and articles that they would like to. Then I suggest that they, as their bosses' good right arms, cover these various responsibilities and then bring back, in report form, a summary that presents the picture succinctly.

For all the beforehand dread, these students have done excellent jobs, and they admit that "it wasn't so bad, after all." My gratification comes from graduates who make the effort to tell me that this training has helped immeasurably on the job.

Remember that good report writers are rare. This means that the demand is greater than the supply; so the supplier is often in a position to name his price. Honestly!

The reports at the end of this chapter are representative of those handed in by students as assignments. Some are essay, some are outlines; they are presented here just as they were turned in to me.

The same general qualities that identify good business letters characterize the report and memorandum. Members of an organization do not speak TO their co-workers; they speak WITH them. Communication is a two-way route, and whether it goes up or down or across, it should be friendly and sincere.

Included in the next several pages are some actual reports that were completed as assignments. The categories are the survey report, the report on a talk or lecture, and the summary report of an article. Because it is almost impossible to determine in advance of employment just what kind of report you might be called on to make, practice in making various kinds of reports is excellent experience; for your information, therefore, in addition to the actual reports, I list here other subjects upon which students reported.

Interview reports

An interview on smoking to try to determine the effects of educational programs to cut down smoking by exposing the harmful effects on health. Some of the questions asked were:

1.   Do you smoke?

2.   Do you enjoy smoking? (Some who did not smoke said, "Yes.")

3.   Do you think smoking causes cancer?

4.   If you are convinced that smoking actually is a cause of cancer, would you quit?

An interview on "How Can We Improve Our Welfare Program?"

An interview on "How Can Our Educational System be Improved?"

An interview of young people in the 18 to 25 age bracket to determine whether they feel that they had a good background in English grammar. A correlation between public and private or parochial schools was made. Here are some of the questions asked: Where did you attend school? When did you graduate (if you did)? Were your grades in English good, average, or poor? Did you like English? If not, why not? Do you feel you received a good background in English grammar? (Most answers indicated that the seventh grade was the last year grammar was taught and that high schools emphasize literature.) What work are you in, or what work do you hope to be in? Do you feel that a knowledge of English will be important to you and your work? Why or why not?

As an assignment, students were asked to make a summary or outline reports of suitable business articles. Following are titles of appropriate articles summarized for these reports:

America the Inefficient   (*Time*)

Why You Buy   (*Family Circle*)

Why New Businesses Succeed   (*Nation's Business*)

You, Too, Can Be a Certified Professional Secretary   (*The Secretary*)

The Charge-It Plan That Really Took Off   (*Business Week*)

The $25 Billion-A-Year Accent on Youth   (*Newsweek*)

Don't Be Gypped By Mail Order Firms   (*Consumer's Bulletin*)

How to Look For the Job You Want   (*Reader's Digest*)

> (Normally, I discourage summaries from the *Reader's Digest* because this magazine is one of summaries. However, if the article is extensive and particularly pertinent, it is acceptable.)

The Punchcard Store   (*Nargus Bulletin*)

Tomorrow's Executive—New Dimensions You'll Need   (*Nation's Business*)

Don't Sell Your Shorthand Short   (*Today's Secretary*)

> This article encouraged men to study shorthand.

The Art of the Resume   (*Careers Today*)

Ten Ways to Sell Ideas   (*American Home*)

Job Hunting   (*Today's Secretary*)

The Frantic Future   (*Nation's Business*)

When Job Tensions Get You Down   (*Changing Times*)

Frequently, oral reports were made on articles, and reports were made available to students in the class. It is easy to see how much was gained by the class as a whole from this project.

Sample Report No. 1:

BUSINESS SCHOOLS

This report is the result of a survey assignment:

This survey is based on six questions pertaining to business schools. The ten people interviewed were from all walks of life, from professional men and women to the layman.

The questions posed to the various people interviewed seemed to catch them off guard. Many thought for quite a while before they answered, saying, "Why, I've never given it any thought." However, the more questions asked, the more interest became aroused. After the questioning was over, 30% wanted to change their answers.

This survey has tried to keep things clear and simple by asking questions that could be answered by yes or no.

The following should give a good hard look at how uninformed the public is in respect to business schools.

The questions and responses are as follows:

1. If you were an employer would you have a preference in employing a college graduate over a business school graduate?

    > Of the ten people interviewed, only one gave a definite answer, and his answer was strongly in favor of the college graduate. The only basis for his answer seemed to be the fact that he went to college, and felt some sort of loyalty to college graduates. Most of the people, however, felt that the preference should depend more on the individual than the difference in educational backgrounds.

2. Would you object to your children's going to a business school if this is what they want?

    > The general consensus of this question was that almost any college would be all right, but that a business school would have to be more carefully checked before giving the final OK. However, if a business school education was what the children really wanted, most of the parents said they wouldn't refuse to cooperate.

3. Do you know that academic subjects are taught in the business schools—subjects such as psychology, English, spelling and penmanship?

    > The answer—almost overwhelmingly no! Only 20 percent had even an inkling that academic subjects are taught in business schools. Of the other 80 percent, two people wouldn't believe it until they were shown in black and white.

4. Do you know the real difference between colleges and business schools?

    Thirty percent actually had some idea of the difference, and one person had previously attended a business school. Twenty percent thought there was no significant difference, and the remaining 50 percent thought that business schools merely eliminated quite a number of college courses.

5. Do you feel that a business school can prepare a person for today's business world?

    About half the people interviewed thought a business school could prepare an individual for some sort of position in business. However, most of the people thought that a business school education could prepare people only for such jobs as bookkeepers, accountants, and secretaries.

6. Does a position in business usually offer higher prestige than positions that are not part of the business world?

    100 percent Yes!

In general, the public seemed to share a sincere interest in modern business schools. But, as this report indicates, most of the people are drastically misinformed. They seem to share the idea that business schools are inclined to narrow their students rather than to broaden them.

What can be done to enlighten the public? Many things.

RECOMMENDATIONS

As most people admit, a position in the business world carries with it a certain amount of dignity.

Therefore, the advertising material that a business school puts out should maintain that dignity. Newspaper advertisements should state very simply the name of the school, what it has to offer, and what a graduate would have to offer to the business world.

Business school instructors should visit high schools in order to confer with counselors and teachers and to talk with junior and senior students. High school students should know that one year in a business school is better than two or three years at a four-year college. Since fewer than half of those who enroll in college finish the four-year curriculum, they could better spend their time and money on a terminal education which requires less time. Students should be reminded that the education they receive in a business college could well mean that they could be prepared to earn their way through a four-year college, and they should be told that many students do just this.

I suggest that speakers be made available to service clubs and business organizations so that the public may be better educated about the opportunities available at a business college or a community college.

In general, why not be a little more business-like in advertising a business school?

(This report was accompanied by suggested brochures for use in mail advertising. Bold letters on the cover of one blared: USE YOUR HEAD AND PLAN AHEAD. Then inside: Choose a Business Career. Do Yourself a Favor. Come In and See Us.)

CREDIT

Report based on a talk by a credit expert

(Frequently, employees are asked to "cover" a talk and report on the highlights. This talk was made to the correspondence class.)

Date: April 2, 1970

Speaker: Mr. Joe Blank

If you like to spend money, the secret is to continue your education. Recent statistics show that college graduates make and spend $444,000; high school students, $303,000; and high school dropouts, $219,000. To get the most out of the money you do earn, you should do two things.

First, you should prepare a budget, a guide to take you where you want to go. A fixed budget is not the answer; don't use a budget prepared by someone else. Tailor a budget to your own needs, prepare it yourself, for yourself. When preparing a budget do not base it on gross income, but on take-home pay, as this is the amount of money upon which you have control.

Second, use credit wisely. It can be a friend or an enemy. Credit has allowed Americans to have the high standard of living they have. Of all the automobiles bought, 95% are purchased on credit; 85% of all appliances, and 50% of all clothing are credit purchases. Credit is a valuable tool. It allows you to enjoy things while you are paying for them. If credit is abused, though, it can be harmful to you, to the community in which you live, and to the nation.

You must have control in buying on credit. Young couples want to live as their parents do. One of the easiest appliances to sell these couples is the electric dishwasher—something they do not need and cannot afford.

Everyone should follow these ten steps when buying on credit:

1. Make as large a down payment as possible. You will not have to pay so much interest this way, and you will take better care of a product if you have invested money in it.

2. Never sign any contract not completely filled out. You may not agree with the things that are typed in later. Yet, with your signature at the bottom, you are held responsible for all terms in the contract.

3. Read and thoroughly understand the contract.

4. Ask questions.

5. Check the contract over for amount, dates, and terms. If any changes are to be made, make sure they are made on all copies.

6. Know the cost of financing. Shop around for credit at banks, finance companies, and credit unions. Find the lowest rate of interest. Buying on credit costs more because of the extra cost of handling the paper work, although in times of inflation, waiting to buy with cash may cost more because of the continuing rise in prices.

7. Be sure to get a copy of the contract and keep it in a safe place. You might need to refer to it in the future.

8. Make payments on time. If something interferes with making a payment, always go down and explain the situation to your creditors.

9. Notify the seller of any change in address. (Be aware that it could be illegal to take your purchase out of the state without permission or notification.)

10. Deal only with reputable companies. They will make good the guarantees on the merchandise.

Each person makes his own credit rating. A credit bureau is a warehouse of credit information. Used right, credit can be the best friend you have.

Sample Report No. 3:

SURVEY REPORT ON SALES TAX

(This is a verbatim report made by a student as an assignment. Figures have changed since this was made in 1970.)

This survey has been made in accordance with the laws and bylaws of the State of Oregon, to be presented to the Legislative Interim Committee on Taxation.

The results of this survey show how the public feels about a uniform sales tax in the State of Oregon and the effects such a tax would have.

This survey is based on the interviews made by a committee of five. Each member of the committee interviewed ten persons in various predetermined and representative economic brackets.

A sales tax is a tax collected at the time of the sale placed on merchandise. The persons interviewed were asked the following questions with the idea of a possibility of implementing a sales tax in the State of Oregon.

1. Do you think we should have a sales tax?

    Answers: YES 40%   NO 60%

2. Do you feel that a sales tax would reduce property taxes?

    Answers: YES 30%   NO 70%

3. Do you think that a sales tax would reduce the income tax?

    Answers: YES 30%   NO 70%

4. Do you think, in view of administration costs, that the state would gain materially by the implementation of such a tax?

    Answers: YES 30%   NO 40%   UNDECIDED 30%

5. Do you think the state would gain very much from the tourists?

    Answers: YES 70%   NO 30%

6. What suggestions or ideas do you have concerning the implementation of this tax in the State of Oregon?

Following are some of the ideas expressed:

Those who felt that we should not have a sales tax based their opinions on the fact that they felt it would be unfair to those in the lower income bracket because this would mean a higher percentage of their incomes to be paid in this form. They felt that it would not be feasible for those who are on welfare to be forced to pay a sales tax when the government (Federal and State) was already supporting them.

Those in favor of the sales tax felt it should not be higher than four percent.

Employers based their opposition to the tax on the cost of implementing it in their businesses. Overhead would go up and hence prices would go up, too. The consumer would be paying, then, more than the actual percentage set for the tax.

Many thought that the tourists should help in paying taxes, and this was a redeeming feature of the tax.

Most of them felt that if a sales tax were to be enacted, neither property tax nor income tax would be reduced. Some of those opposed to the tax indicated that they would be in favor of it if they could be sure that other taxes would be lowered.

RECOMMENDATIONS

1. If a sales tax is enacted, it should not be higher than four percent, and it should exclude food and drugs.

2. If the sales tax is enacted, it should offset or lower materially the property tax and/or the income tax.

3. An alternative to a general sales tax to be considered is a luxury tax on such items as sports equipment, jewelry, colored TV's, furs, cosmetics, etc.

4. If a sales tax is enacted, a large percentage of it should go to school and education costs.

Sample Report No. 4:

REPORT ON A TALK

Speaker: Mrs. Jane Webber
                Office Manager, Brown and Owens Co.
                Member, Retail Credit Association

Subject: Family Credit and Financial Management

The word "credit" comes from the Latin word "credare," meaning "to have faith in." Basically, credit is an agreement between the buyer and a customer. The buyer agrees to supply merchandise, with terms stated, and the customer agrees to supply the money he owes, on time.

The four types of credit are:

1. Service credit: Our light, heat, electricity, water, etc. fall into this category. This credit is based almost entirely on faith.

2. Thirty-day open account credit: Department stores, gas, travel, etc. charge accounts are examples of this particular type of credit. The debtors receive bills at the end of the month and are expected to pay within thirty days.

3. Installment credit: This credit plan applies to larger purchases, such as homes, automobiles, and appliances. Interest is involved in payment.

4. Personal Loan Credit: This is the system of borrowing money from banks or finance companies. Interest is also involved in this credit plan.

The Budget

The budget is one of the most important parts of earning and spending money. The worker must work out a plan by which he spends money that he hasn't earned yet, through credit buying. A sound, yet flexible, budget will help the "bread-winner" manage his money, rather than have his money manage him.

Before planning a budget, it is wise to establish good credit and to determine just how good a credit risk you may be. (See the six C's used to determine a credit rating at the end of this report.)

Establishing Credit

It is important to be truthful in filling out credit applications. Creditors find out all the facts eventually, and a misrepresentation on an application undermines a good rating. The Credit Bureau is a nationwide organization, and it analyzes credit applications and determines credit ratings. The Credit Bureau has records of all business and personal credit standings and it sends them out to its members upon request.

The six C's which are used to determine a personal credit rating are:

1. Character: Is the applicant honest, conscientious, responsible, etc.?

2. Capital: What are the applicant's financial resources?

3. Capacity: What job does the applicant hold? How long has he held it, and how long can he be expected to keep it?

4. Conditions: Is his job seasonal or unstable?

5. Collateral: What cashable property does the applicant own? If he could not pay, is there some way we could get our money back?

6. Common sense: Can the applicant think? Will he have enough sense to pay his bills when they are due?

As these six C's protect the creditor's interest, there are a few things the person taking out credit should keep in mind to protect himself. They are as follows:

1. Choose the type of account that will meet his needs.

2. Keep a close check on the amount of purchases he makes each month.

3. Make sure he is getting what he pays for.

4. Don't be an easy mark for fast talking salesmen.

5. Don't buy thoughtlessly.

6. Always keep his credit record in mind when determining what he should buy on credit.

7. Go to creditors before payment is overdue, if he can't make his payments on time.

8. Know how much the item costs, complete, before he buys it.
(How much will he be paying for interest?)

Sample Report No. 5:

POLICE SERGEANT SPEAKS TO THE SALEM MD CORRESPONDENCE CLASSES

This is a report made by student Joan Mackenzie of a talk made in 1968 by Police Sergeant Marion Valburg. In granting permission to use this report Marion Valburg has changed only the statistics. Otherwise it is verbatim as Joan submitted the report for a class assignment. Marion Valburg is now involved with police training for the Oregon State Police.

Sergeant Marion Valburg, who was a police officer in Los Angeles for eight years prior to joining the Salem City Police force, gave an interesting talk on traffic safety to the Salem correspondence classes.

He pointed out that in order to have traffic safety, people must be good drivers as well as good passengers. To be a good driver involves many aspects. Sergeant Valburg stated five characteristics a driver must have before he is really considered a responsible and successful driver. They are:

1) to be a good citizen

2) to be a good neighbor

3) to think of the other people on the highways and streets

4) to realize that other people have just as much right and as many privileges as he does

5) to feel that other drivers must be considered at all times

A passenger's responsibility lies in the area of not distracting the driver and conducting himself in a manner that leaves the driver in complete control of the car—which means there is to be no embracing!!

When an accident occurs, however, the prime responsibility lies on the shoulders of the driver, so it is important to be a courteous passenger.

Sergeant Valburg clearly explained the consequences that occur as far as financial responsibility is concerned after an accident or traffic violation. When an accident is concerned, a person must post a bond with the Department of Motor Vehicles if he has no insurance. Until this is done, his license is suspended. If a violation is observed by a police officer, he may issue a warning or a ticket, depending upon the circumstances.

The three most common violations within the city limits of Salem are:

1) Improper turns—his experience shows that 85-90 percent of these turns are left turns.

2) Violation of the Basic Rule (He suggested, "Jar yourself loose and think!")

3) Following traffic too closely—He mentioned that it is best to allow 1 car length for every 10 miles of speed.

In 1970 Salem had 3917 accidents, but in 1971 there were fewer accidents. However, the number of fatalities in 1971 was higher (11) than the 3 recorded in 1970. There were 1340 injuries inflicted due to Salem traffic accidents in 1970 according to Sergeant Valburg.

The five major traffic violations with the bail that must be posted for the first three violations are:

1) Reckless driving—bail, $155

2) Driving while under the influence of intoxicating liquor, $305 for the first offense; $355, the second offense; and $505 for two or more convictions

3) Attempting to elude a police officer, $455

4) Leaving the scene of an accident:

   $155 — property damage only

   $255 — personal injury

5) Driving while operator's license is suspended—$255

Because of the above violations and others, there were 72,305 accidents reported in the state of Oregon in 1971, resulting in 35,679 injuries, and 695 fatalities.

Sergeant Valburg said, "If you practice good driving habits, you have nothing to worry about." He also stated, "Always drive your vehicle as you would have your neighbor drive his."

MONEY MANAGEMENT AND MISMANAGEMENT

BY

C. D. Stevens

Example of a report in semi-outline format

From a talk by Mr. C. D. Stevens, Executive Director of the Consumer Credit Counseling Service of the Mid-Willamette Valley, Inc. This report is just as it was written by student Margaret P.

Money management plays a vital role in everyone's life. It includes family planning, budgeting, intelligent use of credit.

A successful business needs two things:

1. A plan of operation

2. A budget to accomplish this

Individuals and families need the same things.

The Consumer Credit Counseling Service of the Mid-Willamette Valley, Inc. was founded in 1969. It gives free counseling service to people with credit and debt problems. Most people wait too long to come for help. Then, the need arises to prorate their accounts. There is a small charge for this. Both local and national businesses contribute to this service. There are 139 offices in this country and Canada; each is independent and locally controlled.

CCCS, which is doing a good job, covers all heavily populated areas in Oregon (and in the Northwest). This service is a definite contribution to the locality. Bankruptcy rate has dropped since CCCS started and the Service feels partially responsible for this.

Some of the reasons people get into trouble financially are:

1. Overbuying due to ease of credit and the pressure on all to buy, buy, buy on credit

2. Younger persons wanting luxury items sooner

3. Families becoming dependent on two incomes and buying accordingly until one income stops. (Then they are in trouble. Besides the regular monthly bills, many times larger than one take-home check, they are possibly complicated by doctor and hospital bills and perhaps a new baby with all the attendant expenses.)

Most families are said to be only 30 days from bankruptcy. The average person has no savings and many credit obligations. Every budget needs two things:

1. A savings account (to tide over).

2. Adequate hospital and medical program

The average person has the cart before the horse. He buys first and then tries to live on what is left. This won't work.

Also there are some things over which we have no control as:

1. strikes

2. layoffs

A man makes excellent wages working a six-day week and lives accordingly. Then one day there is a cutback due to business slump, or perhaps the weather slows business as in logging or construction, and the earner is in financial trouble.

Financial problems cause most marital problems, many times leading to divorce. Then the creditors suffer, the family suffers, the taxpayer suffers.

The CCCS, since starting locally in August, 1969, has counseled 1971 families. It has 435 active accounts prorating in excess of $2,400,000. Creditors generally go along with prorating. CCCS can do these things because it is, basically, a disinterested party doing what is best for both debtor and creditor.

People are generally advised against bankruptcy with rare exceptions. There are many wage assignments taken if a person is having trouble. Collection agencies are notified of wage assignments to reassure them. The wages are paid directly to CCCS which pays the creditors after determining how to prorate the money. The average head of the household is 32.5 years old; his wife is 30 years old; there are 4.4 persons in the family; they have 11 creditors; average take home pay is $465 a month, and average indebtedness is $3800.

The CCCS is governed by a board of directors who set up the policies.

The consumers dealt with are:

1. A few on public assistance

2. A few earning from $17,000 to $18,000 a year

3. A few illiterates

4. A few with masters degrees

Education and income have little to do with insolvency—poor management does. Many of these people actually live on less than welfare standards, but they do this to get out of debt. Many take on moonlighting jobs to supplement wages; others simply cut down on living expenses; some do both.

Ways of preventing this tragic mess are to improve skills or learn to budget—or both.

Everyone should follow the Ten Commandments of Credit listed here:

1. Do remember that credit costs money—always find out how much.

2. Don't buy on credit from a door-to-door salesman—deal with an established dealer.

3. Do plan credit together as a family, and use it for family goals.

4. Don't expect to square a debt by "letting it go back."

5. Do plan how credit will be repaid—before you sign a credit contract.

6. Don't be a "captive" of a credit store.

7. Do compare costs—of goods and credit.

8. Don't buy things you don't need—for cash OR credit.

9. Do read the contract BEFORE you sign it—don't be anybody's fool.

10. Don't be afraid to ask for advice.

Sample Report No. 7:

CONSUMER PROTECTION
(From a talk by Wanda Merrill)

Report on Talk
Essay type report
Talk by Wanda Merrill, Administrator, Consumer Services Division, Department of Commerce, State of Oregon

Diogenes coined the phrase "caveat emptor" 23 centuries ago, and the first voluntary consumer league was founded in New York in 1891. In 1967 the Consumer Organization of America was founded.

President Kennedy said the consumer should have the right to safety, the right to be informed, and the right to be heard.

Forty-five states have consumer protection agencies which have set up a variety of regulations. Oregon has a Consumer Protection Act that makes it no longer legal to sell a used or old item as new. If a person goes into a store for an item advertised on sale, and the item is not available, he can ask for a rain check. The store is expected to have enough of the item for reasonable public demand for the duration of the sale.

A door-to-door contract can be canceled by midnight of the third day. Salesmen are good talkers and if after they have left, a person decides that he does not want to purchase the article, he is permitted by law to void the contract.

It is simple to go to Small Claims Court if a person has the need to do so. To qualify for Small Claims, the amount must be under $500. Filing fees cost $6, and an attorney is not necessary. The judge, the plaintiff, and the defendent sit at a table and each is given a chance to tell his story. After all has been said, the judge hands down a decision. There is no waiting.

The Consumer Credit Counseling Service helps an individual learn to budget his money. If a person has financial difficulties, the Service will take over his bills and paycheck, talk to the creditors and help straighten things out. This organization is supported by the local businessmen. It was certified August 1, 1971.

The Federal Trade Commission is considering a ruling that if an article is ordered it must be delivered within 21 days after the order has reached its destination unless notice has been sent that it is not possible to fill the order in that length of time and if this is agreeable.

Dozens of toys are being taken off the market every day because of the hazards. Four different companies are going to modify car seats for infants; as of August 15, aspirin products will have a new package to prevent children from opening them and getting poisoned.

Dog food has to be free of insects, but so far little has been done for the food that humans eat. State and Federal agencies are being alerted, however.

Of course, not always is the consumer being taken advantage of. Sometimes it is the businessman. The consumer has been known to falsify when all of the facts are right in front of him in the way of receipts and guarantees or warranties. The law should work both ways.

Sample Report No. 8:

CONSUMER PROTECTION

Example of Outline Report

(Report on talk by Wanda Merrill, Executive Director, Consumer Services, Oregon State Department of Commerce.)

I. Brief History of Consumerism

    A. First consumerism 23 centuries ago—when Diogenes said, "Caveat emptor"

    B. 1891 — first consumer league

    C. 1900 — 1930, consumer fighting

        1. Meat packing business

    D. World War II consumer research lapsed

    E. 1938 Federal Drug Administration started watch on labeling

    F. Today

        1. 750 bills in Congress

        2. Consumer rights (first stated by President Kennedy)

            a. Right to choose

            b. Right to safety

            c. Right to be informed

            d. Right to be heard

II. Various National Agencies and Their Concerns

    A. Federal Trade Commission

        1. Permanent clothing labels as to care

        2. Listing octane percentage in gasoline

        3. Listing ingredients in cold and cough medicines

        4. No consumer responsibility for unsolicited packages received in the mail

    B. Federal Drug Administration

        1. List iodine level in salt

III. Protection for Children

    A. Regulation of safety of toys

        1. 700,000 children injured each year by unsafe toys

B.   Regulation of car carriers for children

C.   Regulation of children's drugs

      1.   Safe packaging of aspirin

IV. State Level

A.   Consumer Protection in 45 of the 50 states

B.   Consumer Protection Act in Oregon

      1.   Passed by Legislature in 1971

      2.   Department of Agriculture

            a.   Inspection of food

      3.   Public Utilities Commission

            a.   Available for utility complaints of consumers

      4.   Department of Education

            a.   Education of students on possible irregularities

      5.   Extension Service

            a.   Consumer education

      6.   Private business

            a.   Consumer Credit Counseling Service

      7.   Licensing bureaus

            a.   TV repairmen

            b.   Builders

            c.   Mobile homes

      8.   Legal help

            a.   Legal Aid for low income

      9.   Current projects

            a.   Full labeling

            b.   Good warranties

    10.   Consumer Services, Department of Commerce

            a.   Investigates legitimate consumer complaints

                  (1) P.O. Box 444, Salem, Oregon 97308

COMBINATION INTERVIEW AND RESEARCH
(This report was made on the basis of interviews with several personnel supervisors and information put out by the Employment Service.)

Deciding to quit a job is one of the most important steps you can take, for every resignation requires thorough consideration. If you follow today's normal pattern, you will probably make such decisions more than once in the remainder of your career.

There are many reasons why, if you leave your job, you should keep as good a relationship as possible with all employers: You never know when you will want to come back to work for your present company again; you may need a recommendation, and your prospective employer may call your former employer to ask about you.

You should actually quit a job when you are in good standing with your present firm, when you have outgrown your position and chances for advancement are severely limited, when you are young enough, when you seriously disagree with policies of your firm, or when another firm offers you a substantial salary increase. Other reasons may include being with a company long enough so that leaving will not result in your being classified as a job-hopper, when you feel you cannot adjust to changes introduced by new management, when you seem to be inhibited by your job, or when health requirements make the firm's location difficult for you or some member of your family.

When you do quit your job, the first step is to discuss the matter with your immediate supervisor, then with someone from the personnel department. Occasionally, you should talk with other company officials, and then be quite sure to write your letter of resignation. A letter of resignation should always be written, even when everyone in your office knows that you are leaving. This precludes someone's saying later that you were asked to resign.

Reasons for leaving usually will be accepted with little comment by the firm you want to join if these reasons involve your wanting additional challenge, responsibility, recognition, the desire to get more experience in a new field, or perhaps that another company has offered you such a substantial salary increase that you cannot refuse.

Other reasons may include the opportunity to travel more on the new job, or to travel less (if that is what you object to); your health, or that of a member of the family, requires that you relocate in a different climate; or you have a personality conflict with some member of your firm. This latter is a real reason, but be very careful not to complain to a prospective boss about previous employers. If you talk disparagingly about one boss, you will about another.

The length of time required after giving notice may vary with your position and with company practice. You should be prepared to remain from two weeks to 30 days, or for one full pay period.

Some companies schedule exit interviews whenever any employee leaves. These interviews, usually requested by the personnel department, are designed to determine why the employee is leaving. Personnel supervisors are eager to learn his attitudes toward the company and toward his fellow workers, what type of concern he is joining, and what opportunities it offers, and to alert the company about matters of which it should be aware.

It may be difficult to leave surroundings with which you have become familiar. This can be as true of uncomfortable conditions as of enjoyable ones. If you are security minded and considered your old job a sure thing, you may have difficulty in adapting to a new position in which you are not so secure. But if leaving a position may allow you to breathe a sigh of relief and feel that you can be yourself again, you probably will have little doubt regarding the wisdom of your decision. Remember that security can be the very thing that keeps you from a position you really enjoy. If switching jobs is not just another case of the grass being greener on the other side of the fence—if it offers challenge and excitement, don't hesitate to make the change. Actually, nothing is more secure than being engaged in work that you would do for free if you didn't have to work.

FOOTNOTES AND BIBLIOGRAPHY

This course does not cover extensive research papers which require footnotes. However, for your convenience, here is a list of those most commonly used. If the paper has many footnotes, the numbers start with "1" on each page. If there are few footnotes, the numbers continue from "1" to the end of the manuscript. The number in the writing itself is placed just to the right and slightly above the last word to which the reference is made. The footnotes at the bottom of each page are separated from the manuscript by a continuous line.

Reference to books are noted in this order: author, title of the book (italicized in print, underscored on the typewriter), place, the publisher, year of publication and page or pages of reference. For example:

[1] Eric Hoffer, *The Temper of Our Time,* New York, Harper & Row, 1967, p.84

References to articles are noted as follows: author, title of article (enclosed in quotation marks), name of the magazine (underscored), volume, if any, date (month or week, and year), page or pages of reference. For example:

[1] Robert O'Brien, "Ring Out, Liberty Bell!" Reader's Digest, July, 1972, pp.50-51

References to encyclopedias are as follows: name of article (enclosed in quotation marks), name of encyclopedia, edition year, volume, and page or pages. For example:

[1] "Constitution and Constitution Law," Encyclopedia Brittanica, 1971 edition, Vol. 6, p. 402

When the same reference is cited without the interruption of another footnote, the term Ibid. (*ibidem,* in the same place) is used followed by the specific page number.

[2] Ibid. p. 234

If a reference is repeated with an intervening footnote, indicate the author, followed by op. cit. (*opere citato,* in the work cited) then the page number or numbers.

When a reference is made to the same place previously noted, the footnote indicates loc. cit. (*loco citato,* in the place cited).

These are the most common footnote references. Following is a more complete list.

ed.	editor, edition
f.	and the following page (or pages, ff.)
ibid	in the same reference just cited
l.	line (ll., lines)
loc. cit.	in the place cited

MS	manuscript
n.	note
n.d.	no date given
n.p.	no publisher given
op. cit.	in the work cited
p.	page (pp., pages)
sic.	This indicates an error or irregularity in the original, and is inserted immediately after the irregularity enclosed in brackets.
tr.	translater, translator
vol.	volume (vols., volumes)

The bibliography, placed at the end of the manuscript, is an alphabetical list of references. Note that since the list is alphabetical, the surname of the author comes first. Examples:

Magazine:

Abercrombie, Thomas J., "The Sword and the Sermon," National Geographic, July, 1972, pp. 4-7

Book:

Eckstein, Gustav, *The Body Has a Head,* New York, Harper and Row, 1970

Encyclopedia:

"Origin of Meteors" Encyclopedia Brittanica, 1971 edition, Vol. 15, p. 333

Pages may or may not be indicated in the bibliography.

1. Interview ten persons on a predetermined and contemporary subject in order to arrive at a conclusion of public opinion.

2. Interview ten persons concerning their opinions to determine the feasibility of producing a product or setting up a new service. Arrive at a conclusion and make recommendations on the basis of your findings.

3. Report on a lecture or talk that would be pertinent to the business world. This may be either an essay summary or an outline format.

4. Report on a contemporary article of some length pertinent to the business world. Assume that your employer has handed this writing to you with instructions to summarize it because he does not have the time to read or evaluate it.

5. With permission from the administration, interview a representative cross section of the student body on some suggestion or improvement which would be under the jurisdiction of the student council. Make a report tabulating answers and describing reactions, and on the basis of the interviews make a recommendation to the student council.

chapter fourteen

the personal touch

Success in business does not mean profit alone. Those who have been successful in terms of money are the first to admit that money, in itself, is insufficient without the feeling of service to others. Too often young people starting out in business have dollar signs before their eyes, whereas the more mature and experienced businessman freely admits that his supreme satisfaction lies in the feeling of having contributed something to his fellow man. This contribution may be in the impersonal form of a product or service which makes life easier for others, but the process of becoming a success almost always involves the PERSONAL TOUCH. The pseudo-sophisticate, of course, is almost sure to say that this idea is naive.

O.K., take the case of the rise of the Bank of Troy. How many businessmen do you know who would personally "bat out" 25 letters a day following working hours just because they liked people? Frank Brocke of Troy, Idaho, has done this for 35 years. According to Associated Press and Washington Post stories (late 1971), Mr. Brocke joined the Bank of Troy in 1926, when he was 20. Deposits had dropped to $250,000, but the bank managed to squeak by the depression largely because Mr. Brocke gave personal attention to customers. This attention has meant, through the years, a personal letter to every new account and a prompt answer to every letter from a serviceman.

Although Troy, a small farming community in northern Idaho, has a population of only 514, the Bank of Troy has more than 8000 accounts, many of them from out of state. Current deposits are in excess of $15 million. One California depositor explained that he had started his account years ago when he was in charge of a CCC Camp near Troy. Through the years he has received such good service that he saw no reason for changing banks when he moved out of state. He explained that he has received a personal note at least once a month from Frank Brocke asking about his family and telling tidbits of news about Troy. A Portland, Oregon, businessman told me that he had established an account at the Bank of Troy when he was a student at nearby Washington State University. He received financial help without question when he needed it most, and he, like many other long-time depositors, feels a sense of loyalty and appreciation for good service.

This remarkable banker is proof that SERVICE is more important than profit. This is the order; it is never the other way around. Frank Brocke, through the years, has given individual service to his clientele, and since most of his depositors are not residents of tiny Troy, this has meant personal letters to most of them. He cannot understand why this is unusual. He is quoted as saying there is something wrong with the banking industry.

The papers are full of advertisements of savings and loan companies and other banking institutions which are offering all manner of inducements to gain depositors—rare Indian head pennies, uncirculated silver dollars, two-dollar bills, trading stamps, and even jewelry set with fake diamonds. These ploys may be effective in gaining customers, but how about keeping them?

On the other hand, one large bank, realizing the importance of letter writing, has employed the services of a correspondent consultant to provide instruction in written communication and to spot-check the files for an in-depth study of current practices with suggestions for improvement. While this is good, by applying the techniques and suggestions of this text, every individual who has the responsibility of writing or dictating any letter could readily develop his own expertise without sounding stereotyped.

By becoming familiar with the formulas, and by creating his own set of guide letters, a businessman would write letters because he wants to and not because he has to. His letters then would exude that personal interest which is genuine and sincere—the kind Frank Brocke has had which has brought such a large and loyal clientele. The problem, of course, is time. The personal touch takes time, and this is where a Girl Friday or an executive assistant could come into the picture. Either of these could compose letters and type them for the executive's signature. These letters could easily be adapted from one composed by the executive himself so that they would exude his personality and so that he would be familiar with each letter that goes out. The person qualified to carry out this correspondence policy could easily be one who has completed this course in correspondence.

Over a period of 14 years, the research behind this text has involved writing some 1800 letters and receiving answers to approximately 90 percent of them. It is interesting to note that there appears to be direct correlation between effective letter writing and success.

During this research, one student, a young lady bent on becoming an executive secretary in a bank, wrote identical letters to the managers of five banks, inquiring about the requirements for a position in a bank and asking for advice in pursuing her studies to be best qualified.

Although she wrote to well established, large banks, she received no answer from one, a second one literally brushed her off, another wrote a stereotyped letter, a fourth wrote a brief informative letter suggesting that she apply for a position upon completion of her secretarial course. But the fifth was a jewel. The manager of this bank answered the letter himself with a single-spaced page-and-a-half letter, not only giving the girl suggestions about her courses but offering her hints about human relations and personality which indicated that to him these were as important as skills. One piece of advice he gave to the girl, which has been accepted by subsequent students, was that any person writing to an executive should always find out his name and use it in the address and the salutation instead of resorting to the impersonal "Dear Sir." Letters, he said, are appreciated and considered much more readily when they are directed to a person and not to a nebulous Dear Sir. In this case, he suggested, it would have been a very simple matter for her to call the bank and ask for the name of the manager. This, you see, adds the personal touch. This fine letter carried a handwritten postscript suggesting that the young lady call for an appointment to discuss with him her future employment plans. This girl, who lived in a dormitory, was so impressed with the answer to her letter that she recommended this bank to her schoolmates and to her parents who, it seems, liked the idea of a bank whose manager showed interest in their daughter. This bank manager was interested enough and astute enough to realize that even though the girl's letter could be regarded as a nuisance, and answering it was time consuming, a courteous, interested reply could have wide influence.

Any type of organization, large or small, could increase its volume of business by a concentrated and sincere effort to be of more service through writing letters. Recently, a woman was advised to have her car diagnosed and serviced by a car lab. This, she found, offered her a complete diagnosis with an estimate of the cost of servicing all adjustments necessary. She was so pleased with the results of this service that she wondered why she hadn't heard of it before. The owner of the business admitted that two-thirds of his clientele were women who seemed pleased to know that their cars could be put in good running order and made safe for them to drive.

Women who pay little attention to ads about such a business would read a personal letter explaining its service, something like the following:

Dear Mrs. Bennett:

Would you like to feel that your car is absolutely safe for you to drive? I'm not much at writing letters, so I'll make this brief.

I run the Wagner Car Lab Service, and by using an apparatus called a dynometer, I can diagnose your car as thoroughly as a physician could give a person a complete physical. For this service, I charge $9.95. You will receive a profile telling the precise condition of your car's motor, its brakes, transmission, battery, spark plugs—the whole works. I can give you an estimate of the cost of taking care of all the adjustments indicated. After such a service, you could drive your car with assurance that it is in good safe running order. Besides this, you will like the way it runs—like a new car.

Call 581-9090 and ask for me so that we can arrange the best time to pick your car up.

Sincerely,

Jake Wagner

Since you are by this time thoroughly familiar with the basic formula, you may have observed how this letter follows it.

Jake may have asked himself, "What do I want to accomplish?" And his answer is, of course, "I want to get another new customer."

How can he do this? Here he emphasized the YOU attitude. He likely said to himself, "I can offer a clear explanation of what my service is, and I can influence Mrs. Bennett to feel that it is to her advantage to accept this service I have to offer."

232

A woman, usually, is not a mechanic. She drives her car, but she doesn't understand its mechanism. There are exceptions, of course, but if she is like me, if kicking the four tires doesn't help, she has had it. Of prime importance to any woman is a trouble-free, safe car which can give her peace of mind. Notice that there are no "ifs" in this letter. Jake doesn't say, "IF you would like my services. . ." He says, ". .call me. . .", but while the letter indicates confidence, it displays no arrogance.

Clearly, as Jake rereads his letter, he can be sure that Mrs. Bennett would be so favorably impressed that she would call him.

Chances are that Jake would get referrals from a satisfied Mrs. Bennett, so that the volume of his business would be virtually determined by the number of letters he would write. A follow-up letter would assure repeat business. How about something like this:

Dear Mrs. Bennett:

To keep in top shape physically, a person gets a yearly physical. A car needs a yearly checkup, too.

This is to remind you that it's been nearly a year, Mrs. Bennett, since we last checked your car. After last year's checkup, any adjustments now would likely be minor, but it's better to be sure. You'll get better service from your car if you give it regular attention. It's good to feel safe.

Call me at 581-9090. Since you are a former client, I'll give your car preferred handling. We'll arrange an appointment to suit you.

Sincerely,

Jake Wagner
Wagner's Car Lab

Satisfied customers and repeat business are the life blood of any organization. Personal interest by way of letters will increase the volume of any business. The competition game in business can be won by this simple technique.

Insurance is a very personal service which is particularly adaptable to an indication of personal interest. A periodic letter to a policyholder and perhaps handwritten notes from the agent enclosed with premium notices would work wonders. One policyholder noted that promotion literature enclosed with a premium notice stated clearly, "If you have any questions, don't hesitate to call your agent." When she called her agent for an explanation of some handwritten figures and notations on her notice, he didn't know the answer and seemed annoyed at her request. He finally found the answers for her and added that he was glad all his policyholders didn't ask a lot of questions. Clearly, this man is more interested in profit than in service. He'll never reach the million-dollar club this way. His policyholders would never recommend him or his company to their friends. He is literally sending business to his competitor—the one who does take time to write letters and personal notes.

The owner of a small dress shop tripled her business after she started taking the time to show personal interest in her customers. What woman could resist the following note:

233

Dear Mrs. Griffith:

I have just returned from a buying trip, and I selected two dresses in your size which look just like you. I know you will love both of them. My advance shipment will be here Thursday. Come in soon, won't you?

Sincerely,

Jan Lewis
The Silver Door

P.S.   I selected a lot of other goodies, too.

An experienced buyer, whether in her own shop or not, will select items with specific customers in mind. This technique would have to involve personal notes. Nothing makes a customer feel more important or pleases him more than this type of personal consideration and service. The technique is just as effective with men as with women, but the correspondence approach would be of course, more masculine, something like this:

Dear Leo:

Since you are one of our most discriminating customers. I feel sure you will like to know that Stanley Strand, a representative of Frank Hobbs custom-made suits, will be in our Men's Department next Thursday and Friday, June 10 and 11. He will have a wide selection of fine fabrics and he can measure you for the style you select.

If you choose a summer fabric, delivery will be assured in three weeks. The fall suits will be shipped the second week in August in plenty of time for cooler weather. We'll make every effort to suit your convenience for an appointment, but do call soon (675-9800).

Sincerely,

P.S.   We have a fine selection of top quality shirts and ties so that you will be able to accessorize your suit on the spot.

Any businessman could make his service or product seem special and unusual through personal communication, even if this is a very short note. People are sick of being one of many; they are fed up with junk mail and duplicated sales pitches; they are resistant to wheeler dealer types. They respond readily to testimonies of their friends and acquaintances who are favorably impressed with personal service they have received. This spreading the word through satisfied customers is the most effective sales appeal in existence, and customers can readily be made satisfied through the practice of personal written communication.

While the price of the average business letter may be $3.27 (or higher), this figure is far in excess of the cost to the businessman who makes a habit of writing friendly personal letters. The more he writes, the less the cost of each letter. This is a far more economical and efficient medium of advertising than the conventional methods. Those men who make a production of dictating the stuffy stereotyped letter add to the overhead of written communication. Too often businessmen avoid writing letters because they imagine that it is a chore, or their communication is so different from their natural personalities that they are artificial. Too often they write the kinds of letters that prompt a client to say, "I don't know what you are trying to say. If you will just tell me what you want, I'll try to respond." Many insurance men, lawyers, bankers, and top executives too often fall into a pattern of professional vernacular which is completely foreign to a layman. This kind of gobbledegook impresses no one but the writer. The really big man not only has time for the little man, he has the ability to communicate with him on his level.

One television dealer who specializes in good service has a word-of-mouth following because, after he makes a service call, he sends a handwritten note on a postal card saying, "How's your TV working? If you are having a problem be sure to let me know." If a problem develops within two or three weeks after he has serviced the TV, he doesn't charge for the extra call. You would imagine that he would be sticking his neck out and inviting complaints, but because his clients know that he is not the prototype of a gyppo TV serviceman, he has built a large clientele which trusts him.

A car salesman I know keeps a file of all of his customers, the dates of their purchases, and the kinds of cars they bought. Periodically, he sends handwritten notes reminding them that he is ready to serve them, or he informs them of cars, new or used, that he has on the floor or on the lot. He plants the idea in the minds of his former clients, and if they are the least susceptible to new-car-itis, this personal note will do the trick. He has customers who wouldn't buy a car from anyone else, even though he has changed dealers several times. As you can imagine, he is in demand by car dealers. However, his first thought is service, and he is completely honest.

A business school whose representatives are alert to newspaper items about special news of honors of high school students sends personal notes of congratulation to these students with no sales message included.

Alert textbook salesmen, whose business inevitably involves duplicated letters describing new publications, remember names of teachers, department heads, and administrators responsible for selection, and they add personal notes to these individuals in routine communications.

Sharp realtors search the business pages of newspapers to learn names of personnel changes and send notes offering to sell a house or find a suitable new one for those moving from one town to another.

Positive habits are just as easily formed as negative ones. Results of writing personal letters are so rewarding that businessmen feel encouraged to try again and again, and thus a habit is formed. As letter writing becomes a habit, it is a pleasure instead of the chore that it could well have been.

Large companies have become larger and have remained successful because of their interest in serving their customers—and this service has originated largely with their letter-writing policies. One large cosmetic company wrote (in answer to an "out" letter), "We cannot overstress the importance of written communication in connection with public relations. In many cases it is the only method we have of contacting the consumer. We try to be personally interested."

Too busy to write the personal type letters? Frank Brocke with his First Bank of Troy wasn't too busy. J. C. Penney, in spite of his business acumen and his financial success, was never too busy. The men who are really on top in business are not too busy.

The reaction of one small bank in answering an inquiry about letter-writing policies is quite likely the reason that it has remained very small. The secretary of the manager wrote that her boss disliked writing or dictating letters. Here is a direct quotation from her letter, "Mr. Blank also said to tell you that if we fail to answer a letter for a long enough period, they usually seem to take care of themselves without a letter being necessary." The difference between Mr. Blank and Mr. Brocke of Troy is obvious. One man is a drudge who regards personal service as being dispensable; the other man has found excitement and prosperity in being genuinely interested in his depositors. THERE IS A DIRECT CORRELATION BETWEEN A GOOD PERSONAL LETTER WRITING POLICY AND SUCCESS. This has been proved time and time again.

The bank manager who advised the young lady about qualifications as a bank secretary and suggested that she avoid the Dear Sir routine—this same man habitually wrote a personal letter of appreciation to each new depositor. It is no wonder that he was promoted to the position of bank manager in a large city bank. He literally _wrote_ his own ticket to success.

How about you? Are you willing to show enough PERSONAL interest in people to write your ticket to success? Remember, upon its correspondence shall a business rise or fall.

Review Study — Capitalization

The review study in Chapter 2 covered the capitalization of schools, courses, and classes, but this subject deserves further review. I tell my students that they are "capital happy." They capitalize every word that seems important to them. Relative importance is so varied that rules seem more uniform and dependable, so I prefer following the rules. I do admit, however, that even grammarians seem not to agree, and it is quite true that even capitalization and punctuation rules are subject to change. Here are some rules for easy reference:

Any historical event or document is capitalized:

World War II, Magna Charta, Civil War, Declaration of Independence

Specific churches or denominations are capitalized:

Church of the Good Shepherd, The First Baptist Church,
Lutheran, St. Luke's, Mormon, etc.

The word _church_, unless it is specific or unless it refers to a particular church, is lower case.

He went to church every Sunday.

236

According to the dictionary, the word <u>president</u> is capitalized only when it refers to the President of the United States. However, in business, the word <u>president</u> is important to the person who holds the title, and respect is accorded to him by others within and outside his own company. Consequently, I suggest that we let the psychology of human relations take precedence over rules of capitalization. I always capitalize the title of any officer in any company, especially in written communication to his own company. By the same token I would capitalize designated departments and the titles of any executives such as Credit Manager, Personnel Director, etc. Technically these need not be capitalized unless they are used in place of a name or are attached to a name as Supervisor Jones, Director Smith.

I find that students frequently capitalize the words <u>Mother</u>, <u>Father</u>, <u>Uncle</u>, <u>Grandfather</u>, etc. These people are important to them, and to deny this capitalization privilege would be nit picking. These words are actually not to be capitalized unless they stand for the name of the person or are attached to the name—the same rule that applies to the titles of executives. By the same token, plurals or generalities should not be capitalized no matter how important the words may seem:

The presidents of the companies met to discuss the matter.

The managers met with department heads to discuss the policy.

Capitalization of proper nouns and their derivatives.

Proper nouns (the names of particular places, persons, or things) should be capitalized. It follows that adjectives that come from these nouns should also be capitalized. So we have France and French, Spain and Spanish, America and American.

However, so many words that originally were derived from specific proper nouns no longer have any direct connection to that noun, or have become so commonly used, that capitalization is no longer necessary. We do not think of turkish towels, for instance, as coming from Turkey, or of india ink as coming from India. Our dishes come from many places besides China—some of the best china comes from France. Observe the following:

She wore French perfume.   They installed french doors.

Eash of these is correct. The perfume is from France; the doors are not. Yet, inconsistently, Danish and French pastries are almost always capitalized. If in doubt consult an up-to-date dictionary.

Many trade names have been accepted—incorrectly—as products. You may hear someone say that she has a new Philco frigidaire. Correctly, Frigidaire is the trade name of a particular kind of electric refrigerator. Facial tissues are Kleenex; cola drinks are Cokes, and so it goes—but not correctly.

In business writing capitalize a particular product, especially in communication with the company that produces it. One of my students received from a large oil company a manual listing the correct spelling of the dozens of products put out by the company. Each one is capitalized. I was interested to note that this same manual (loose leaf, to permit updating) listed the names and titles of all the executives in the company—there were two pages of these. Anyone is sensitive about the correct spelling of his own name, and secretaries and typists in this large company were instructed to refer to the manual for the spelling of names and products.

Words or names that are used frequently should be learned, and the only way to learn how to spell words is to type or write them. The same goes for capitals. Once you get the correct form, learn it.

Assignments

1. As a banker, write a letter to a new depositor whose account has been transferred to your bank from another branch of the same bank. While this letter will be adapted to each new depositor, it will be used as a guide letter.

2. Revise the following letter from a printer:

Dear Mr. Tabor:

Last time you placed an order with us, you asked me to let you know when we got in a stock of erasable bond paper suitable for letterheads. This is to let you know that we now have some in.

Yours truly,

3. As an interior designer, write a letter to Mrs. Delbert James for whose new home you planned and furnished the major decor. Express your appreciation for the privilege of designing the decor of her new home and for her cooperation in working so well with you. Tell her you have just received a shipment of imports from Finland which would complement her home, and suggest that she visit your shop to see this new stock.

4. As an insurance agent write a personal note to Mr. and Mrs. Don Kasterline thanking them for their new car and homeowner comprehensive insurance policies which you have just written. Offer to be of any help in answering questions they may have or to assist them in the event of an emergency.

chapter fifteen

the over-and-above-and-beyond-the-call-of-duty letter

At this point you have the idea that every letter you write should incorporate the YOU attitude, should use the TRI-ASK TECHNIQUE, and should exude the PERSONAL TOUCH. Isn't that enough? Well, not quite. There's the letter you don't <u>have</u> to write—the over-and-above-and-beyond-the-call-of-duty letter. Oh, come now, you mean that we have to think up letters to write in addition to all those duty letters? That's it exactly. These are the very letters—the ones that don't have to be written—that frequently create an aura of friendliness and human interest that sets an individual or organization apart from the run of the mill.

What kinds of letters are these, and how can they be written? The important question to answer is the third one of the TRI-ASK TECHNIQUE: How would I feel if I were to receive this letter? When you ask this question, the answer is so obvious that you will never feel that this kind of letter is a chore or a duty.

How about a sympathy letter? This is the letter you don't have to write, certainly. When you hear of the death of a business acquaintance or a death in the family of an associate you very likely have a deep feeling of sympathy, but the chances are that, besides sending the customary funeral flowers, you do nothing because you "just don't know what to say." When you ask yourself, "What do I want to accomplish, your answer is, "I'd like to express sympathy, but I don't quite know how." It is always difficult to know how to express sympathy with words—it's the feeling that counts. Just say, very simply, what you feel. Something like this:

Dear Joe,

I was shocked to hear of the sudden death of your wife. It is so very hard to know what to say, but I wanted you to know that my thoughts are with you at this difficult time.

If there is anything at all that I can do, please don't hesitate to let me know.

Sincerely,

Max

Normally, this would be handwritten. When Joe recovers from the shock of his loss, he will likely write a short note telling Max how much he appreciated his thoughtfulness. These brief notes between businessmen can do much to create a lasting rapport. Women are less self-conscious about this kind of emotional expression, and quite often a secretary may suggest such an expression to her employer. I remember my boss's gratitude when I took the initiative in sending such an expression in his behalf when he was out of town.

Concern for business associates is further shown by sympathy notes at a time of illness. Hospitalized patients enjoy commercial cards, but if the patient is very ill, his sense of humor may be frayed to the point that he fails to appreciate the funny ones. In any event, a handwritten note will be more effective. This personal note is sure to be more appreciated than a conventional card.

Dear Rick,

I was sorry to hear from your office that you are in the hospital. We always look forward to your visits, and we hope to see you back on the job soon. Joe took care of our order all right, but it just didn't seem quite the same not to have you on hand giving us your good service. You are one representative we really enjoy seeing.

Get well. Do what the doctors say so that we'll see you again soon.

Fred

Men of long acquaintance frequently show their friendliness by sarcasm. Generally, this is strictly a masculine propensity, so use it cautiously, if at all, with a woman. Men who have a strong rapport frequently "kid" each other mercilessly. In this event Fred's note might go like this:

Rick,

Well, so you decided to take a few days off, did you? Playing "sick" is a sneaky way of getting a vacation. Pretty soft. Good service, pretty nurses! You want sympathy, I suppose. Well, you're not getting it from this direction. Better get back on the job, or we'll give our account to Curt. Don't stay away too long.

Fred

P.S. We do sorta miss you, you old so-and-so.

If you send a sarcastic note, be sure it is kept in the same vein as personal kidding. If Fred and Rick rib each other hard, and enjoy it, then a pseudo-nasty note is appropriate. Be sure to adapt the tone of the letter or note to the recipient.

Never fail to send letters of congratulations to business associates, and frequently to competitors. The following letter might be one to a business associate:

Dear Mr. Belding: (or Dear Steve: — if you know him that well.)

I have just read in the Journal of Commerce of your advancement to the presidency of your company. I congratulate you on a promotion which is well deserved. You are most capable of coping with the problems of such a prestigious company as Taggart and Stratton.

In all the years that our organization has been associated with you, we have always been most impressed with your service. We know we can depend on you.

Everyone in our company is delighted with your good news. We look forward to our continued association.

Sincerely,

Here is an example of a letter to a competitor:

Dear Ralph,

I have just read of your promotion to General Manager of Mason and Edmonds. My heartiest congratulations! Through the years you and your company have been our most formidable competition, but I will say that you have always been fair—even though you have kept us on our toes.

Your company made a fine choice, and I wish you every success in your new position.

Sincerely,

Too seldom do people express their appreciation other than with a perfunctory and hasty personal thank you. Some service clubs do not even express appreciation to speakers who perform without a fee. Unless a person is a politician or is promoting his own service, he certainly deserves a sincere thank-you note when he donates his time and effort to make a talk at any organization. This note of appreciation should not follow a pattern but should be personal in referring specifically to the talk, so that the recipient will at least know that he had been heard.

Sometimes a thoughtful gesture is to include in the thank-you note a newspaper clipping describing a talk, an article, or some other accomplishment. A person always appreciates an extra copy of something written about him.

Letters of congratulations and appreciation are so varied that it would be impossible to give examples of all of them, but here are some types of letters that really should be written: congratulations on being elected president or other important officer in any business or civic organization, on any awards or honors, such as being chosen junior or senior citizen of the year, on a business anniversary, and on the opening of a new branch or business (with best wishes for success). Don't assume because the persons involved are what you might think of as dignitaries that they appreciate any less a word of appreciation or congratulation. When one well-known platform speaker is asked by a nonprofit organization to speak without fee, he says, very frankly, "I'll be happy to if you will write me a letter telling me how you liked my talk." He uses these letters and others like them as recommendations to add to his resume when his agent books him for paid lectures.

A thoughtful employer will write, without having to be asked, a letter of recommendation—a To Whom It May Concern Letter which, in spite of the contentions of some self-appointed authorities on written communication, are not at all passé. Many times valued employees leave an employer regretfully for reasons other than dissatisfaction, and a letter of recommendation can be used by the departing employee when he needs help in obtaining another position. Since the average employee stays for only three and a half years on one job, chances are that any such letter will be most useful at some time in the future. Here is an example:

To Whom It May Concern:

Mrs. Lynn Larsen was employed as my secretary for two and a half years from June, 1971, through December, 1973. During that time she served as head secretary in the personnel department of more than 100 professional and clerical employees. Her duties included arranging appointments, shorthand and dictaphone stenography, typing, telephone and personal reception, payroll, filing, and providing information and counsel to the staff concerning a wide variety of personnel matters.

Mrs. Larsen always took pride in producing work which would be a credit to her and the department. She accepted suggestions gracefully and demonstrated a commendable capacity for improvement. She was prompt and conscientious in her working habits. She was loyal to her employers and the company, and completely circumspect with respect to the professional confidences with which she dealt regularly as my personal secretary.

Well-groomed, poised in manner, and well-modulated in voice, Mrs. Larsen developed and maintained exceptionally fine relationships with both the professional and secretarial office staff, and with the community. Her telephone and personal reception courtesy were often commended to me by callers. I especially appreciated her calm presence and good humor in the face of various pressures of time and demand.

It was a pleasure to have had Mrs. Larsen as my secretary. She left my employ because of her husband's transfer. I am pleased to recommend her for any top-level secretarial position.

Sincerely,

This fine letter may seem a little flowery, but it is taken from an actual letter an employer voluntarily handed to his secretary when she resigned her position. His recommendation explained fully his appreciation of her fine services. Such a letter could very well be the determining factor in her getting a position.

It is perfectly ethical for an employee to request such a letter, for most employers, with their aversions to letter writing, simply do not think of it themselves.

A much simpler letter could be something like this:

242

To Whom It May Concern:

Ben Harris has been in my employ for the last five years, and I am happy to recommend him as a fine, dependable employee. He had complete charge of our accounting department, and his work was exemplary.

He is leaving our employ to move to Portland so that he and his family may be near Children's Hospital, where his young son must be confined for some time.

I should be happy to complete a recommendation form or to answer any questions you may have regarding his personality or his work.

Albert Goldsmith
Goldsmith and Son

What if an employee whom you feel you cannot give an unqualified recommendation asks for a To Whom It May Concern letter? One employer handled this by making it clear to all new employees that he would be happy to give them whatever recommendation he felt they earned—that he would accentuate the positive, but he would always tell the truth or his word would be worth nothing. He explained that in filling out a recommendation form or answering questions, he would have to adhere strictly to facts. Now a letter of recommendation for Mr. Average could be something like this:

To Whom It May Concern:

Dale Garrett was employed by our firm from December, 1970, to March, 1971. During that time he was promoted from trainee to bookkeeper in the payroll department. His supervisor reports that his work was quite acceptable. His salary here was $5700 at the time he left to accept a position which paid more than this.

I shall be glad to complete your regular recommendation questionnaire if you wish.

Robert Smyth, Manager

Note that this does not exude the enthusiasm that a more outstanding employee would have received. Writing this kind of note saved Mr. Smyth the embarrassment of turning down a mediocre employee. Dale might not even use this letter unless, indeed, he were desperate.

How about a letter to a new employee? Silly? Not at all. Suppose the manager of a large company is apprised by Personnel of all new employees. A short handwritten note from him could easily dispel new employee jitters. Something like this:

To Norman Chase:

I have just heard, Norman, that you have joined our company, and as soon as I return from San Francisco, I'll stop by your desk to chat with you. I have heard nothing but the best about you, and I feel sure you will enjoy your position with Hamilton's. Don't hesitate to call on Bruce Long if you need answers to any questions.

I'll look forward to meeting you.

Baird Gordon

A new employee in a smaller company would appreciate a short personal welcoming note, or a note of appreciation for doing some specific job well. The best recommendation any company can have is from its own employees. It is said that the quality of an organization can easily be determined by asking an employee where he works. It isn't even necessary to ask how he likes his job, just where he works. Haven't you heard it said, "It must be a very fine company. Even the employees like it." Communicating by written memo, note, or letter to your own employees can contribute to the rapport of your organization.

How about the other way around? It is not brash for an employee to write a note to her boss or her supervisor. I am not suggesting any hanky panky or soft soap, but bosses are human, and a discreet note of appreciation is not at all out of line. How about a thank-you note for a new piece of equipment or for a promotion or raise? People are often too reluctant or too lazy to initiate this kind of written communication, which can do wonders to nurture good feelings.

A gift and accolades at a banquet are all very fine for the retiring employee, but don't forget that personal handwritten note. This will always soften the shock of employment separation.

Nothing is more impersonal than an imprinted Christmas greeting. Businessmen should realize that their associates and patrons would likely appreciate short, personal, handwritten greetings more than elaborate imprinted cards or gifts.

Other courtesies handled by personal written communications are the following: A letter of introduction for a friend to someone in another city; expression of appreciation to a travel bureau for good service in helping with tickets and itineraries; appreciation for hospitality; appreciation for any kind of service well done—even to a profit making organization such as to a hotel for fine accommodation; to a printer for getting out a good job in record time; letters to an editor for good coverage of your company or club. Just think how you would express your thanks in person and transfer this expression to paper. That's all there is to it.

Letters to the editor to be published? Fine. Never hesitate to express yourself, but avoid personal innuendoes or negative criticism. It's OK to be firm and even biased, but never lose your dignity. Many people read the letters to the editor first, and what you say as a person can be a reflection or a credit to your company.

Make a habit of taking five minutes every day to ask yourself: "What can I write today that would make the world seem brighter for someone else? What letter can I write that I really don't have to?" Making someone else feel good is always reflex—businesswise and personally. You won't even have to ask yourself, "How would I feel if I were to receive this letter?" You'll know before you ever write it. And there you have it. Become that rare individual whose written communication policy includes those letters that don't HAVE to be written.

Assignments

1. Jerry Brandon, the representative of Acme Building Supplies who visits your construction company regularly and who gives you excellent service, has been involved in an accident. His wife was killed and he is hospitalized with a broken leg. Write a letter expressing your sympathy.

2. As her employer, write a letter to your secretary expressing your appreciation for doing a commendable job of getting out in record time a very involved and lengthy report which was very important to you. Mention that she may expect, in her next pay envelope, a bonus.

3. Write a To Whom It May Concern letter for the secretary in assignment 2 who is leaving her position to get married. Assume that she has been in your employ for the last three and a half years, first as a file clerk, then as a general secretary, and later as your executive secretary.

4. As outgoing president of your service club, write a note of appreciation to your program chairman who has been largely responsible for making your year in office a success.

5. As a secretary whose Air Force husband is being transferred, write a letter of resignation expressing your appreciation for a position you have thoroughly enjoyed for the last two and a half years.

Sample Over-and-Above-and-Beyond-the-Call-of-Duty-Letters:

BOB PACKWOOD
OREGON

United States Senate
WASHINGTON, D.C. 20510

April 13, 1972

Mr. Robert M. Leonard
c/o Mr. and Mrs. Joseph Leonard
725 Sumner Street, N.E.
Salem, Oregon 97308

Dear Bob:

Best wishes on being elected student
body president of Merritt Davis School of
Commerce. You have every right to be proud
of this honor and I'm delighted for you.

Congratulations.

Cordially,

Bob Packwood

BOB PACKWOOD

BP/gjr

TOM McCALL
GOVERNOR

OFFICE OF THE GOVERNOR
STATE CAPITOL
SALEM 97310

December 23, 1971

Ms. Joyce Cox
3794 Center Street
Salem, Oregon   97301

Dear Ms. Cox:

Your warm letter of Thanksgiving Day is just as heartening to me on Christmas.

It was good to hear from you and to learn of your steady progress toward new and exciting accomplishments.

I remember the day of your visit and I am pleased to know that your plans have proceeded according to schedule and that your hopes are still high.

May I join you in your anthem of thanksgiving? Where, indeed, but in this kind of a nation could one continue to move with the tides and make a life of beauty and meaning through the impact of his effort and desire!

I, too, am grateful for being able to live in this country and in our most beautiful State of Oregon. Thank you for thinking of me on Thanksgiving and thank you for sending me the optimistic and buoyant letter. Best wishes for continued success and happiness.

Sincerely,

Tom McCall
Governor

TM:sv

247

June 26, 1972

TOM McCALL
GOVERNOR

Mrs. Lester Herigstad
2550 Broadway N. E.
Apartment 21
Salem, Oregon 97303

Dear Mrs. Herigstad:

Belated thanks for your warmly welcome letter about voluntarism, our respective families and related subjects. Some communications go into my "precious pile" for special pondering by my family -- and yours got this treatment. Sam, Audrey and I enjoyed it very much.

You recalled a number of fond memories, and we shall try to continue to live up to the examples of compassion with which you credited us. Your existence obviously reflects to same sensitive responses to human wants and needs.

Appreciatively,

Tom McCall

Governor

TM:cm

MASP   23 June 1972

Mrs. E. D. Hallock
Salem, Oregon 97301

Dear Mrs. Hallock:

Since I last communicated with you, I became the Superintendent at
West Point, where I have been stationed for over two years. It was
a delightful surprise to receive your letter.

By all means, feel free to use my letter in your text. I am pleased
that Cheryl found it helpful and that she has retained it.

I might say in passing that in most of the Army staff positions which
I have held, I have encountered the conditions which you mention and
which are so common in America. Unskilled writers often feel that
the longer a letter is, the better it is. It is also a bureaucratic
tendency to use jargon of many syllables when simple English would
do the job better. Many draft letters which have come to me over the
years gave no indication that the author had read the incoming letter
to which his work was a response. I hope you are able to persuade
people to use simple English in preference to jargon, to answer the
points raised by the incoming letter, and to write simply.

With best wishes,

                                        Sincerely,

Incl   WILLIAM A. KNOWLTON
Ltr, 6 Mar 70   Lieutenant General, USA
                                        Superintendent

PORTLAND GENERAL ELECTRIC COMPANY

WILLAMETTE VALLEY DIVISION
136 High Street S. E.
P. O. Box 191
Salem, Oregon 97308

January 28, 1971

Mrs. Virginia Lee Hallock
Salem, Oregon   97301

Dear Mrs. Hallock:

Every cloud has a silver lining, they say. Furthermore,
the silver lining comes in many forms, I realize.

One of the most delightful forms is an all too infrequent
note from a customer to reassure us that the service which
we provide has value and is appreciated by those who use
it.

Thank you very much for taking the time to put your little
note in with your last bill payment. We held off a rate
increase for ten years, asked for one reluctantly, and
still feel that "electricity is your biggest bargain."
I'm glad you do too.

Sincerely,

Leo E. Chaffin
Division Manager

chapter sixteen

once over lightly

I am not about to suggest that letter writing be taken lightly, but I do suggest that it should never be a drudgery. Many communications in business are routine—I readily admit this—and they need not involve what we normally consider the "full route." However, the most efficient time saver in the area of routine and frequent messages is the triple-sheet, double carbon form referred to under a number of trade names such as Speed-Reply, Speedrite, Quick-Reply, Speed Memo, etc. Two of these with messages are reproduced at the end of this chapter. The size of this form varies from about 7 by 8½ inches to about 8½ by 9 inches. It is divided into thirds, usually horizontally, with the top third devoted to the name and address of the recipient on the left and the name and address of the sender printed at the right. The middle third of the form is reserved for the message, and the lower third, for the reply. The top sheet, usually white, and the two colored sheets are separated by light carbons. The sender keeps the second carbon to have a record of his message. The recipient is instructed to write his answer on the lower third of the form and return the original to the sender keeping the first carbon as his record of the communication. Messages may be typed, but brief communications may well be handwritten.

These are most efficient and time saving, and friendliness need not be sacrificed for brevity. Actually, companies that communicate frequently by this method usually reflect more effectively the personalities of the writers than by longer letters. This is so primarily because too many people still equate business letters with stuffiness.

Some of the most successful and progressive organizations are using the simplified letter. While business demands a certain degree of dignity and restraint, there should be no hesitation in deviating from the conventional structure. Eliminating the formal salutation and complimentary closing is progressive and efficient as long as the context of the letter itself is friendly. I predict that the day will come in the not too far distant future when we will look back with amusement on what we shall consider stuffy and ridiculous such usages as Dear Mr. Jones, Yours truly, Cordially yours, etc. Since the inside address, which is used mainly for reference, is of no interest to the recipient of the letter (he knows his own address), this is more conveniently placed at the lower left of the letter. Attention lines will be used rarely, and, at the direction of the Postal Service, such a line will be placed just under the company name in the address. Envelopes with any type of printing, typing, or writing at the lower left will be thrown out by electronic scanners and delayed. Accept readily these very efficient changes, and dare to be up to date as long as the context of the letter follows the TRI-ASK TECHNIQUE.

Bear in mind that your written communication reflects you and your organization and that any time your letters include such time worn and meaningless clichés as Thank you for your letter, Enclosed please find, This is to advise you, Hoping to hear from you soon, or such snarl words as unfortunately, refuse, regret, etc., the reader of that letter has every right to suspect that you and your organization are not up to date (you are just not with it).

While the appearance of a letter is important, you will find, after you or your place of business has established a pattern of attractiveness, that the process of format will come naturally. The number of carbons, the placement of date, the inside address, the type of salutation and complimenta closing, etc. will become automatic. However, if you have any part in the determination of these details, don't be resistant to change. If you decide that you like the simplified letter and you feel comfortable with it, don't hesitate to adopt this policy simply because it is not being widely used. Be among the first with practicable innovations.

Periodically, act as your own correspondent evaluator. Study the carbon copies in your files. Consider improvements. Ask yourself whether each letter accomplished its purpose. File for convenient access copies of guide letters—those letters from which you can adapt specific communications. It is not always necessary to "start from scratch" in composing a letter.

Here is a quick review for easy reference:

General Rules

1. Choose the type of letterhead that not only will suit you and your organization but that will be acceptable to most people who receive your letters. It should tell who you are, what you do, where you are located, and how you may be reached by telephone and cable. Avoid the cluttered look of too many names or too much advertising. Consult a reliable printer for advice. Be sensitive to comments, positive or negative, about your letterhead, and never hesitate to make a change if you come across an attractive letterhead which you might adapt for your own use. Remember that erasable bond paper is practical if it is carefully used. It could relieve tension for typists who are less than perfect.

2. For efficiency and convenience select a format which will be attractive and consistent.

3. Answer letters promptly, preferably within 24 hours. Answer ALL letters, even nuisance inquiries, but give priorities to those which ask about your service or product.

4. Take care to use correct English and spelling. Use passive voice sparingly.

5. Eliminate all gobbledegook, clichés, snarl words and redundancies from your correspondence. Review, if necessary, Chapter 2 until your thinking habits are conditioned to easy, positive, YOU attitude expressions. Don't be a stuffed shirt.

6. With every letter you write, USE THE TRI-ASK TECHNIQUE:

What do I want to accomplish?

How can I do this?

(Soften the blow before you lower the boom.)

Write the letter; then ask:

How would I feel if I were to receive this letter?

The Letter of Inquiry
(Ask and You Shall Receive)

1. Make the inquiry easy to answer.

2. Make the recipient of the letter feel that it is to his advantage to do what you ask.

Answer to an Inquiry

1. Answer the inquiry (or request) promptly.

2. If the inquiry has to do with your service or product, give it priority.

3. Answer the inquiry in terms of the advantage to the inquirer.

4. Expect the inquirer to accept your answer.

Refusing an Inquiry or Request

1. The formula

    a. Soften the blow.

    b. Explain.

    c. Refuse.

    d. Offer an alternative, if possible.

    e. Create good will.

The Claim Letter

1. Don't ever hesitate to scream if you are hurt.

2. State claim clearly; be specific; include all facts.

3. The formula

    a. Soften the blow.

    b. Explain the claim.

    c. Tell how you have been inconvenienced (if you have been).

    d. Indicate the adjustment expected (unless you feel the adjuster might include punitive damages).

4. Don't hesitate to go to the top (the president, the manager, the manufacturer, etc.)

5. If you do not get satisfaction, pursue the claim; use the service of one of the following:

    a. the local chamber of commerce

    b. the Better Business Bureau

    c. the Director of Consumer Affairs

    d. Small Claims Court

    e. an attorney

Granting an Adjustment

1. The formula

    a. Apologize.

    b. Explain.

    c. Adjust.

    d. Create goodwill.

Refusing a Claim
(virtually the same as refusing a request)

1. The formula

    a. Soften the blow.

    b. Refuse.

    c. Explain.

    d. Offer an alternative (if possible).

    e. Create goodwill.

The "Out" Letter

1. Think of an effective letter that "needs" to be written.

2. Write it.

The Biography

1. Prepare in advance interview questions.

2. Conduct the interview.

3. Listen carefully to the answers.

   a. Read between the lines to supplement the interview with questions not previously planned.

4. Outline the information.

5. Write the biography.

   a. Open with an attention-getter.

The Application Letter
(and related writings)

1. The letter itself

   a. The conventional application   (3 paragraphs)

      (1) qualification of education and/or experience
      (2) specific detail on qualification
      (3) request for interview

   b. The name beginning

      (1) use of name as an opener

   c. The gimmick letter

      (1) the different, original approach

2. The resume

   a. cover page
   b. education
   c. experience
   d. personal data and interests
   e. references

3.　The precis

    a.　a one-page summary of the resume

4.　The follow-up letter

    a.　expression of appreciation

    b.　specific reference to discussion during interview

    c.　expression of hope that application and qualifications are being considered favorably

5.　Refusal of job offer

    a.　appreciation

    b.　refusal

    c.　explanation

    d.　sign-off, goodwill

6.　Rushing an answer

(note:　This letter is ethical if it is diplomatic, and if it does not appear to censure the recipient for not having answered sooner. This letter usually indicates another offer.)

    a.　reference to discussion during interview—usually an expression of confidence in ability to handle the position discussed

    b.　explanation of reason for answer (another job offer—?)

    c.　expression of admiration for company, an earnest desire to fulfill the position (if this is the truth)

7.　Letter of resignation

    a.　Never express dissatisfaction with the job.

    b.　State date of termination (allow two weeks' notice if salary is received twice a month; allow one month's notice if pay is received monthly).

    c.　Date the letter and keep a copy (for protection).

    d.　Express appreciation if this can be a sincere expression.

8.　Reminders:　Do's

    a.　Keep resume up to date.

    b.　Record dates of starting and terminating jobs.

    c.　Record salaries chronologically.

    d.　Ask references for permission (annually).

    e.   Keep a record of honors, activities, and interests.

    f.   Tell the absolute truth. (Remember that your resume and your application letter may be carefully checked.)

9. Reminders: Don'ts

    a.   Don't appeal to emotion in applying for a job.

    b.   Don't express opinions about yourself—be objective.

    c.   Never speak disparagingly of a former employer.

    d.   Don't commit yourself on salary. (Leave this to the employer.)

    e.   Don't be arrogant, but don't hesitate to be confident.

The Sales Letter

1. The conventional sales letter

    a.   attention

    b.   desire

    c.   conviction

    d.   action

2. The PERSONAL sales letter (the selective approach)

    a.   sincerity

    b.   enthusiasm

    c.   knowledge of the service or product

    d.   YOU approach

The Credit Letter

1. Requesting credit information

    a.   Make the letter easy to answer.

    b.   Give assurance that information will be confidential.

2. Acknowledging a request for credit

    a.   The formula

        (1) a welcome or appreciation

        (2) request for information or references

        (3) an incentive to action

3. Giving credit information

   (1) Express facts — be absolutely objective.

4. Granting credit

   a. The formula

      (1) Express appreciation — welcome the new customer.

      (2) Encourage him to use his credit (sell).

      (3) Explain credit terms and payment policies.

      (4) Goodwill — sign-off

5. Refusing credit

   a. The formula

      (1) Soften the blow.

      (2) Refuse.

      (3) Explain.

      (4) Suggest an alternative to cash basis.

The Collection Letter

1. The series (adapted to the specific situation and based on the credit standing of the debtor)

   a. Send duplicate statements (with handwritten reminders).

   b. Did you forget? Do you want to be reminded?

   c. Is anything wrong?

   d. Don't jeopardize your credit.

   e. Pay or else.

   f. Use humor with caution.

The Memorandum

This intra-office communication is up and down and across. There is no sub-formula—only the TRI-ASK TECHNIQUE. Adapt the memorandum to the recipient. This mode of communication means that the right hand knows what the left hand is doing.

The Report

1. Ask these questions:

    a. For whom is this report to be prepared?

    b. What does he want—what is the purpose of the report?

    c. Stick to the purpose—don't pad.

2. Reasoning

    a. deductive—reasoning from a known or assumed conclusion

    b. inductive—determining a conclusion from research

The Personal Touch

1. Remember that a big person has time for little people.

2. The secret of personality development (and success) is interest in others.

3. Service comes <u>before</u> profit.

The Over-and-Above-and-Beyond-the-Call-of-Duty Letter

Get in the habit of writing the letter you don't have to write.

I urge you to keep this text as your reference when you are on the job. Refer to it often until using the TRI-ASK TECHNIQUE and writing the YOU attitude letter become second nature. File copies of your best letters and your guide letters in this text. WRITE YOUR TICKET TO SUCCESS.

1. Revise the following letter:

   Dear Mr. Andrews:

   The bill that we received for hotel accommodations for our convention guests is in error.

   You quoted a price of $14 a day for single rooms and $20 a day for double occupancy. If you will check your records, you will find that you provided four single occupancies and two doubles, making our bill for rooms $96 instead of $114.

   The banquet was quoted at $4.50 each including gratuities, and you have added $20 for gratuities. Since ours is a nonprofit organization, we must adhere to our preplanned budget.

   As soon as I receive an adjusted statement for our records, I shall have our treasurer issue a check in payment.

   Yours truly,

2. Answer a letter to Mrs. Joe Brock who has written to tell you that she has not received shipment of furniture which she was expecting on Thursday. On checking, you found that the shipping department held up shipment because a chair appeared to have been scratched. This was returned to the furniture department to be replaced or refinished, hence the delay. Shipment will be made next Tuesday.

3. Compose a form letter to be sent out to new students at a local private university soliciting them as depositors at your bank. Point out "no check charge" service, regardless of the size of the account, the friendly personal service, the convenient drive-in window service, and the night depository.

4. The local paper has carried the story of the appointment of a new city manager, giving details about his family (wife, college son, two high school daughters). As a department store manager, write an appropriate letter welcoming him to the city and invite him to avail himself of the services of your store.

Note: One more type of correspondence—the Speed-Reply!

FORM SR-101

656

Speed-Reply

TO KIM LON Wallcoverings

555 Dock Street

Portland, Oregon 97---

FROM

The Interior Design Shop

P. O. BOX 1

ALBANY, OREGON 97321

Phone (503) 926-6446

SUBJECT

— FOLD

MESSAGE   DATE July 7   19

Ken: This morning I talked to you about our PO#3375. Everything is fine now,

but could we still get the 10? Sorry to change minds again, but we couldn't

find a good match. Hope to receive our PO#3376 for 6 #G-436 soon.

Thanks,

SIGNED Alli

REPLY   DATE 7/12   19

ALLI — YES THE 10 S/R's ARE STILL AVAILABLE &
YOU CAN GET THAT IN A COUPLE OF DAYS. LET
ME KNOW IF YOU CANNOT USE THE 10 S/R's I
WILL SHIP UNLESS I HEAR FROM YOU.
SORRY I COULDN'T ANSWER SOONER
SIGNED KEN

RETAIN WHITE COPY, RETURN PINK COPY

DETACH THIS COPY—RETAIN FOR ANSWER

Speed-Reply

TO *Import/Export Service Co., Inc.* FROM **LÄNDIA**

155 Commerce Bldg.

Portland, Oregon 97 - - -

IMPORTS FROM FINLAND

P.O. Box 55
562 Springhill Rd.
Albany, Oregon 97321—U.S.A.
Phone (503) 926-0047

SUBJECT

— FOLD   MESSAGE   DATE *Feb 20*   19

Dear Ruth: I need to know the duty on the various items we import. Can you supply me with information showing these %'s?

SIGNED *Jo Anne*

REPLY   DATE   19

Jo Anne: Furniture is 5% , wood chairs are 8.5% , other furniture (metal) is 12%..

The glass articles are: Value over 30¢ not over $1.00 = 30%
                         Value over $1.00 to $3.00 ea = 30%
                         Value over $3.00   = 15%
                         Value over $3.00 cut or
                                   engraved   =15%

I believe this covers the majority of the articles you import at present,

if not please let me know the specific items you are questioning.

SIGNED Ruth

RETAIN WHITE COPY, RETURN PINK COPY

DETACH THIS COPY—RETAIN FOR ANSWER

TYPICAL ERRORS TO AVOID

The following errors were found in one set of English essays (35 papers).

Spelling

definetly (definitely)

alot (two words—I like him a lot)

occured (occurred)

cryed (cried)

typanies (timpani)

to — as in to far (too)

English errors

The reason I worked there was because it was good money.
(Never say the reason was because; rather, say the reason was that)

I lived in Albany Oregon the first year or so of my life.
(When the state is preceded by the city, the state is set off by commas: . . .Albany, Oregon,. . .)

Clubs are a Freshmans security blanket.
(Freshman should not be capitalized, and there should be an apostrophe before the s: freshman's.)

My parents worked in the shipyards during world war 2.
[As a (an) historical event, World War II should be capitalized and used with a Roman numeral. (By the way, British usage dictates the article an before the word history or historical. American usage follows the rule of placing an before words with consonant sounds; so it is an hour, but a house.)]

My life wasn't as exciting as most children's.
(The rule dictates that so should be used with negative expressions.
 She is as pretty as her sister, but she is not so tall.)

There were some bad times for my friend and I.
(. . .for my friend and me.)

We went down south.
(South as an area of the country should be capitalized.)

Remember that periods are always inside the quotation marks.

Punctuate correctly or correct any grammatical errors in the following sentences:

1. Of we two girls my sister was by far the prettiest.

2. During his Senior year of High school he only missed two days of school.

3. She always gave her assistance to whomever asked for help.

4. He was forced therefore to withdraw from school before the end of the year; he was of course reluctant to do this.

5. Her grades were as follows, English, A, Algebra, B+, Modern Problems, B, Typing, A-, Art, A.

6. The team was devoting all their efforts to winning the game.

7. She had to make her choice between three things; college, business school, or to get married.

8. The first ones to take advantage of the student loan fund were my brother and me.

9. A comparison of their salaries show a marked difference.

10. The possibility of him getting a job was excellent.

11. The president together with the council members were to meet with the school staff.

12. Included among his many talents is singing, acting and playing the piano.

13. She asked whether I had a job?

14. His job, as well as his civic activities, have made his life a challenge.

15. His main responsibility are his younger brothers and sisters.

16. Every man and woman in the company are expected to do their part.

17. The chance of him winning the scholarship is very remote.

18. A keen appreciation of art, music, and handcraft are necessary for membership in the art association.

19.   Who did you give your report to?

20.   Her books were laying on the table right where she put them.

21.   Her assignment of November 12, as well as the two previous ones, were turned in late.

22.   A report, made on the basis of an interview, is more interesting than one made from a magazine article.

23.   A student like Jim, who turns their assignments in on time, makes the instructor's job much more pleasant.

24.   Enclosed in the sales letter was a brochure, a return envelope, and the letter itself.

25.   Neither the report nor the daily assignment were turned in on time.

SPELLING STUDY

Here is a list of words that are used in business. Many of them are misspelled, mispronounced, or misused. By referring to a reliable dictionary, rewrite each word by dividing it into syllables, indicating the accented syllable. Indicate the business meaning of each word, and be able to pronounce each one.

1. abatement

2. acceptance

3. accommodation

4. accountant

5. accretion

6. accrual

7. accrue

8. accrued

9. accruing

10. accumulated

11. accuracy

12. acquire

13. acquisition

14. actuarial

15. administrator

16. affiliate

17. allocate

18. amortize

19. analyze

20. annuitant

21. anticipate

22. apportionment

23. appraise

24. appraisal

25. appreciation

26. appropriation

27. arbitrary

28. authorized

29. bankruptcy

30. bookkeeper

31. budgetary

32. capacity

33. carrying

34. certificate

35. certified

36. certification

37.   codicil

38.   coefficient

39.   commodity

40.   comparable

41.   composite

42.   comptroller

43.   computed

44.   consignment

45.   consistency

46.   consolidated

47.   constituent

48.   contingency

49. convertible

50. coordinate

51. corporate

52. cumulative

53. debenture

54. defalcation

55. defer

56. deferred (v. or adj.)

57. deferral

58. deficiency

59. deficit

60. delinquent

61. demurrage

62. depletable

63. depletion

64. depositary

65. depository

66. depreciable

67. depreciation

68. digit

69. effective

70. diminution

71. embezzlement

72. encumbrance

73. entity

74. equity

75. exhibit

76. expectance

77. facility

78. factor

79. fiduciary

80. fiscal

81. graph

82. hypothecated

83. impairment

84. imprest

85. increment

86. incur

87. incurred

88. insolvency

89. intangible

90. interim

91. lapse

92. leasehold

93. legacy

94. lien

95. liquidation

96. maintenance

97. maturity

98. merger

99. minority

100. mortgage

101. municipal

102. narrative

103. negotiable

104. nominal

105. obsolescence

106. opinion

107. option

108. parity

109. participating

110. periodic

111. perpetual

112. physical

113. pledged

114. preferred

115. principal

116. principle

117. promissory

118. proprietary

119. proxy

120. recapitulation

121. reconciliation

122. recoup

123. redemption

124. registrar

125. remittance

126. renegotiaion

127. replacement

128. replacing

129. requisition

130. requisite

131. residual

132. residuary

133. restricted

134. specific

135. statistic

136. statute

137. subsidiary

138. supplemental

139. tangible

140. testamentary

141. testator

141. traveling

143. validity

144. variable

145. variance

146. verification

147. warranty

148. warrant

149. withholding

150. yield

CREDITS